THE REVOLUTION THAT WASN'T

Kennikat Press
National University Publications
Series in American Studies

THE REVOLUTION
THAT WASN'T

A Contemporary Assessment of 1776

Edited with introduction by

Richard M. Fulton

National University Publications
KENNIKAT PRESS // 1981
Port Washington, N.Y. // London

To Karen
for her love and for her help

Manufactured in the United States of America

Published by
Kennikat Press Corp.
Port Washington, N.Y. / London

Library of Congress Cataloging in Publication Data
Main entry under title:

The Revolution that wasn't.

(National university publications: American studies series)

Includes index.
1. United States—History—Revolution, 1775–1783—Historiography—Addresses, essays, lectures.
2. United States—History—Revolution, 1775–1783—Causes—Addresses, essays, lectures. 3. Revolutions—Addresses, essays, lectures. I. Fulton, Richard M., 1940–
E209.R438   973.3'1   79-27395
E209.R438
ISBN 0-8046-9259-9

CONTENTS

ACKNOWLEDGMENTS

Grateful acknowledgment is given to the following for permission to reprint materials.

Perez Zagorin, "Theories of Revolution in Contemporary Historiography." Reprinted with permission from the *Political Science Quarterly* 88 (March 1973). 23-52.

Peter Amann, "Revolution: A Redefinition." Reprinted with permission from the *Political Science Quarterly* 77 (March 1962): 36-44, 53.

Samuel P. Huntington, "Revolution and Political Change." Reprinted with permission from *Political Order in Changing Societies* by Samuel P. Huntington (New Haven. Yale University Press, 1968), 264-78.

Claude Welch, Jr., and Mavis B. Taintor, "What Is Political Revolution?" From *Revolution and Political Change* by Claude Welch, Jr., and Mavis Taintor. Copyright 1972 by Wadsworth Pub. Co., Inc., Belmont, CA 94002. Reprinted by permission of the publisher, Duxbury Press.

Hannah Arendt, "The Meaning of Revolution." From *On Revolution* by Hannah Arendt. Copyright Hannah Arendt 1963, 1965. All rights reserved. Reprinted by permission of Viking Penguin, Inc.

Robert Brown, "Reinterpretation of the Revolution and Constitution." Reprinted with permission of the National Council for the Social Studies and Robert Brown from *Social Education*, March 1957, 102-4, 114.

Jack P. Greene, "The Social Origins of the American Revolution: An Evaluation and an Interpretation." Reprinted with permission from the *Political Science Quarterly* 88 (March 1973): 1-22.

Gordon S. Wood, "Rhetoric and Reality in the American Revolution." Reprinted with permission of the author from the *William and Mary Quarterly* 23 (January 1966): 3-32. Copyright Gordon Wood.

Marc Egnal and Joseph A. Ernst, "An Economic Interpretation of the American Revolution." Reprinted with permission from the *William and Mary Quarterly* 29 (January 1972): 3-32.

Jack P. Greene, "From Resistance to Revolution." Reprinted with permission from the *Times Literary Supplement,* August 6, 1976, 971-72.

Max Savelle, "Nationalism and Other Loyalties in the American Revolution." Reprinted with permission from the *American Historical Review* 67 (July 1962), 901-7, portions of 908-23.

Rhys Isaac, "Dramatizing the Ideology of Revolution: Popular Mobilization in Virginia, 1774-1776." Reprinted with permission from the *William and Mary Quarterly* 91 (July 1976): 357-85.

Bernard Bailyn, "Political Experience and Enlightenment Ideas in Eighteenth-Century America." Reprinted with permission of the author from the *American Historical Review* 672 (January 1962), 339-51. Copyright Bernard Bailyn.

Winthrop Jordan, "Familial Politics: Thomas Paine and the Killing of the King, 1776." Reprinted with permission from the *Journal of American History* 60 (September 1973): 294-308.

Thomas C. Barrow, "The American Revolution as a Colonial War for Independence." Reprinted with permission of the author from the *William and Mary Quarterly* 83 (July 1968):452-64. Copyright Thomas Barrow.

This book was made possible in part by a grant from the Northwest Missouri State University Faculty Research Committee. Their help is gratefully acknowledged.

THE REVOLUTION THAT WASN'T

CONTRIBUTORS

Peter Amann
University of Michigan

Hannah Arendt

Bernard Bailyn
Harvard University

Thomas C. Barrow
Clark University

Robert Brown
Michigan State University

Harry Eckstein
Princeton University

Marc Egnal
York University

Joseph A. Ernst
York University

Richard M. Fulton
Northwest Missouri State University

Jack P. Greene
The Johns Hopkins University

Samuel P. Huntington
Harvard University

Rhys Isaac
La Trobe University

Winthrop Jordan
University of California, Berkeley

Max Savelle
University of Washington

Mavis B. Taintor
Citibank of New York

Claude Welch, Jr.
State University of New York,
    Buffalo

Gordon S. Wood
Brown University

Perez Zagorin
University of Rochester

Richard M. Fulton

INTRODUCTION

Most authors insist, whether out of psychological, intellectual, historical, or nationalistic motivation, upon perceiving the events of 1776 in America as a classic revolution. Academic conflict and stress might be greatly relieved and understanding might come more rapidly if there were to be a general recognition that the so-called American Revolution was really a struggle for socioeconomic, political, and psychological independence from the British imperial system—a colonial war of independence.

This is not to denigrate the event; indeed, the rationale used for separating from Britain and the historical documents that were produced remain important in the development of the Western mind and of man's political organization. For the first time a connection was forged between the theory of natural rights and the equality of all men on the one hand and political practice on the other. Revolution, however, was not the means.

The fundamental argument of this work, then, is that by 1763 the British colonies in America were so economically and politically mature that the contradiction between the legal and moral birthrights of British citizen-subjects and the second-class conditions of colonial status was apparent; and that by the end of the Seven Years' War (French and Indian War in North America) a significantly new political consensus had come to the British colonies so that "one can speak, not inaccurately, of the emergence by 1763 of an American civilization."[1] The inherent trade-offs accepted by settler colonials within the imperial system—psychic security and physical protection for dependency and economic tutelage—were no longer viable. The consequence of this fundamental division was a need to redefine the sovereign unit by way of revolt, a war for independence, and not a revolution. The context of the work, then, is the political scientist's view of the concept of revolution applied to the historic American case.

To substantiate this view of the American war for independence, we will search for a rational perception of the concept of revolution; discuss the interpretive historiography built around the so-called revolution; evaluate the Anglo-American war in relation to its revolutionary character, dealing first with potential long-term causes of revolution and then with the immediate precipitants of a potential revolutionary struggle; and then within the context of the accumulated evidence affirm that struggle as a war for independence.

There is little contemporary consensus on the precise usage or meaning of the term "revolution." Its classic political meaning comes from astrological roots—the concept to revolve implying the revolution of government and its institutions from one form to another within a relatively set framework of possibilities, as in the revolving of the heavens. The classic political emphasis was upon "restoring a just state of affairs." Aristotle, for example, postulated a typology of the one, the few, and the many with revolving ascendencies of forms of each type. Plato saw revolution in this classic sense of revolving forms of change in the context of a just but decaying utopian state.

Through Hobbes, Locke, and Rousseau came the idea of natural rights and popular sovereignty, and thus also the concept of wresting power from the ancien régime, which was founded upon limited sovereignty and divine right, in favor of a new regime based upon some form of popular sovereignty. Dramatic changes in modern violent revolutions were inevitable within institutions and within the relationship patterns between the government and the citizens that bound the fabric of the state. In this context "revolution" has become intertwined with socioeconomic and psychological change within the polity and not with structural and leadership interchange alone.

By intrinsically and directly linking the political with the social, economic, and even psychological characteristics of society, we complicated the definition of revolution. The fundamental problem has been differentiating from amongst a variety of phenomena all of which produce within a polity internal change in a relatively short time, usually with some accompanying violence or threat thereof. Because this broad concept of revolution can in fact encompass coups, rebellions, peasant revolts, mob violence, nativism, wars of independence, secession movements, or combinations of these, "the main feature that may be noted about much of the theoretical analysis of revolutions is its thinness and triviality."[2] Indeed, some writers prefer to establish rebellion as the generic historic force, leaving revolution as merely one of the species.[3] Substituting "rebellion" for "revolution" is hardly a cure for a conceptual problem. Others, perhaps with more foresight, have perceived revolution as a possible consequence of a lesser phenomenon like a rebellion (defined as any violent attempt to overthrow the government) which has produced "substantial social change."[4] Rebellion can lead to revolution, which, frustratingly, can profitably be identified only after the fact.

The broader picture shows a continuum of contemporary usages of the term "revolution" that goes from the *strict constructionists*, who define revolution solely in terms of significant and deep societal change, to the *loose constructionists*, who perceive any nonsystemic change within the polity as a revolution. The strict pole perceives a specific term with finite characteristics defining limited historical cases; the loose pole provides a generic term for nearly any challenge to constitutional legitimacy.

Representative of the hard-line strict constructionists are such writers as Samuel P. Huntington, Barrington Moore, Karl Marx in his theoretical works, Claude Welch, Jr. and Mavis B. Taintor, and Mark Hagopian.[5] Representative loose constructionists include Harry Eckstein, Chalmers Johnson, Alexander Groth, and a host of others.[6]

Huntington perceives revolution as a fundamental change in society: "A revolution is a rapid, fundamental, and violent domestic change in the dominant values and myths of a society, in its political institutions, social structure, leadership, and government activity and policies."[7] This hard-line insistence upon change in values, myths, institutions, structures, and leadership as well as in government leaves us a legacy of precious few successful revolutions. Its strictness distinguishes the classic revolutions of France, Russia, and perhaps those of China and Cuba from all other systemic change. For Huntington revolutions are "historically limited phenomena" connected to the contemporary (occurring in the last two hundred years) processes of modernization.

Hagopian, less insistent upon change across the board, will allow for fundamental change in only one of the areas of stratification. He calls revolution "an acute, prolonged crisis in one or more of the traditional systems of stratification (class, status, power) of a political community, which involves a purposive, elite-directed attempt to abolish or to reconstruct one or more of said systems by means of an intensification of political power and recourse to violence."[8] We might conjecture that surely change in one, however, will eventuate in further change sooner or later. He still excludes limited change represented by coups, rebellions, secessions, and the like. He would add the English Revolution to Huntington's list.

Marx, of course, prescribes a revolution arising out of the historical dialectic that produces a proletarian attack upon a collapsing bourgeoisie, the capitalist infrastructure. The resulting triumph of the proletariat creates the requisite fundamental change in the functioning of the entire society. Revolution is a specific event produced by specific historic forces, and it is inevitable.

Welch and Taintor see revolution primarily as a rapid tearing down of existing political institutions and a building anew on different foundations. They list four elements of a strictly defined revolution:

1. a change in the means of selecting political leaders, and the creation of new political elites, usually by extra-constitutional or non-systemic means;
2. new and expanded channels for access to positions of political power;
3. expanded political participation, possibly temporarily; and
4. the creation and solidification of a new political order on a different basis of political legitimacy.[9]

Many contemporary writers confuse the root word "revolve" with the term "revolt." Perceiving "revolt" as the root, they find "revolution" in almost any simple opposition to authority. For these loose constructionists revolution is "any resort to violence within a political order to change its constitution, rulers, or policies."[10] Chalmers Johnson in his classic work favors this generic approach. He perceives revolution as violence directed at one or more of the following goals: a change of government; a change of regime; a change of a society. Johnson then wants to subdivide these generic revolutionary phenomena into peasant outbreaks, rebellions, and coups as well as "great revolutions" which lead to far-reaching change (a category the hard liners would take for the exclusive use of the term). Wherever there is a lack of harmony between the social and political systems (multiple dysfunction), there is revolution.[11] Johnson's overall viewpoint is quite valuable in its concentration on the social system as a barometer of political problems, but its broad definition of "revolution" merely subdivides the term rather than helping to produce a useful concept that is inclusive and precise and that provides an element of predictability (the prerequisites of good scientific usage).

It would seem obvious that the events of 1776 can be called a revolution if the term is loosely construed to include many categories of non-systemic change; the question is whether or not the American case can qualify as a strictly defined classic or great revolution. Although no one argues that the event was not at least a rebellion in the form of a war for independence, some specifically argue that it definitely was not a "great revolution."[12]

In the modern world the term "revolution" satisfies the psychological demand to identify so-called great accomplishments in politics, technical achievements, social mores, even product development and merchandising. Thus it is that any change in political status must be called revolutionary to be legitimate in the eyes of political activists, their constituents, and, they hope, their posterity. Certainly the American War of Independence provided significant achievements in democratic theory, in political organization and subsequent power and prestige, and in pragmatic utilization of the concepts of natural rights and liberty. Could such results be accomplished by anything less than a full-fledged revolution? Not in the minds of most Americans—scholar and citizen alike.

This simple psychological need is strikingly demonstrated by American political scholars' nearly wholesale acceptance of Hannah Arendt's rationale. At base, Arendt has conceptualized revolution from its singular ability to produce a specific end result, freedom understood as political participation. This neat philosophic packaging reinforces that basic need to aggrandize the American experience,[13] yet Arendt's concept "is narrow and tendentious because it defines revolution in terms of certain moral values."[14] It is narrow not in its definition of revolution but in its predetermined value content. An anomaly among our polar definitions, it is a philosophical approach. Arendt in effect defines revolution to fit but one successful situation—the American one. However, to insist as she does upon republican values as a moral base to sustain a revolution is to subvert the substantial research that portrays real events of substantial dislocation, change, and upheaval like the French, Russian, Chinese, Cuban, and perhaps the Mexican revolutions and to reduce them to mere rebellions against socioeconomic conditions.

We should examine the Anglo-American war of 1776, then, not as a revolution simply because it had nonsystemic change accompanied by violence; nor because it produced (or maintained) a republican form of government; it meets these criteria all too easily. Rather it must be evaluated as a fundamental change in the dominant values and myths of the society accompanied by a purposive, elite-directed attempt to abolish or reconstruct one or more of the traditional systems of stratification (class, status, power) by means of violence. That is to say, we must at the very least accept as useful only the strictly construed definition of revolution. To do otherwise would be like calling all volatile substances dynamite simply because they can create explosive destruction.

Most historians identify the Anglo-American conflict of 1775-1784 as the American Revolution whether they believe it to be revolutionary or not; and naturally enough, historians provide several approaches to the interpretation of the event. However, there are two basic schools: the Progressives, who view the revolution as a consequence of internal strife with social and economic causations; and the neo-Whigs (or conservatives) who perceive it to be a political struggle of ideas and principles, a constitutional conflict for liberty by united colonials against colonial imperialism.

The neo-Whigs see a conflict caused by British oppression—an external cause; the Progressives view a dual conflict: Americans fought for independence from British rule, and simultaneously "unenfranchised and underprivileged lower classes wrested democratic rights from a privileged local aristocracy."[15] In the political scientist's terms, the neo-Whigs perceive the events as a war of independence fought against an external foe, notwithstanding their propensity to give credence to revolutionary rhetoric and argumentation for the idea of liberty as sufficient ground to identify revolution: "For them as for nineteenth-century interpreters, the fight was over constitutional principles expressed in the rhetoric of the period and they minimalize the internal divisions among the people."[16]

The Progressives lean much more heavily towards the view that "there was a real revolution in America, and that it was a painful conflict, in which many were injured."[17] They hold that "the significant story of the Revolution was found more in the internal conflict of social classes based upon economic power than in the external struggle with England."[18]

There are problems both within and between these two general views, however. While many of the Progressives' assumptions seem to have been shattered by thorough research since 1945, there remain champions of the "class conflict" view[19] who rely on the good data supporting social and economic causation.[20] The interpretations of the neo-Whigs, on the other hand, leave most of this substantive data on socioeconomic dislocation unanswered and ignore the Tory sentiment in 20 percent of the populace. Clearly, there is enough specific data substantiating at least parts of both basic approaches to keep the controversy very much alive. Perhaps, as Gordon Wood has argued, new intellectual historians and old Progressives should synthesize an interpretation of the war that accepts the basic growth of social classes and also puts the conflicts that flowed from this within the political context.[21]

If our interpretation of the events of 1776 is to be upheld, then the Progressives must be proven fundamentally incorrect. Yet this does not mean that the neo-Whigs must be accepted wholeheartedly. Class conflict and social dislocation accompany many types of socially dysfunctiona?

activity, from simple coups to international war; it can well accompany a rebellion against colonial rule. The question must be whether the causes of the Anglo-American conflict were primarily external (a war of colonial secession) or internal (a revolutionary change of social-political values and myths); and if internal whether they were sufficient to produce what could be called a revolution.

What, then, happened in America? To explain the events, we need to investigate first the long-term preconditions for revolution in the colonies and then the immediate precipitants of the events of 1775-76 that culminated in the Declaration of Independence and stimulated the war that is too easily called the American Revolution. While we will examine what historians usually discuss under the heading of "causes" of the Revolution, our goal will be the political one of evaluating its revolutionary character.

Long-term developments in several areas could contribute to genuine revolution: economic growth, technological and scientific advances, secularization, formation of a modern state, nationalism, and democratization.[22] In the American case a strong argument can be made that historical developments in most of these areas contributed not to dysfunctional conflict but to the fusion of a relatively egalitarian society based on consensus (à la the neo-Whig arguments) and founded upon, for most, a common English heritage distinguished from that of the motherland by geographic isolation, the frontier, the lack of an aristocratic class, and imperial tensions. With this in mind we shall briefly scan these long-term potential causes of revolution in the American context. Given the disruptive potential of each of these categories of historic development, it is prudent to judge well how these developments affected America in the seventeenth and eighteenth centuries up to the 1760s.

Most historians would agree that America saw the gradual *growth of a strong economic system* through the seventeenth and the first half of the eighteenth centuries. Economic growth was especially strong beginning in the 1720s; the expansion between 1745 and 1775 was unprecedented. Irving Kristol notes that this growth produced the most prosperous people on earth,[23] and Hannah Arendt uses it as a key argument to substantiate her view of the unique formation of the American democratic society. Until the end of the French and Indian War, this growth was not much hampered by British mercantile laws. Enacted in response to a successful industry or trade that had been initiated by private citizens, these laws often suppressed profitable colonial industry, but they were not strictly enforced and they often encouraged other colonial industry. After 1763 the situation was to change: existing laws were more strictly enforced and new ones were passed; long-term attitudes may well have been affected by this abrupt change. Further, while there is some argument over the fact, the relative availability of land probably contributed to the steady economic growth of the colonies.

If these bullish long-term economic preconditions were to arouse a pattern of expectations that were then frustrated by conditions and British policy after 1763—and particularly in the 1770s—some theorists indicate that the scene could be set for political activity. This so-called revolutionary gap between rising expectations and frustrated achievement could quickly become a precipitant for political change: this is the J-curve theory.[24]

Technical and scientific developments in the eighteenth century produced the industrial revolution in England (the beginning usually placed arbitrarily at 1760) and the explosion of scientific thought and methodology of the Enlightenment. Developments in England, especially laws protective of industry, surely affected the colonies, and it is clear that educated colonists were as aware of science and its development as were their European counterparts.[25] For a variety of reasons—the frontier, geographic limitations, the mercantile system—these movements took more pragmatic forms in the New World, for tasks were immediately at hand and there was room for initiative. Technology was applied directly to economic problems. Preconditions for societal change were thus present, but there was no dramatic incentive for change.

Although religion had always played a significant role in the colonies, in governmental terms America had for some time been significantly more *secularized* than most of the rest of the world. From the very beginning religious pluralism had encouraged differentiation between the religious and the secular in most of the colonies. Although some colonies maintained connections between church and state even after the 1770s, these connections were more formal than real. In addition, the Great Awakening in the 1740s tended to encourage individualized religion rather than to support established religious institutions.

The colonists' possible belief that the Church of England was a manifestation of an active British conspiracy against liberty, as Bernard Bailyn theorizes,[26] also promoted secularization. The Anglican church was using its Society for the Propagation of the Gospel to convert not the pagan Indians and Negroes, its stated targets, but the nonconformists, the latter believed. For example, there were missions in places like Cambridge, Massachusetts, where not a single Indian had resided since the seventeenth century. The secularization process is documented by the end results—a complete separation of church and state in the federal constitution of 1787 and consequent disestablishment of the remaining state relationships shortly thereafter. Religion was thus secularized by adaptation to the social environment, but this was a long-term process and, like scientific developments, not a dramatic precipitant of change.

The *development of the modern state* in the colonies can best be illustrated by the growth of strong governmental institutions. Because the colonies had grown from settlements, local governance had always been strong, but the dominance of colonial structures hampered the growth of indigenous centralized structures. Until the 1770s executive power was greater everywhere in the colonies (except in Rhode Island and Connecticut) than it was in England itself. Governors could and did veto colonial legislation, which no English monarch had done since Queen Anne in 1707, and sometimes they prorogued and dissolved the lower house of assembly. Furthermore, the colonial executive had a power over the judiciary which was denied even to the crown—the dismissal of judges. More pragmatically, executive power could be used to control the politics of the colonies through patronage systems that often became hereditary. Obviously, these trends are part of what the Progressives point to when they discuss the growth of socioeconomic elites in the colonies.

Even given these relatively strong executive powers, however, indigenous legislatures did prosper, for the British Parliament neglected to provide the local governors with sufficiently flexible guidelines and support to compete with the influence of the local notables who populated the legislatures. By the mid-eighteenth century the local assemblies checked the colonial governors in the exercise of their powers and even in the effect of their patronage. This was the most signficant political and constitutional development in the colonies prior to independence. By 1763 the lower houses of Rhode Island and Connecticut had virtually complete authority, while those in Pennsylvania and Massachusetts were almost as powerful. The others were virtually equal in power with the governor and the council.[27] Is it any wonder that most of these legislative bodies felt themselves appendages to the House of Commons? Clearly, these self-governing institutions and the economic-philosophic baggage that accompanied them provided, by the 1760s, a mature society fully qualified for nationhood. "In effect by 1760 self-government in America, while still incomplete, had gone far."[28] These trends undercut a significant base for political revolution in 1776, for by then the local units already possessed important powers. The only point left is whether or not there was a local elite that controlled the system and was displaced in 1776.

Modern *nationalism* followed closely behind the building of the state socially, economically, and politically. Over a century and a half of prosperous development in all these areas accompanied by benign neglect from England inevitably fostered a feeling of separate identification within the hearts and minds of the colonists. While ostensibly parochial in the earlier periods, the colonials began in the 1760s and 1770s to perceive themselves as separate and unique, whether there was a growing Whig elite that fostered powerful local economic and political institutions, as the Progressive hard liners hold, or a broader egalitarian society of virtual social equals, as seen by the neo-Whigs. American patriotism was growing well before the idea of independence became viable. Note the prerevolutionary poem "The Rising Glory of America" and the sermons of Samual Davies and Jonathan Mayhew. Rossiter could write, "The colonial mind was growing steadily less English and more American."[29] It would still take the crisis of the 1770s to galvanize the united nationalism of the thirteen colonies, but over a hundred years of separate development and relative isolation from England had taken their toll. Is it revolution to recognize the fact of nationalism?

The neo-Whigs and the Progressives differ on the degree of *democratization* that took place. Certainly participation in the political process was limited even amongst the free, white population, but the process of broadening participation differed in each colony. There was probably an egalitarian aspect to the early colonial period, but social cohesion may possibly have eroded between 1690 and 1760. The waters remain muddied on the point.

If Merrill Jensen claims that by the mid-eighteenth century the colonies were politically controlled by a Whig elite allied politically, economically, or consanguineously,[30] then Bernard Bailyn will say that by the early 1700s every colony had representative assemblies elected under more or less popular suffrage.[31] Perhaps the truth lies, as it often does, somewhere in the middle. Jackson Main has written, "few colonials in British North America believed in a government by the people, and . . . they were content to be ruled by local elites."[32] Yet most people—and here is the basis for a probably growing consensus in the colonies—believed in a somewhat broadened Whig view of democracy, i.e., wide nominal participation within a context of individual liberties and limited government. Everyone maintained the rights of Englishmen, and everyone believed in a degree of participation, but most believed that men of substance should probably be the actual representatives. Social strain there may well have been—though the specifics were drastically different in each colony—but the consensus was based on expectations of citizen participation and the protection of natural rights—not on specified egalitarian views of democratic structures that might provide a philosophic base for class or sociological conflict that might lead to revolution.

All this evidence could point to a possible dysfunctional break with Great Britain, a colonial war of independence, but on these bases it was not inevitable. Clearly, the colonies were maturing independently of, though not outside the traditions of, Great Britain. Although there is evidence of socioeconomic dislocation and change, evidence for the seeds of a hard-line revolution seems thin. Consensus and relative egalitarianism based on common views of the New World society predominated within a system of relative prosperity. There were no socioeconomic gaps like those symptomatic of the Russian and French societies prior to their revolutions, no dramatic rises and sudden dips in fortunes or expectations. Only within the slave population could we begin to find blatant long-term causes for classic revolution from within North American society.

Rather, the internal situation probably was one of gathering consensus about colonial identity. Even though internal divisions were many and great, they fell well within the pattern of a maturing polity. As Thomas Barrow put it, "A firm basis for unity obviously existed within American society, which, naturally, suggests the reverse, too, was true—that such tensions and divisions as did exist within American society were relatively minor and harmless."[33]

Long-term external causes for revolution seem stronger, although the British imperial system was applied to the colonies only intermittently until after 1763; but the American economy was outgrowing imperial restraints, colonial institutions were achieving self-sufficiency and autonomy, and secularization had progressed more significantly than in Europe. In short, the state was growing but was also feeling the newly heavy hand of England.

The Progressive scholars demonstrate that national maturation necessitated internal colonial adjustments; however, these adjustments did not find, within the white community at least, a focus in class polarization, dramatic economic disparity, nor ingrained social gaps. Indeed, most historians emphasize the relative classlessness and socioeconomic fluidity, particularly in contrast to reasonable contemporary expectations and practice in Europe.

Short-term causes of revolution are the precipitants of the actual events. Therefore evidence of a strictly defined American Revolution must be found within the years following the French and Indian War of 1763 and particularly between 1774 and 1776, directly preceding the break with Great Britain. Neo-Whig historians concentrate on the constitutional issues that grew in this period in conjunction with the long-term trends towards nationalism and nation building in the colonies to explain the independence movement. They see a growing consensus that American identity was unique. While this reasoning seems fundamentally correct, it falls short of a full explanation. The Progressives have illuminated the socioeconomic basis for many of these issues, which often had internal consequences; they should not be ignored.

1763-1772

At the close of the great war in 1763, Great Britain found herself the center of an expanded empire. She also found herself in financial trouble. It seemed logical to assume that since America benefited so from the war she should help pay for it—or at least help defray costs that were the result of that war. George Grenville, who took office after the war and stayed until 1765, articulated British policies and attitudes that were to persist to the end. The Revenue Act ("Sugar Act") of 1764, the Currency Act of 1764, the Stamp Act of 1765, and the Quartering Act of 1765 as well as the Royal Proclamation of 1763 closing the western frontier all illustrated the new British approach. Parliament chose economic measures supporting these policies to reassert its authority over the colonies. The colonists were shocked and dismayed, particularly the northern merchants and the southern land speculators. Under decades of benign neglect the colonies had formed a view of themselves as equal Englishmen under basically local control. For Parliament to suddenly assert its powers was a rude awakening. If the years before the 1760s in British North America could be characterized by a loose general consensus built upon common citizenship within the empire, the approximate period from 1763 to 1772 became a time of increased constitutional questioning of the relationship of colony and Parliament; the motivations were often economic and self-serving. In the end virtually everyone joined a new, more definite consensus built upon feelings of incipient nationalism and centered on the relationship of the colonies to the Parliament. The consensus was rooted not yet in rebellion but in defiance of an unreasonable government with errant policies. The only significant dissenters over contemporary politics and the rights of British citizens were the colonial agents and a few ardent Tories. (See chart.) This discontent was focused particularly upon the measures of Parliament listed above. Active politics was aimed at the policies of the government, the British Parliament, and colonial acts.

It is instructive to note that until 1775 little mention is made of the culpability in these measures of the king—the head of state, the seat of legitimacy, the focus of loyalty. The conflict was between the British political leadership and the citizenry of a particular constituency, the American colonies. Because of the imperial nature of this constituency, however, the discussion inevitably turned to the constitutional relationships that heretofore were assumed to be adequate. Between 1763 and

1772 political differences and economic discontent on both sides defined the arena of conflict that, when sharpened in focus, would lead to serious questions of the legitimacy of British parliamentary rule.

PRIOR TO 1763

Loose General Consensus
(Colonists as co-equal citizens within the empire)

1763-1772

90%	10%
Unifying Consensus	*Imperialists*
(Unity over the status of	(British officials, Tories,
colonies in re parliament)	portions of Whig elite)

1770-1774
Division within Consensus

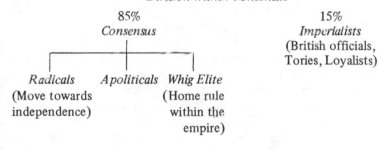

85%	15%
Consensus	*Imperialists*
	(British officials,
	Tories, Loyalists)

Radicals	*Apoliticals*	*Whig Elite*
(Move towards		(Home rule
independence)		within the
		empire)

1774-1776+
Hardened Consensus

50%-60%	20%-30%	20%
Consensus	*Apoliticals*	*Imperialists*
(Independence		(British officials,
radicals and		Tories, Loyalists,
Whigs)		home rule Whigs)

By 1770 opposition to Parliament had spread within most geographical areas and classes of people. Remedies for the most part were still sought in parliamentary policy. But Parliament would not understand, it was intractable, even compromises were laced with sour pills; it administered existing policies more strictly, renewed acts for revenue and punishment of boycotts, sent troops to support colonial regimes. Most colonists believed that all the colonies were in the same boat (though most reserved primary loyalty for their home colony), and a stronger consensus solidified over the need for a more equitable relationship with Parliament. This consensus, built upon the long-term forces of nationalism discussed earlier, solidified by the bitter realities of the post-1760 world, was never to falter; it was the foundation of all that was to come, the magnet that continually drew the colonists together regardless of more specific differences in outlook, economic condition, and policy.

Within the consensus, however, there was divergence on the means to achieve self-determination. In the 1760s and early 1770s most wanted to follow the Whig elite in demanding some sort of home rule or some degree of autonomy within the empire. They wanted to be left alone to run their affairs through the homegrown assemblies with help and guidance but not significant interference from the imperial governors. The Whig elite were comfortable within their system of limited republicanism. Most colonists, even the non-English, perceived themselves to have the rights of British citizenry, protected within the framework of general control by the merchants, landowners, and planters who were the Whig political elite in the colonies.

As early as the 1760s, of course, there were radicals calling for more drastic measures to counter the British attacks on American liberties, but these men were few and only intermittently did they make a serious impact upon the conflict. They were continually pushing, though—especially men like Samuel Adams in Boston.

The longer the conflict continued without satisfactory resolution, the more deeply and extensively rooted grew the general consensus and the more rational became the appeals of the radicals. Independence was barely uttered in political tracts in the 1760s even by the radicals, for that was treason; but their arguments moved closer to it by the early 1770s. The radicals' tools were increasingly successful, especially boycotts of British goods. Local committees kept their communities informed and enforced boycotts. The radicals (and increasing numbers of moderates) set up Committees of Correspondence throughout the colonies, formally initiated in Massachusetts in 1772. The Whig elite supported much of this agitation, but feeling strongly that mobs should not rule, they became increasingly wary of mobilizing numbers of people. Mobs, of course, were early tools against acts of the British government. Citizen groups in some areas were even chastising the local Whig elite for breaking boycotts or for flagging in loyalty to what was beginning to be perceived as their cause. Worst of all was the possibility of mob action against British officials. That scared even John Adams, whose view of democracy was, "The people must constitute government; they need not actually run government."[34]

By 1770, then, the general consensus had within it a majority who wanted to work for reconciliation through constitutional adjustments and a minority of radicals trying to force the issues as far and as fast as possible. Neither faction was very cohesive.

1772-1774

By 1773 when Lord North became head of the British government there had been a lull in the conflict for about three years. It seemed to be a balancing point. Could some compromise be forged that would satisfy the bulk of the colonists and a hard-pressed Parliament? Lord North sincerely hoped so. An America fundamentally committed to the British system and basically unified in its loyalty to the empire but also to a concept of coequal status as British citizens and dependents was ready to accommodate itself to England. But Parliament was to err again. It pushed too hard for subservience. The Tea Act of May 16, 1773, and then the acts known as the Intolerable Acts upset the balance. The British tried to bail out a financially troubled East India Company at the expense of the Americans. American merchants cried, "Monopoly," and the radicals took up the chant. Moderates and radicals were beginning to sound alike. The Boston Tea Party was symbolic of American resistance. Lord North responded by closing Boston harbor, a shocking demonstration of the deterioration of relationships between colony and British government. The quarrel became an open break characterized by defiance on one side and coercion on the other. For the first time the radicals, who became even bolder, and the moderates, who perceived that their economic base was being undermined by arbitrary British policy, had a common interest. Economic and constitutional issues had merged; the crisis had begun.

Reactions to the Intolerable Acts were varied, but the radicals and a growing number of moderates in all the colonies were outraged enough to call for a congress to deal with the problem in a united way. Newspapers blossomed as they had not for five years. The general theme was some form of home rule within the empire: "Jefferson argued (in *A Summary View of the Rights of British America*) that the power exercised by parliament over the colonies was a 'usurped' power, that the British Empire consisted of separate 'states' with equal and independent legislatures, united only by the crown and that the Americans were a free people."[35] He went further than most were ready to go in 1773, but his views pointed the way.

The split within the earlier consensus manifested itself more forcefully at the First Continental Congress and was to persist until the victory of the radicals in 1776. (See chart.) On the one hand were the radicals or "popular leaders," who represented the push for strenuous opposition to British policy and for serious remedies to the constitutional status quo. The opposition to the radicals' probably minority initiative were the Whig elite, who opposed British policy but wanted the door left open for reconciliation. The Tories were not represented at the Congress and were on the defensive everywhere, harassed by local committees of citizens and unprotected in most localities by a slowly disintegrating colonial administration.

The radicals or popular leaders dominated the first Congress and forced the adoption of the Acts of Association by Congress. In effect the Congress laid the groundwork for the eventual break by authorizing extra-legal bodies to check the colonial governments. The decision for independence seems to have been sealed here, but there was still great division within the American people as to the correct course of action. Many feared war or economic ruin.

Arguments deepened, though still within a general agreement over the American position. The split remained between those calling for radical opposition to British policy (even to the use of force) and those who counseled care, still hoping for a plan of reconciliation that would ensure home rule within the empire. The British, however, continued policies that made this moderate position increasingly untenable.

1774-1776

The period 1774-76 was crucial to the anti-British movement. For those who call the events a revolution, it represents the transition from the imperial colonial administration to government by American bodies. The call by Congress for a series of local committees increased enthusiasm for the cause, and the slow disintegration of central colonial authority transferred real power to local entities and colonial assemblies and there was a surge of local democratic participatory governance.

Each colony had its own variation on the process. By and large, however, at least temporarily new leadership replaced even the old reluctant Whig elite. There was broad citizen support of the localized committees that policed the boycotts, secured support for the anti-British movement, and even provided militia to counter British troops. The committees had become the local government, sometimes rather independently, sometimes in coordination with state assemblies. By the time enthusiasm reached a peak after Lexington and Concord (1775), the radicals had produced throughout the colonies a network of support based upon the local committees and broad public concurrence, which was encouraged by pamphlets and newspapers. Further, they had enlisted the support of many moderates.

In some colonies democratization produced a new leadership that would predominate until after the constitutional period. This was especially the case in Pennsylvania, where radicals seized control in 1775-76 and dominated until 1790. In other colonies the extensive localized democratic surge could not be sustained past 1774-75. By late 1776 in North Carolina, for example, "with the complexity and scope, and sheer number of problems demanding public attention, the county committees seem to have withered away."[36] A North Carolina provincial government was instituted formally in December, 1776, and it assumed most of the responsibilities held since 1774 by the local county committees. Most colonies were to follow a road more akin to the North Carolina experience than to that of Pennsylvania. In some areas the conservative Whig elite or even Tories maintained control well into the war.

Pennsylvania's constitution of 1776 was more democratic (participatory) in its provisions, the state convention being dominated by radicals, than that of North Carolina, where moderates provided key leadership again; but both documents reflect philosophies and structures well within the Anglo-American political tradition. That is, neither was revolutionary in its socioeconomic or political effects. Indeed, the Pennsylvania constitution that brought new constituencies into the active political arena was flexible enough to allow for the continued participation of moderates. Their resurgence in 1790 even tempered the ultrademocratic elements of the constitution. Was there revolution in 1774-76 and counterrevolution in 1790 in Pennsylvania and in other places by implication? Hardly. There was domestic change brought about by the emerging war for independence but no change in the dominant values or myths of the society, no class, status, or power reconstruction of any fundamental nature. There was only a shift in power from one faction to another—well within the bounds of domestic political differentiation. The question involved loyalty to the empire—a question of nationalism and pragmatic remedies rather than socioeconomic condition.

Even with the collapse of colonial government and the assumption of power by colonial assemblies, local entities, and the Continental Congress, as late as 1775 there was still no clear call for independence. John Adams denied vociferously in *Novanglus* (February 13, 1775) that his aim was independence. Independence probably was his aim, but evidently the public was still not ready for the break. Moderates still restrained the call for independence.

Thomas Paine saw the stumbling block to the call for independence more clearly. His *Common Sense* raised the call for independence in such a way as to make it seem rational and reasonable, even inevitable, to a majority of politically active Americans, moderates as well as radicals. The mechanism was simple. The final step was to transfer anti-British sentiment from Parliament alone and government itself (which kept the argument within the fragile bounds of legitimacy) to the king—a break with the symbol of legitimacy and of loyalty to the imperial state itself. To argue for rights in relation to the government and Parliament is still politics, albeit radical in this case; to attack the king in the context of home rule and liberty is one step beyond: it is treason.

The themes that raced through public discussion in 1775 and 1776 were heartfelt. People felt:

an utmost necessity for union among the colonies;

that the British government had mounted a conspiracy to deprive American colonials of their rights;

that Great Britain and especially the British government was steeped in corruption and degeneracy;

that Americans were truly threatened with outright enslavement.[37]

Yet most historians agree that "the Americans were not an oppressed people; they had no crushing imperial shackles to throw off. In fact, the Americans knew they were probably freer and less burdened with cumbersome feudal and monarchical restraints than any part of mankind in the eighteenth century."[38] The Progressives argue that socioeconomic causes elicited excessive, self-serving rhetoric. The neo-Whigs argue that the constitutional issues fanned the flames of emotions. Perhaps socioeconomic conditions, the long-term growth of nationalism, and the immediate precipitant, the Intolerable Acts, caused the colonists to believe that Britain was tyrannical and that they had to fight for freedom. The propaganda perhaps reflected what the radicals and then the moderates had convinced themselves were real situations: "Their repeated overstatements of reality, their incessant talk of 'tyranny' when there seems to have been no real oppression, their obsession with virtue, luxury, and 'corruption' their devotion to 'liberty' and 'equality'—all these notions were neither manipulated propaganda nor borrowed empty abstractions, but ideas with real personal and social significance for those who used them."[39]

The final straw was Paine's denunciation of the throne itself. Everyone read it. From January to March, 1776, at least two hundred thousand copies were sold; three to four times as many people surely read it. With a population of 2.5 million that left few adults who did not come into contact with *Common Sense* in early 1776,[40] and the majority of politicized Americans responded.

The line had been crossed. Support was sufficient for the Declaration of Independence at last. For the first time the colonists had answered affirmatively to a clear, broad call for independence. The moderates were forced to accept the inevitability of the struggle, and the radicals found their views vindicated. The apolitical, of course, remained neutral to the end but the conflict had been squarely joined.

The break with the empire demanded even stronger consensus in the colonies, and most of those who sought self-determination did support independence. In the end, however, about 20 percent of the white population felt the tug of the homeland, the legitimacy of the empire; they remained loyal, many reluctantly. An equal number, perhaps more, remained apolitical or neutral. Thus the majority of Americans were swept actively or passively into the struggle for independence. It must be noted, however, that many of the loyalists continued to work for and believe in home rule for America even if they opposed independence as illegitimate and rash.

These precipitating events immediately preceded the struggle, but its causes had accumulated during at least the previous decade. There had been no mechanism to stop what Grenville and North had begun, and later events seemed to have their own momentum. These precipitant events of 1774-76 did not include socioeconomic conflict. Although some of the Tory elite were perceived as being of a separate social status and were a target for some violence, most of these were dependent families—bureaucrats, officials, and protected merchants—greatly reliant upon direct connections to the British imperial government. They were agents of its external force. There were some loyalist well-to-do Whigs who held privileged positions in the local hierarchy or under the imperial arrangements, but what distinguished loyalty to Britain from responsiveness to the call for independence was not socioeconomic status. Most backed the independence movement, and some of the middle class and poor remained loyal to Britain.

The focus of the conflict was external control—the need for a separate American identity, the reality of separate development in the New World, the desire for independence and self-defined freedom; these were the causes of colonial unrest. The immediate trigger for the war of 1776-83 was political reaction to acts of Parliament, but many Americans had long felt the necessity for self-determination.

The American colonies found themselves after 1763 relatively free of threats from foreign powers and Indians (with some exceptions on the

frontiers, e.g., Georgia); increasingly stifled by Britain's economic dominance of the growing market economy, and unable to accept the reemergence
of British active political involvement and military presence in colonial
affairs resulting from the Parliament's new pay-as-you-go policy towards
the colonies. The costs had grown too high, the benefits no longer
sufficient. The closing of the frontier rubbed salt into the wounds.

The real benefits of empire had diminished, especially for the older
colonies. Political and geopolitical opportunities were being limited by
British policy, not expanded as was the general case before 1763. Trade
policies limited a healthy economy that was capable of initiating its own
full cycle of economic development. The colonists had come to expect
full political representation as the right of free men (especially free
Englishmen); thus limits placed by virtual representation in Parliament,
symbolic and substantive heavier taxation, colonial governors with their
continuing (at least in theory) significant powers, and the increased use
of the British army (and worse, German mercenaries) to check the exercise of the colonies' independent options became increasingly intolerable.

Americans perceived the options of freedom and tyranny, but did they
perceive that the remedy would include significant changes in the myths
and values of their society, a readjustment of the system of class, status,
or power stratification? Were they trying to turn the world upside down
or merely to kick out the British imperial system?

The argument then is that an American society that had outgrown
its need for external patronage and dominance threw off the protective overlayer of British imperial rule. Internal social stratification of
power, status, and class changed only to accommodate the loss of the
appendages of the imperial government and its sympathizers. The process
was devastating to individuals; it dislocated the normal flow of events
and processes. In the end, however, the first modern war for independence
was won. But it was not the first modern revolution.

This is not to say that there were no elements of revolution within
the rebellion. The American case is not only negative in response to Welch
and Taintor's four aspects of political revolution. The Anglo-American
conflict produced several incipient aspects of revolution, if not revolution
itself. As a conclusion let us look at these four aspects of revolution—
strict-constructionist revolution—and briefly evaluate the Anglo-American
war in light of our fundamental question: is it a revolution or a revolution
that never was?

Criterion number one concerns change in the means of selecting leaders
and the creation of a new political elite. The Americans found extra-
constitutional methods to expel the imperial leadership, but there was no
basic change in the internal system for creation of leadership nor in its

overall character. Local and state processes changed little when constitutions were created as a result of the independence movement. Imperial executives were replaced with elected ones, but the system of politics was adjusted structurally in minor ways only; substantively it was adjusted somewhat in scope but not in form. Many of the loyalist Whig elite left the country, but many stayed, and some reasserted their claims to local prominence. External forces were removed, while internal political dynamics developed in adjustment to the removal of the external force. The means of selecting leaders changed hardly at all for the legislatures and the judiciaries and, indeed, for the more informal leadership roles of the community.

New leaders were inevitably created. Yet a surprisingly large segment of the preindependence leadership maintained itself after the war. The war itself brought dislocation and some socioeconomic mobility. Most of this was well within the parameters of the myths and values of social and political continuity that had grown in the New World. The only real nonsystemic change came within the top crust of imperial officialdom. The rebellion removed all except those unrehabilitated loyalists who stuck with the British even in defeat, and even these removed themselves from the new state and thus from any calculations of new leadership. This means that some communities lost their sociopolitical leaders; however, others easily took their places.

Republicanism became official, though it had been a de facto force in the colonies for some time. Some new people rose to leadership, but no new class of people.

The second criterion is that new and expanded channels for access to positions of political power are to be created. Since there was little change in the process for leadership selection in the colonies, there was little change in the structural access to political power. Radical politics did expand political access to power somewhat. Any dysfunctional change provides some increased channels for political input merely because it shakes the system. This happened with remarkably frugal results. Again, leadership remained in the hands of the stable, middle class radicals and those Whigs who were for independence. Even where expanded participation involved others, their stay tended to be short and their effects moderate and generally compatible with the group.

The Progressive historians have given unmistakable evidence for revolutionary activity in this category. There were localized mass mobilizations that do smack of hard-line change. In the end, however, and usually without much hesitation, these tendencies were overwhelmed by moderate and even conservative majorities. The fight was for full British rights, even at the price of leaving the British empire, but for *British* rights universalized. The radical egalitarians were to assert themselves periodically—Shay's Rebellion being a good example of their staying power—but they were not to hold center stage or to change the direction of the rebellion towards revolution. In fact, the fear of mob rule that they instilled in the dominant middle class strengthened the conservatives.

Criterion three is expanded political participation, possibly temporary. As is hinted above, this aspect of the revolt shows significant revolutionary content. As Hannah Arendt particularly argues, the American revolt produced a rush of popular action and participation and a loosening of the franchise. Particularly during 1774-76 there was great mobilization for the cause. The crucial point, however, is that the cause was a nationalist one— conflict with a perceived external enemy. The target of mobilization was not the internal system nor internally developed institutions and processes. On the contrary, the mobilization was meant to protect the internal system against a perceived threat to its continued free existence.

Expanded citizen participation was meant to preserve the system, not to tear down and replace it. Whenever that participation became too radical, the consensus within the movement took over to maintain moderate internal goals and leadership. One benefit of the rebellion was a somewhat more participatory system; it was a benefit of degree, however, not of basic change. Perhaps the Progressive can successfully argue that the rebellion changed most people's concept of democracy to include a more active role for themselves in affecting institutions and policies. In this sense of the development of participatory democracy as a foundation for a state, the rebellion did have revolutionary content. Still, the advance was merely developmental, it was not of a new political order. The revolt (or rebellion) was directed at self-determination at base and not at systemic change. If the concept of participatory democracy in a mass society was advanced as a result, so much the better.

Criterion four is creation and solidification of a new political order on a different basis of political legitimacy. As a result of the events of 1776-83, there was a change of political legitimacy in America. That change was in relation to an external source, not an internal one, and that is the difference between a war of independence and a strictly defined revolution. If an American entity was formed by 1763, then the fundamental legitimacy of British rights founded upon Enlightenment assumptions within a framework of homegrown republican institutions (legislative, judicial, and even to a degree executive) was not disturbed by the war with Britian. To look at the political order prior to independence and after is to see identical twins. Only the crown and its imperial appendages are missing. There were refinements of the system but not fundamental distortions. Some states had to change their constitutions scarce at all. Broadened participation was the most important change, and even this was relative rather than absolute.

The war for independence was fought to preserve a political system (or more accurately a series of thirteen similar systems) that grew within the bounds of a permissive empire—a system that under pressure of resurgent empirical control sought freedom from the imperial restrictions. If revolution is anything like "tearing down . . . existing political institutions and building them anew on different foundations,"[41] then the American experience was definitely not a revolution. The changes that throwing off British restraint brought were really opportunities to grow and to produce a mature national entity. Change came with release from the restrictive hand of British imperialism, not from the reformation of the body politic. Change came for the reasons independence was sought: lack of independence limited the psychological and physical growth and vitality of the New World. The War of Independence was successful precisely because it was not a revolution. The new entity survived because it had not lost the security of a well-founded internal system of socioeconomic and (mostly) political institutions developed and matured for a century on the foundation of a strong British heritage.

Part One

THE CONCEPT OF REVOLUTION

Understanding the concept of revolution has been a major endeavor of countless philosophers, historians, sociologists, political scientists, and other students of political phenomena. Agreement on what constitutes a revolution, its quantifiable characteristics, and its qualitative distinctions remains elusive. The readings in this section illustrate the three branches of scholarly investigation discussed in the introduction.

The loose constructionists are represented by Perez Zagorin's discussion of Chalmers Johnson's approach and then by Peter Amann's definition. Zagorin's article outlines historical thought on the concept of revolution and presents Johnson's "most useful" classic definition. While Johnson's definition is broad, it is specific in its delineation of a variety of violent phenomena that change government, regime, or society. Peter Amann says simply, "Revolution prevails when the state's monopoly of power is effectively challenged and persists until a monopoly of power is reestablished." Its lack of specificity is, of course, its problem.

The strict constructionists prefer a more specific definition which includes basic societal change. Samuel Huntington sees revolution as a recent development connected with the processes of modernization, a process which produces rapid fundamental changes in the "dominant values and myths of a society" as well as its institutions and politics. Claude Welch and Mavis Taintor provide more detailed means to identify revolutions and factors that precipitate them. These specifics might be useful to keep in mind when later chapters examine the particulars of the American experience.

Chapter 5 provides a portion of Hannah Arendt's widely influential ook On Revolution. It illustrates a philosophic view of revolutions per ived as mass mobilizations toward liberation and freedom based on ·ticipation.

Perez Zagorin

1 THEORIES OF REVOLUTION

Revolution has been the subject of investigation by philosophers and historians since almost the beginning of the Western intellectual tradition. Plato and Aristotle were the first to deal with revolution as a theoretical problem and Thucydides the first to give it reflective historical treatment. No one who reads it is likely to forget Thucydides' penetrating account of revolutionary psychology and the effects of class war upon the Greek states. It is highly critical of revolution, yet is, on the whole, the fruit of profound insight and detached observation. From the time of Thucydides to the eighteenth century, a succession of historians, most of them men of affairs who wrote on history and politics as an avocation or as the occupation of exile or retirement, have thrown fitful light upon revolution and civil war. To this company belong Sallust, Machiavelli, Commines, Davila, de Retz, Harrington, Clarendon, and Montesquieu, together with some other well or little known authors. It was not until the nineteenth and twentieth centuries, however, that revolution became one of the supreme and central preoccupations of historiography. Since the French Revolution, the volume of work devoted to various revolutions of the Western countries has increased enormously, while, more recently, interest has extended farther to include the revolutions of Asia and Africa as well.

The prominence that revolution has assumed in historical study is generally thought to be mainly due to the influence of revolutions themselves in shaping the modern world. This influence became powerful with the French Revolution, which both by its actual character and by mythologies it inspired, opened an era of profound change in hu affairs. In 1850, Alexis de Tocqueville, commented on the extent of the change:

> For sixty years we have been deceiving ourselves by imagining that we saw the end of the Revolution. It was supposed to be finished on the 18th Brumaire, and again in 1814; I myself thought in 1830, that it might be over when I saw that democracy, having in its march passed over and destroyed every other privilege, had stopped before the ancient and necessary privilege of property. I thought that, like the ocean, it had at last found its shore. I was wrong. It is now evident that the tide is rising, and that the sea is still enlarging its bed; that not only have we not seen the end of the stupendous revolution which began before our day, but that the infant just born will scarcely see it. Society is not in process of modification, but of transformation.[1]

These words were written more than a century ago, but who would say that they are no longer applicable? Although the revolution of which Tocqueville spoke has constantly assumed fresh forms, although it has metamorphosed into communist, fascist, racial, and colonial revolutions, the process that he recognized has nevertheless retained all of its dynamism.

During the last few years the word "revolution" has also been heard a great deal in the United States. The American postwar consensus, which some had imagined to be permanent, broke down in the 1960s. The so called "end of ideology," happily celebrated in the 1950s by many academic intellectuals, turned out to be an illusion. Various revolutionaries, both real and merely self-styled, came upon the scene, and in the angry babble of argument that followed the possibility of a revolution in the United States also began to be discussed for the first time since the 1930s.

A number of revolutions have recently proclaimed themselves in America: the black revolution, the student revolution, the women's revolution, and that miraculous occurrence prophesied by Professor Reich and known as Consciousness III or the youth revolution. There have been manifestations of a similar kind in Europe and Japan. The belief in the necessity of a redemptive revolution that will cleanse the advanced industrial world of its accumulated evils has taken root in various quarters. At the same time, significant developments have occurred also in revolutionary strategy. The teachings of Mao Tse-tung and General Giap have gained disciples in the West. Régis Debray's important book about Latin America, *Revolution in the Revolution?*, contains a rationale for the ideas of Castro and Guevara, which are intended to shake up the Communist parties, launch guerilla insurgencies, and thereby create revolutionary ations capable of bringing Communists to power.

Admittedly, much of what passes for revolution nowadays is only light-minded talk and frivolous posturing. Some of it, however, deserves to be taken seriously. Moreover, the increasing frequency of violent episodes of protest and repression has aroused questions about the stability of American institutions and their adaptiveness to peaceful change. Connected with this questioning has been a sudden outburst of writings and studies dealing with the causes of violence in America. Partly for the same reasons and partly because of the revolutionary challenges operating in the underdeveloped world, there has also been a marked revival of intellectual interest in the problem of revolution. Thus, revolutions, which the revolutionist Leon Trotsky called "the mad inspirations of history," have acquired a fresh pertinence. It is therefore worth seeing the place of revolution at present in the intellectual landscape of history and the social sciences.

To proceed, we must raise the important and controversial question of the definition of *revolution*, the source of considerable disagreement. A glance at the history of the word itself may provide us with some help in this matter. It still seems not to be generally realized that before the seventeenth century, *revolution* possessed quite different connotations from those associated with it today. The word was scarcely used at all in a political sense, but referred mainly to the circular motion of planets. During the seventeenth century it gradually acquired a political meaning also, but retained the idea of circularity. Thus, even as a political occurrence, *revolution* was understood merely as a synonym for the cycle of change in states, a cycle of turbulent ups and downs. The first rebellion of modern times widely called a revolution by its contemporaries was the English Revolution of 1688. Nevertheless, these same contemporaries, as well as many later writers, did their best to depict the revolution against James II as conforming to the circular model—as a "restoration," a "return" to a system of legality that had been violated by a tyrannical king. Accordingly, what is noticeably absent from the meaning of *revolution*, even at the end of the seventeenth century, is any connection with innovation and the inauguration of a new order. For the purposes of this discussion, let it suffice to say that after 1789, *revolution* vastly enlarged its reference. The upheaval in France infused the term with a new potency and made it a call to action, a shibboleth, a mystique. Marxism in due course reinforced this significance. It became linked with ideas of progress and the conscious shaping of history. It began to signify the willed deliberate effort to create a new society, a new humanity, and a new world. Nineteenth-century thinkers, whether conservative, liberal, socialist, were largely in accord in viewing revolution as a phenome of epochal change and innovation.

Thus, by an indefinite process of extension, *revolution* has come to contain a vague, assorted medley of meanings and to be applied to developments of the most varied kinds. Historians, in consequence, have given us an almost endless number of different revolutions, such as, for instance, the industrial, commercial, scientific, and Protestant revolutions; the intellectual, educational, and military revolutions; and the urban, neolithic, population, second industrial, and sexual revolutions. This loose and confusing use of the term merely illustrates how closely the idea of revolution has become equated with change. It would seem that all macroprocesses of change, whatever they are, must be described as revolutions. Nevertheless, few of these revolutions have anything in common with one another or with the concept of revolution itself defined in any precise sense. Hence, although I have little hope that they will do so, historians would add greatly to clarity if they ceased the proliferation of revolutions and reserved the term for a single reasonably well marked class of events.

What should its definition be? A recent suggestion, adopted by some political scientists, is to substitute for *revolution* the term *internal war*, defined as "any resort to violence within a political order to change its constitution, rulers, or policies."[2] While the use of *internal war* has provoked some illuminating discussion, it is hard to see the superior merit claimed for it. It also has the defect that certain kinds of revolutions, such as some colonial revolts or military coups d'état, would not normally be called internal wars. In addition, internal war is analogous to civil war and, therefore, rather than being sui generis, is best seen as one possible phase or stage in the development of a number of different types of revolution. Hence it seems preferable to retain the well established word *revolution* in a clearly delimited context describing change which is characterized by violence as a means and a specifiable range of goals as ends.

A well known line of thought proposes to restrict the term *revolution* solely to movements with goals involving far-reaching changes in social structure, class domination, institutions, and ideology. This view has been characteristic of the Marxist approach although it is held by non-Marxists as well. In effect, it accepts only the greatest revolutions as revolutions. A recent version of this opinion is advanced by S. P. Huntington: "A revolution is a rapid, fundamental and violent domestic change in the dominant values and myths of society, in its political institutions, social structure, leadership, government activity, and policies."[3] This definition, however, is arbitrary in what it excludes and is, therefore, of little use to the historian. It has no room for most peasant revolts, urban insurrections, and provincial or national separatist rebellions, to mention only a few. To adopt it would only result in a pointless narrowing of the field for both the comparative and theoretical study of revolution.

Perhaps it is impossible to establish a completely satisfactory definition of the term, so complex are the phenomena and variables to be included. Of the definitions available, the most useful appears to be the one adopted by Chalmers Johnson in his two books.[4] It conceives a revolution as violence directed toward one or more of the following goals: a change of government (personnel and leadership), of regime (form of government and distribution of political power), or of society (social structure, system of property control and class domination, dominant values, and the like). It would be desirable to add to this list a change of governmental policy as well. With that addition, Johnson's formulation seems reasonably exact and appropriate to all or most varieties of revolution, whatever their differences in aim, scale, or social character.

Accepting this working definition, we are in a position to ask in what ways the problem of revolution has been attacked. Three possible lines of inquiry exist, which even though they may overlap, can nonetheless be clearly distinguished from one another. The first, which is also the best worked and most familiar, is historical in the strictest sense. It is directed to the investigation of a specific individual revolution like the French or the English Revolution or the Fronde. Historians taking this approach have achieved outstanding successes, with the result that almost everything we know about revolutions comes from their detailed researches and general accounts. The second kind of inquiry is comparative. Its procedure is to deal with revolutions as a class, selecting from this class two or more instances in order to investigate any significant relationship between them. In this field, like that of comparative history in general, historians and social scientists have accomplished something, but not a great deal so far. Finally, the kind of inquiry is theoretical. Its purpose is to establish a theory of revolution capable of explaining its causes, processes, and effects as a type of change. Various hypotheses have been advanced within the social sciences, but despite the suggestiveness of some of these, nothing has appeared that qualifies as a general theory of revolution. Furthermore, among theorists there has been little progressive accumulation of ideas. The general theory of revolution remains subject to confusion, doubt, and disagreement. Even elementary questions of definition, terminology, and delimitation of the field to be explained are still not settled.

Before looking at recent work on the theory of revolution, it is usefu to mention some earlier attempts to deal with the subject. Previous effo to establish a theory of revolution have concentrated primarily causation. Other problems, such as the classification of revolutions, the investigation of the dynamic processes involved in revolutions, and the study of the long-range consequences of revolutions, have been neglected by comparison. To account for revolution, many factors and conditions have been adduced. In European history, the French Revolution affords the classic case in which causal primacy has been imputed to factors of the most diverse kinds—social, economic, intellectual, psychological, and so on. Tocqueville thought that revolution was likeliest to happen when oppression was being lightened. Marx, on the other hand, connected the development of revolution with intensified oppression or exploitation. In 1944, the American historian Louis Gottschalk published an article proposing five general causes of revolutions, such as provocation by regimes, solidified public opinion, hopefulness of change.[5] A list of this kind, however, is too nebulous to contribute much to the development of a theory of revolutionary causation.

Between the two world wars, prior to the recent renewal of interest, some writings of considerable merit dealing with the theory of revolution appeared in the United States. Among these were the works of two sociologists, Pitirim Sorokin and Lyford P. Edwards, and a political scientist, George S. Pettee.[6] The best known of earlier writings, however, is historian Crane Brinton's *The Anatomy of Revolution*, still probably the most influential as well as the most widely read book on revolution to have been written in this country. Prior to the appearance of his book, in a monograph on the Jacobins, Brinton tested several hypotheses about the role of psychological and economic factors in attracting people to the revolutionary cause. He decided from an analysis of their membership that the Jacobins were neither misfits nor failures and that they included a large cross section of French society. His skeptical conclusion was that the Jacobins were actuated not by material or any other interests, but by a quasi-religious faith. In *The Anatomy of Revolution*, Brinton attempted to discover certain uniformities by systematically comparing the English, American, French, and Russian Revolutions. In selecting these four, he followed most scholarship, which has tended to concentrate on instances drawn from the small class of so called great revolutions. Limiting the comparison to this category, however, affords a dubious basis for establishing uniformities. Even among the great revolutions, moreover, a number, like the Dutch Rebellion or the Mexican and Turkish Revolutions, for instance, are hardly ever considered. For Brinton some of the uniformities in the inception of revolution are an economically advancing society, an inefficient, financially hard-pressed government, class antagonisms, desertion of the existing order by the intellectuals, and loss of self-confidence by the ruling elite. He also perceives additional uniformities in the successive stages of revolution: the control of moderates gives way to the rule of extremists, which, in turn, gives way to a reign of terror followed by a Thermidorean reaction. Further uniformities appear in the effects of revolution, including great property transfers, the replacement of one ruling class by another, and the achievement of more efficient, centralized government.

It is doubtful whether anyone would accept these as uniformities since so many exceptions to them can be found. The English Revolution, for instance, was not caused by class antagonism, was not preceded by the desertion of the intellectuals, and did not produce a reign of terror. Similarly, a political scientist has written of the American Revolution that "we find neither victory of the extremists, nor the terror, nor the Thermidor, nor yet the 'tyrant' dictator who reestablished order. . . ."[7] Furthermore, neither in England nor in America did one ruling class replace another. In my opinion, Brinton's generalizations result from an uncritical tendency to treat the French Revolution as a model, a predisposition he shared with many others. Hence they apply much better to the French than to other revolutions. Although brilliantly suggestive, *The Anatomy of Revolution* seems to me to offer in the main a number of partial resemblances rather than uniformities in any true sense.

Another early attempt to deal with the theory of revolution derives from Marxism, which has remained extremely influential in the historical treatment of revolution. It has dominated the historiography of the French Revolution to such an extent that its interpretation of the Revolution has become virtually canonical.[8] Marxist theories have also been frequently advanced to explain the English Revolution, and they figure as well in current controversies about the so called "general crisis of the seventeenth century." Marxism has been, as well, one of the main influences upon the historical conceptualization of the nineteenth-century revolutions in France and other European countries. The much discussed question of the *rivoluzione mancata*, or failed revolution of the Italian Risorgimento has its origin in Marxist conceptions of the historical process. And although it contains no statement of a formal theory of revolution, Marxist ideas have provided a considerable part of the explanatory framework of E. H. Carr's great *History of Soviet Russia*.

Marxism has been a source of insight to historians of widely different views. In speaking of the Marxist theory of revolution, however, we are referring to Marxism in its integral character, not to Marxist ideas diluted in eclectic mixtures nor to those of Marx's ideas that are accepted by nearly all students of society. The outstanding merit of the Marxist model is its systematic integration of the factors of the economy, the social structure, the state, and ideology in order to explain revolution. Its defects include the attribution of ultimate causal determination, largely or wholly, to economic factors; its mistaken assumptions that economic class is always the dominant collectivity in social structure and that class conflict is the sole source of revolutionary change; finally, its grossly simplified notion of an evolutionary succession of societies, with primitive communism giving way, in turn, to slavery, feudalism, capitalism, and so on, to which there corresponds an equally simplified classification of revolutions.

Historically, Marxist scholarship has been most interested in bourgeois revolution and the transition from feudalism to capitalism. Its conceptual and terminological confusions on the subject are notorious. Feudalism has come to include anything from the eleventh to the nineteenth centuries and to designate conditions as far apart as a full-blown seigneurial regime, absolute monarchy, and an order in which landed aristocracies merely enjoy superior social prestige and authority. The bourgeoisie and bourgeois revolution are almost equally elastic categories. When Marxist historians speak of seventeenth and eighteenth-century France as a feudal society or describe the imperialism of Hapsburg Spain as "the highest stage of feudalism," the result can only be confusion. Admittedly, the analysis of class and of social structures presents complicated problems and is a difficult undertaking. Marxist concepts used for this purpose, however, have not been rigorously or even clearly developed.

With the progress of research, the inadequacies of the Marxist theory of revolution have become increasingly evident. Marxist explanations of the English Revolution have fallen into abeyance because of the damaging criticisms to which they have been subjected. In the case of the French Revolution, attempts to preserve the Marxist scheme resemble the addition of epicycles to the Ptolemaic system in order to save the phenomena. The accumulation of knowledge about the complexities of French society has made it clear that the Marxist analysis is far too abstract and too crude. Marxists trace the revolution to a conflict between the aristocracy and the bourgeoisie, but concrete evidence for so reductionist a dichotomy is lacking. A leading French historian, Pierre Goubert, has recently pointed out in a penetrating study of the ancien régime the absurdity of any longer trying to explain the revolution as "the triumph of an unidentifiable capitalist bourgeoisie over an unidentifiable feudal aristocracy."[9] Severe criticisms of the Marxist class analysis have also come from Professors Mousnier and Cobban. Even E. H. Carr, who is more sympathetic to the Marxist view, has pointed out that the French Revolution cannot be described as a bourgeois revolution in the sense that it was begun or led by an identifiable class. When Marxists resort to explanations of a still more general character, the difficulties become even worse. For example, Professor Soboul, who has done important research on the popular movement in revolutionary Paris, locates the ultimate cause of the French Revolution in the contradiction between the productive forces and the relations of production.[10] This proposition is so murky and abstract that it eludes any possibility of verification. Perhaps it should be received as a profession of faith rather than as an historical statement.

If one asks about Marxism the question that Croce in a famous essay asked about the philosophy of Hegel—what is living and what is dead in the Marxist theory of the revolution?—the answer must be that, in large part, it has been superseded. Its inadequacies might have been thought to have been conclusively revealed when Marx's own prediction that revolutions would occur in the most advanced countries of the West did not come true, and, instead, socialism triumphed in the backward peasant societies of Russia and China. With the growth of research on many revolutions, so much of the Marxist model has been disproved or shown to be untenable because of its oversimplifications that it has become in many ways an obstacle to further understanding. What remains of value in this model are some of the problems it poses for investigation and its emphasis upon the importance of economic and social-structural factors in the analysis of change and revolution. These will undoubtedly set challenges to historians, sociologists, and political scientists for a long time to come.

Since about 1960 there has been a noticeable revival of interest among social scientists other than historians in revolution as a theoretical problem. This interest has manifested itself in a number of writings by political scientists and sociologists dealing with revolution in various theoretical contexts. At the same time, the present position of historiography with respect to the investigation of revolution also presents certain features that call for mention. Although I have been referring to history as a social science, many historians would either reject or wish to qualify that description. In addition to the continuous fragmentation of historiography into innumerable specialties, there has been an increasing separation between the humanistic and social-science approaches to historical inquiry. This seems to have reached the point where it may be asked if history remains any longer a single discipline. The same question has been raised in a recent volume edited by David Landes and Charles Tilly which is part of the survey of the behavioral and social sciences conducted under the auspices of the Social Science Research Council and the National Academy of Sciences.[11] There the humanistic and social-science modes are contrasted as quite different types of inquiry. Probably most historians would place themselves somewhere between the two extremes, but nearer the humanistic than the social-science approach. In view of the distinction, however, it is significant that the same survey should indicate that revolution is one of the focal subjects of social-science history. This is certainly true of much of the more interesting work being done. Social-science history is not characterized primarily by the use of quantitative techniques; it is mainly characterized by a certain manner of formulating problems, by its effort at empirical rigor, by its use of theories, models, and ideal types, by its interest in comparative and interdisciplinary studies, and by the orientation of its research toward the understanding of whole societies. In history, as in other fields, most of the current efforts to gain a clearer understanding of revolution proceed from or are influenced by this approach.

An example of current scholarship is the research on what might be called revolutionary populations. The actors in revolutions belong either to elite groups or to the masses. Systematic analysis of the characteristics of each group using comparative data on the individual members can lead to enlightening results. Research of this kind can center on anything from the membership of formal institutions and ruling bodies to the participants in protest incidents as shortlived as a riot. From such work it is possible to gain a much fuller and more precise knowledge than we have ever had before of recruitment, of opposition to revolution, of leadership, of popular activism, and even of individual mentalities. The collective history of the Parisian sans culottes by Albert Soboul is an outstanding example. He reconstructed as far as possible in all its lineaments the mass movement in Paris during the Jacobin ascendancy and the Terror by close investigation of the people who composed it. George Rudé has performed a similar task in his dissection of the crowds and crowd behavior in the French Revolution and other social disturbances.[12] Another instance of a different kind is the detailed elite studies, like the analysis of the Soviet Politburo and of Nazi officialdom, done by political scientists.[13] Still another example is the investigation of the membership of the Long Parliament by Douglas Brunton and D. H. Pennington, from which it appears that the Royalist and Parliamentarian members as a body were socially and economically more or less indistinguishable from one another.[14] This research is not only valuable for the understanding of particular revolutions, but is also relevant to the theory of revolution because it can provide data for models and for the testing of explanations derived from general theories.

Another kind of work is the comparative history of revolution, of which there are various recent examples. A prominent one is R. R. Palmer's *The Age of the Democratic Revolution*, which gives a valuable account of political developments between 1760 and 1800 and also conceives of the French Revolution as the central event in an interrelated upsurge of revolutions extending over America and Western Europe. Most of the discussion provoked by Palmer's book has centered on the question of whether there really was an eighteenth-century revolution of the West. Although Palmer has put much material together with great skill, his work contains little on the wider problem of revolution itself. It touches passingly on the causes of revolution, on revolutionary psychology, on the basis of political allegiances, and similar problems, but these reflections are too vague to be very illuminating. Palmer has also written an essay on generalizations about revolution which is equally cursory and vague in regard to theoretical issues.[15]

Work of more direct theoretical interest has appeared in recent writing dealing with sixteenth and seventeenth-century revolutions and "the crisis of the seventeenth century." The differences arising from these studies, which address themselves to basic questions concerning the societies, governments, and revolutions of early modern Europe, have led to some of the liveliest controversies in contemporary historiography. Contributions to the subject have come from H. R. Trevor-Roper, Eric Hobsbawm, J. H. Elliott, Lawrence Stone, J. H. Hexter, Perez Zagorin, Roland Mousnier, and others, who have provided searching discussions of the determinants of social structure and political differences in connection with the revolutions of the period. Models for these revolutions have also been suggested, such as the court-country opposition or the conflict between the warlike, top-heavy absolutist state and society. One of the most active scholars in all these problems is Professor Mousnier of the Sorbonne. He has compiled an extremely detailed questionnaire to guide research on rebellions in France between the end of the Middle Ages and the French Revolution. In a number of historical and comparative studies, he has also stressed the importance of aristocratic leadership for the type of revolt that occurred in the societies of the ancien régime.

Millenarianism, another large topic, has been the subject of comparative studies, in which the central problem is its relationship to modern revolutionary movements. On this there has been a convergence of research by historians, anthropologists, and sociologists. While by no means uniform in character, millenarian movements in Europe have usually displayed two features: first, the complete rejection of the existing world order and the expectation of a future new world purged of the evils of the old; second, an ideology of total transformation derived from Jewish-Christian apocalyptic beliefs. A further feature frequently associated with millenarianism is the presence of a charismatic leader or a prophet. Many writers have noted the typological resemblance between such religious movements and secular revolutionary movements, and some have also argued the historical dependence or interconnection of the two. One approach to the problem is exemplified in Hobsbawm's *Primitive Rebels*, which treats millenarianism as a prepolitical phenomenon arising in traditional societies and among the backward strata of more advanced societies. Millenarian movements in this view are a revolutionary expression of deprived and oppressed groups who have not yet attained political consciousness and who lack the means of political organization. An alternative approach is taken by Norman Cohn in *The Pursuit of the Millennium*, who stresses not only socioeconomic factors but also the psychological elements in millenarianism which tend toward producing outbreaks of collective hysteria and irrationality. In the case of rebellions such as the German Peasant War of 1525, Cohn is inclined to see millenarianism as a factor injected by a small number of fanatical enthusiasts into a much larger popular movement with realistic aims. He also points out the importance of intellectuals in framing the ideology of millenarian revolts.

Hobsbawm's analysis regards millenarianism both as the expression in mystical terms of social and economic interests and as the precursor of realistic political struggle. It also assumes an evolutionary scheme, distinguishing archaic from modern forms of rebellion, the highest stage of which is revolutionary Marxism. His assumption, however, is questionable. It seems more likely that rather than being a phenomenon peculiar to primitive social forms, futurist fantasies of transformation and perfection are a possibility in any society and are capable of combining with highly realistic beliefs and a sophisticated political organization. They are an important element, for instance, both in Leninist and Maoist thought and in the utopian expectations of contemporary youth revolutionaries. Millenarianism can therefore be considered not only as defining one particular species of rebellion, but also as a possible component in some secular types of revolution as well.

Perhaps the most noteworthy recent comparative study of revolution is Barrington Moore's *Social Origins of Dictatorship and Democracy*. Moore's book exemplifies the current intellectual trend in the study of revolution by being the work of a sociologist concentrating entirely on a set of historical problems. What it seeks to explain is the process of transition from traditional agrarian to modern industrial society as experienced in a number of countries in the East and West; England, France, the United States, Japan, China, and India are examined, with frequent reference made also to Germany and Russia. The balance between the analysis of historical events and the drawing of theoretical generalizations is admirably maintained. Whatever criticisms historians may make, they are not likely to accuse it of the jejune and mechanical treatment often apparent in the writings of nonhistorian social scientists when they use historical materials.

Moore identifies three basic patterns in the modernizing process. The first leads via bourgeois revolution to capitalism and democracy of the Western type. Its instances include England, France, and also the United States whose civil war Moore explains as a revolution caused by the political incompatibility between slavery and a democratic capitalist order. The second, in which the bourgeois revolution fails, leads to capitalism with much weaker democratic features. This was the pattern for Germany and Japan which resulted in fascism. The third leads through great peasant revolutions to communist regimes that force the society into modernization. The examples are Russia and China. To these three basic patterns, Moore adds a fourth, exemplified by the case of India, in which, despite the achievement of parliamentary democracy, the impulse to modernization is weak because there has been neither a bourgeois nor a peasant revolution.

One variable is critical in the patterns described by Moore—namely, the way in which the traditional agrarian sector in each case has been subjected to capitalist relations and modernization, which, he believes, was, in turn, determined by the respective roles of peasants, landed elites, urban bourgeoisies, and the state. Where the process has been carried out by the bourgeoisie and part of the peasants, as in France, or by capitalistic landlords together with the bourgeoisie, as in England, the result is democratic capitalist regimes. Where it has been accomplished by landlords and the state bureaucracy without the presence of a strong bourgeoisie, as in Germany and Japan, the result has been authoritarian and fascist regimes. Finally, where landlords and state bureaucracies inhibited the process and the bourgeoisie was too small and weak to effect it, as in China and Russia, the impetus has come from peasant masses mobilized by communist parties, which then made the peasants their first victims.

Moore does not propose a general theory of revolution; rather he presents some generalizations about a certain range of experience in which revolution occupies the central place. The occurrence or failure of revolution, as well as its specific character, are viewed as crucial for the ensuing type of development. Revolution is thus placed within the historical process as a decisive point of conflict having systemic consequences. Moore dismisses the idea that revolution is necessary to remove the obstacles to modernization. He points out, however, that modernization achieved under conservative auspices retains many old structures and hence leads to quite different results from those produced by a great revolution. He accepts the conception of a bourgeois revolution, though he does not necessarily mean the seizure of power by a bourgeoisie. Revolutions, Moore holds, should be compared and classified with reference to their broad institutional consequences. Consequently, because of the kind of political and social order that resulted from them, he links the English and French Revolutions with the American Civil War as stages in the development of the bourgeois-democratic revolution.

There are a number of serious weaknesses in Moore's work. For one thing, in laying such heavy stress on economic relations, he underestimates or disregards the role of values and even of politics in social change. Thus in the case of Germany, conservative modernization may be a necessary cause of fascism, but it can hardly be a sufficient cause since it does not include other political circumstances and value orientations that were fundamental to the outcome. In the case of England and France, to call both products of a bourgeois revolution does nothing to explain why the subsequent French political order, in contrast to the English, was so unstable and divided against itself. Moreover, German fascism, like Italian, was itself a revolution with broad systemic features. Moore's model, however, cannot include fascism as a type of revolution. Strong reservations also arise in connection with Moore's analysis of the American Civil War. Since he agrees with the conclusion of recent scholarship that Northern capitalism and Southern plantation slavery were not antagonistic, but existed in a profitable relation with one another as economic systems, it is difficult to see what ground there can be for explaining the Civil War as a bourgeois-democratic, capitalist revolution of the same type as the English and French.

Moore's work, nonetheless, must be regarded as a signficant synthesis in the comparative treatment of revolution. It is also notable for its avoidance of excessive abstraction and its firm sense of historical reality. An approach of this kind, linking the comparative and theoretical dimensions of inquiry with the historical, is one of the most likely to lead to a better understanding of the nature and effects of revolution in large-scale processes of social change.

In addition to comparative studies, social scientists have also tried to develop some general theories and explanations of revolution. For instance, the question of how revolution is related to poverty and to economic and social oppression has always been puzzling. Although Marx explained revolutions as the effect of increasing misery and exploitation, Tocqueville, Brinton, and others, while not denying, of course, the importance of poverty, have argued that some of the greatest revolutions occurred in societies where the level of life was improving. Tocqueville is most explicit on this point, declaring that an unprecedented advance in the prosperity of the nation took place before the French Revolution and that this promoted a spirit of unrest and discontent which was highest in those parts of France which had experienced most improvement. Today most students hold that revolution is least likely among populations experiencing static conditions of poverty, low living standards, and economic backwardness. Comparative data assembled by political scientists also indicate a positive correlation between political instability and rapid economic growth. What then is the connection between poverty and oppression, economic development, and revolution?

To this question a political scientist, J. C. Davies, has proposed an answer in the form of a model that combines features of both Marx and Tocqueville.[16] It is based on the view that a situation most favorable to revolution exists when a prolonged period of economic growth is followed by a short period of sharp reversal. New expectations, needs, and standards have then been created that are suddenly checked. With the J-curve, as Davies calls the downward swing, an acute discrepancy appears between mounting wants and expectations and the possibility of their satisfaction which, in turn, establishes the potential for revolution. Revolution is accordingly seen as the effect neither of poverty and misery nor of improvement but of a certain sequence of the two. Davies has tried to fit his model to several cases, and although it cannot be accepted as a general explanation of revolution, it is clearly pertinent to certain revolutions like the French, which began when contraction, bad harvests, and famine succeeded a secular phase of growth. Lawrence Stone has pointed out that the J-curve can also apply to other sectors beside the economic. Thus trouble may arise if a phase of liberal governmental concessions is followed by a phase of political repression or if a phase of easier entry into the elite is followed by a phase of aristocratic reaction and closure.

A much broader approach founded on similar premises has been recently developed in a book by Ted Gurr, *Why Men Rebel*. Gurr's point of departure is the theory of relative deprivation, which may be defined as the discrepancy that individuals perceive between what they expect and what they are likely to obtain. Relative deprivation may exist either because value expectations increase faster than value capabilities or because value expectations remain the same while value capabilities decline. In both cases men will feel anger, frustration, and discontent. If relative deprivation is strong enough and becomes focused on political objects, a situation arises that may lead to violence and revolution. Whether revolution does occur or not depends on a number of variables including the scope and intensity of the relative deprivation and the actions taken by the regime. Gurr has elaborated the logic of this analysis with great thoroughness. Thus the expectations subject to relative deprivation are not necessarily limited to the economic and material. The expectations may be about power and political participation or status, personal development, and belief. Gurr attempts to specify the diverse causes of relative deprivation and to explicate the conditions affecting both regimes and dissidents that may culminate in revolution. The analysis gives close consideration to the role of legitimacy, to the effects of violence under various circumstances, and to the determinants of support for rebels and regimes. It also suggests methods such as opinion surveys to measure some of the variables involved.

Gurr's work is of exceptional interest both in its range and precision. The main question that it raises concerns its fundamentally psychological formulation and treatment of the problem of revolution. The theory of relative deprivation is derived from the studies done by social psychologists on frustration and aggression. It thus begins by locating the cause of dissatisfaction and discontent in the individual. Starting there, it generalizes the process to account for many people's discontent and then by a further progression to the likelihood that these same people will become violent, will direct their violence against political targets, and eventually engage in revolution. The focus is accordingly on the side of personal experience leading to the formation of discontent.

There are several important drawbacks to this view. Apart from the practical difficulties in determining the scope and intensity of relative deprivation both in the present and even more in earlier periods where the data are scanty, a very long distance separates discontent from revolution. In order for the one to lead to the other, many factors must intervene, such as developments in the social and economic structure, conflicts and changes in the political system, the emergence of ideologies, and the like. Such factors are crucial to the dynamic causal process of revolution. Furthermore, they are not attributes of states of mind, but properties of political and social situations or systems. Gurr's theory, however, cannot take account of structural developments or political conflicts except as they are related to the psychological phenomenon of relative deprivation. This inability considerably diminishes both the significance and the possibility of analyzing adequately nonpsychological factors. For that reason, although the relevance of a psychological approach is undeniable, it seems to be in itself a limited and incomplete one.

In explaining revolutions, it is obviously necessary to distinguish long-range preconditions and processes from immediate precipitators which, by chance, act to release revolutionary situations. Only the preconditions can be incorporated into causal theories. Any attempt, however, to elevate a particular set of preconditions into general causes runs into difficulties. Harry Eckstein, a political scientist, has classified the commonly advanced hypotheses dealing with the causes of revolution, or, as he prefers to call it, internal war.[17] Some emphasize conditions of the social structure, like too much or too little social mobility, the emergence of new social classes, and the inadequate circulation of elites. Others emphasize ideological conditions, like the conflict of belief systems and social myths or the existence of corrosive philosophies and unrealizable values. Others stress economic conditions, such as poverty and exploitation or rapid growth. Still others emphasize political conditions such as government oppression, division within governing classes, or the excessive tolerance of alienated groups. With such an abundance of partially inconsistent hypotheses, any of which might yet be valid in a particular case, the obstacles to a causal theory are apparent.

Eckstein offers some suggestions to improve the explanation of the preconditions for revolution. First, he points out that historians and theories have tended to pay more attention to rebels than to incumbents, but that both should receive equal consideration. This can hardly be gainsaid in view of the importance of elite behavior in creating the preconditions. Some writers, like Pareto for instance, have even held that revolutions are largely due to changes in elite characteristics, leading to estrangement from non-elites, incompetence, and the failure of nerve.[18] Second, any explanation should take into account behavioral as well as structural factors. This is contrary to the common approach, which has tended to concentrate on the structural or so called objective conditions of revolutions. The same conditions, however, may and do produce different results because orientations, values, and attitudes mediate between the social environment and action. Hence, culture, ideology, and the role of intellectuals in maintaining the values of legitimacy must also be stressed in the formation of preconditions. Third, explanations should strive for broad propositions describing general social processes which can apply to a large variety of specific preconditions. This last suggestion is no doubt valid, but at the same time there is also the danger that such propositions may become vacuous or trivial through their very generality.

Based on these ideas, Eckstein has proposed an explanatory model containing eight variables which in combination establish the presence and extent of the preconditions for revolution. The negative variables working against revolution are the facilities (especially for coercion) available to incumbents, effective repression, adjustive concessions, and diversionary mechanisms. The positive variables working in favor of revolution are the inefficiency of elites, disorienting social processes, subversion, and the facilities for violence available to insurgents. With this paradigm, Eckstein holds that it is possible to assess the potential for revolution and the balance between the favoring and counterfavoring factors.

Eckstein's model seems a useful one in its ability to incorporate different sets of particular preconditions. At the least it provides an inventory of factors to be checked off in explaining revolutions. It would therefore be of considerable interest to see it applied to an historical case in order to test its fit to the complexity and untidiness of the events.

There are a number of other angles from which recent social-science scholarship has attacked the problem of revolution. For instance, in an historical monograph on the Vendée, Charles Tilly, a sociologist, has based an analysis of a counterrevolution on the effects of urbanism and market penetration in a region of traditional subsistence agriculture.[19] A noticeable trend has also been to subsume revolution under the theories of violence. The assumption implied in such studies is reflected in Gurr's work as well as in the attempts of political scientists to establish precise indices and measures of conflicts within states. The identification of violence and revolution is a mistake, however, for while the use of violence is certainly one of the defining characteristics of revolution, the two are not identical phenomena. A people may be prone to violence, like Americans, without necessarily being revolutionary. Many acts of collective or political violence—such as banditry, labor strife, lynchings, food, race, and antiforeign riots—may bear no relation to revolution or to the formation of the preconditions for revolution. A great deal of violence, moreover, proceeds from agencies of the state both in their "normal" activities and in repressive actions, such as those carried out against peaceful demonstrations with no revolutionary import. Also, the major kind of collective violence is carried out by governments when they make external war. Hence, though revolution and violence have some common features, they are different phenomena requiring different theories for their elucidation.

Revolution is often discussed in connection with theories of modernization. The study of modernization has become one of the preoccupations of current political science and focuses on the problem of stability in societies undergoing rapid social and economic change, its interest being for obvious reasons concentrated mainly on the contemporary scene. Modernization itself is sometimes regarded as a revolution rather than as the possible outcome or characteristic of a certain type of revolution. Thus one writer speaks of "the revolution of modernization," which he calls "the first revolution in history to set a new price upon stability in any system of society; namely, an intrinsic capacity to generate and absorb continuing transformation."[20] This paradoxical observation repeats the familiar mistake of making revolution synonymous with any rapid, large-scale change. It also assumes that a society that has achieved modernization will be free of violent change and can remain stable even if transformation is continuous and incessant. Both assumptions are doubtful and pertain more to the utopia of modernization theorists than to the real world.

Probably the outstanding work devoted to revolution in the context of modernization is Samuel P. Huntington's *Political Order in Changing Societies*, an impressive synthesis of the conditions of stability and instability. As I have previously remarked, Huntington restricts the definition of revolution exclusively to transformations of the most sweeping character which are effected by violence. His argument is that social and economic changes such as urbanization, industrialization, the spread of literacy, of education, and of communication facilities, and so on lead to a rise in political consciousness, the mobilization of new groups into politics, and multiplication of political demands. Traditional societies launched on the process of modernization usually lack the political institutions and organizations capable of bearing the heavy new strains put on them. There is consequently an imbalance between socioeconomic growth and the political capacity to assimilate the new forces mobilized in the process. The result is instability, disorder, and, in certain cases, revolution. Accordingly in Huntington's view, revolution is an aspect of modernization. It is very unlikely to occur either in highly traditional societies or in highly modern ones and is least probable in both democratic and communist political systems because of the capacity of each to absorb new groups. Huntington also distinguishes a Western and an Eastern pattern of revolution. In the Western pattern—of which the French, Russian, and Mexican Revolutions are instances—the decay of political institutions and the collapse of the old regime precedes the process of political mobilization and the creation of a new order. In the Eastern pattern, which includes the Chinese and Vietnamese revolutions, political mobilization and the shaping of new institutions come first and the overthrow of the existing order last.

I will not attempt to assess this challenging thesis in detail, but instead will merely express some critical reservations. Huntington's theory is based on a three-stage classification of societies as traditional, transitional or modernization and modern. While these categories are useful for some purposes, they are much too large and undifferentiated to describe the course of development as the historian sees it. To place French, Russian, and Mexican societies, for example, within this classification and then to treat the revolutions as the effects of modernization adds little to our understanding of them. The contrasts between the societies, economies, cultures, and states concerned are in many respects far too wide to justify such a procedure. It is not clear, moreover, why there should be two patterns of revolution, since Huntington's model appears to require that the political mobilization of new groups must always precede the breakdown of the traditional regime. With only one pattern, however, difficulties arise because certain revolutions cannot be made to fit the historical sequence. Furthermore, throughout, the analysis is continually open to the danger of advancing by a circular argument. Instead of consistently treating revolution and modernization as variables between which, in every case, an empirical connection must be established, Huntington sometimes joins them by definition. Thus, in explaining why China underwent a revolution and Japan did not, he tends to judge whether the political stresses resulting from modernization were severe enough to cause a revolution merely by the fact that a revolution did, indeed, occur.

This problem poses the larger issue of whether modernization, as such, can be accepted as the cause of revolution. There is, to be sure, a good deal of evidence that rapid social and economic change is apt to produce instability. Modernization itself, nevertheless, is merely a name for an ensemble of complex processes. Unless these are disentangled and their effects separately tested and verified, it is difficult to see how reliable conclusions can be drawn as to their connection with revolution. If we follow Huntington, modernization leads to revolution via the political mobilization it engenders. "Revolution," he writes, "is the extreme case of the explosion of political participation."[21] But while it is true that great revolutions are accompanied by unprecedented mass involvement in politics, how can the fact of modernization account for the support of a revolution by groups already involved—by intellectuals, bourgeoisies, and dissident aristocracies, for example, as has often been the case? The alienation of participants in political life, and the withdrawal of their support from existing regimes, is frequently of profound importance in the inception of revolution, yet it is a phenomenon on which Huntington's theory throws little light.

A common feature in explanations of revolutions is to attribute them to some incompatibility or stress within the ongoing institutions and processes of society; the most general theory of this kind has been developed by Chalmers Johnson. Johnson's starting point is the model of a functioning social system in a state of equilibrium. Equilibrium in this case does not mean the absence of change but rather synchronization between the different sectors of the system as change proceeds. Here Johnson is largely dependent for his ideas on the sociological theories of Talcott Parsons concerning the requirements of a functioning social system. The process of revolution accordingly begins with disequilibrium and dysfunction. These may ensue from changes in both values and the environment and such changes may originate either from within the system or be introduced from without. Dysfunction signifies a lack of integration between the sectors or subsystems of the social system as a whole. It occurs when the change taking place is too much for the adaptive and adjustive processes of the system. If dysfunction is not dealt with by purposeful measures to reestablish equilibrium, then it will multiply with widening effects of disorientation and protest within the society. At this point the action of elites is crucial. If the elite relies on force to cope with the pressures of dysfunction, the result will be what Johnson calls a power deflation. On the other hand, if the elite fails to institute policies capable of reintegrating the system, it will suffer a loss of authority. Sheer intransigence on its part may also be fatal. Multiple dysfunction and elite inefficiency create a revolutionary situation. What then makes revolution highly probable or certain, according to Johnson, is the intervention of some unforeseen triggering factor accelerator. This could be an event such as a defeat in war or any other incident that undermines an army's loyalty to a regime and persuades revolutionaries that they have the chance to win power. Johnson's formula can therefore be summarized as follows: change plus disequilibrium plus multiple dysfunction plus elite failure plus an accelerator lead to revolution.

To account for the varieties of revolution, Johnson has also devised a classification based on four criteria: the targets of revolutionary activity, whether government, regime, or society; the identity of the revolutionaries, whether elites, masses, or both; the goals of the revolutionary ideology, whether reformist, nation-building, eschatological, etc.; finally, whether the revolution is a spontaneous or a calculated movement. With the help of these criteria, Johnson then distinguishes six types of revolution. The first is the jacquerie, a spontaneous peasant outbreak that does not challenge the legitimacy of the regime and appeals to traditional authorities for redress of grievances. The second type is the millenarian rebellion, which may be actuated by the same grievances as the jacquerie, but aims at a totally new order with the expected aid of supernatural forces. The third type is the anarchistic rebellion, which is a reaction against change or modernization and seeks to reinstitute an idealized older order. The fourth type, which is also the rarest, is the Jacobin-communist or great revolution and is the one that leads to the most far-reaching changes. The fifth type is the conspiratorial coup d'état, an attempt by a small elite to introduce social change by violence. Finally, the sixth type is the militarized mass insurrection, a creation of the twentieth century, which is a people's war of guerilla insurgency led by a dedicated elite and inspired by nationalist and communist ideologies.

This typology of revolution is the best that has yet been suggested and can be useful in discriminating particular revolutions, which may, of course, possess characteristics of more than one type. It cannot, however, be regarded as complete. There is no place in it, for example, for the religious-civil wars of the sixteenth and seventeenth centuries led by aristocracies nor for the separatist rebellions or urban revolts of the same period. Another flaw is that the Jacobin-communist type of revolution is misleadingly named, since some great revolutions in this category, like the Mexican Revolution or the Nazi conquest of power, were neither Jacobin nor communist. One might also consider whether what Johnson calls the militarized mass insurrection does not really belong to the type of great revolutions and differs only in making use of new political and military strategies.

Turning from the typology to Johnson's model as a whole, it represents the most ambitious attempt made thus far to apply social-systems theory to revolution. Its principal defects are due to its too abstract and overly general character. The assumption, for instance, that a nonrevolutionary society is a system in equilibrium is one that arouses considerable skepticism. Has any such system ever existed? Surely it assumes that societies are far more integrated than they possible can be. A more plausible view is that imperfect integration and some degree of disequilibrium are characteristic of every social system. But such talk is, in any case, unilluminating in the absence of definite criteria for specifying equilibrium and disequilibrium. The criteria that Johnson proposes for this purpose are unfortunately of little help. Thus, equilibrium is described as a condition of synchronization between values and the social division of labor. Such a formula, however, suffers from extreme vagueness unless clear indicators are given by which to identify and distinguish this condition from its opposite. In the case of disequilibrium, Johnson mentions somewhat more precise criteria, such as a rising suicide rate or increased ideological activity. The drawback here, however, is that we have no reason to accept these factors as *necessarily* reflecting disequilibrium unless we first accept the theory they are supposed to confirm. Problems arise as well with regard to the conception of dysfunction. Every social system contains many instances of poor governmental performance, elite failure, and out-of-date institutions. Since these are all presumably dysfunctional, how to recognize dysfunction as a special condition resulting from disequilibrium becomes a puzzling question. Considerations of this kind suggest that equilibrium, understood even as an ideal condition to which actual systems are merely in some approximate relation, is not a good foundation on which to erect a theory of revolution. A final point is that Johnson's work concentrates so heavily on the social system that it is relatively uninformative about the specific conflicts present in revolution, the genesis of revolutionary opposition, or the actions undertaken by governments and rebels. In placing himself on the heights of general theory, he has not avoided the danger of making his fundamental propositions so expansive that they verge toward emptiness and thus fail to entail the concrete correlatives by which their adequacy can be tested.

After this review of theories of revolution, the main conclusion to be drawn is that the subject is in a lively but disorderly state. A number of promising ideas have been propounded, but they do not fit into any coherent scheme. Whether a general theory of revolution is attainable is a question one might well wish to ask, in view of the disagreements and lack of success of past and present efforts. Of course, no answer to this question can be given on a priori grounds, and every theoretical contribution should be assessed on its merits. Nevertheless, I admit to considerable skepticism in the matter. As an historian, I am inclined to believe that above a certain level of generality social-science theory is too remote from reality to be either very interesting or useful. A global approach toward the problem of revolution seems to me, therefore, less likely to be profitable than one that strives, for instance, to clarify the different types of revolution and to develop a model of the causal process of each type. Yet despite the reservations historians are apt to feel about the utility of grand theory, they need to take account of whatever theories are available and to try to use and improve them. In the present position of history, the union of theoretical and comparative investigation with the more traditional methods of inquiry is one of the most important lines of advance toward a deeper understanding of the past.

Peter Amann

2 REVOLUTION: A Redefinition

Historians traditionally insist that they must carry out their work without benefit of presuppositions. In spite of the shadows which Marx, Freud and Mannheim (not to speak of such American historians as Beard and Becker) have cast over "objectivity," the dominant Rankean tradition still requires the historian to enter into his subject with unsullied, if not blank, mind until such time as he is permitted to re-emerge, pure as Botticelli's Venus, clutching history "as it really happened" to his bosom. If this burlesque is unfair, it is not groundless. Although some historians are quietly making good use of concepts borrowed from the social sciences, a majority continue to frown on any schematic approach to history as fraught with prejudice and dogma.

The limitations of the traditional methodology become obvious in the study of political revolution. Aside from assessing the impact of revolution, the historian is surely concerned with a rational understanding of the dynamics of a revolution. Merely "reliving" the chaos "as it really was" is unlikely to provide such an understanding. Actually, though the advocates of Rankean detachment also want to draw conclusions and discover patterns, they feel that they can do this without bringing to their study any conceptual apparatus at all—merely a healthy curiosity and the canons by which they were trained. I believe that they are deceiving themselves. The real alternative lies between a conceptual framework which is never made explicit and therefore remains beyond the reach of criticism, and one which is open to critical inspection.

The aim of this article is to suggest a framework for studying the course of a revolutionary movement, irrespective of its ideological content

51

or specific historical significance. This analytical framework hinges on a redefinition of the term "revolution." This is not to claim some superiority inherent in my particular definition. There is no "true" definition of an abstraction: such a term is a semantic device which may or may not be useful, not a reflection of some absolute Platonic prototype. A term that during the seventeenth century referred to the revolving Wheel of Fortune casting down one prince and raising up another has since been broadened to the point of hopeless imprecision. If I suggest a narrowing of the definition of revolution, it is in order to provide a useful analytical tool for the study of revolutionary politics in the west since the seventeenth century. This definition will in turn permit a schematic approach, helping the historian to distinguish the politically crucial from the insignificant, without attempting to impose the pattern, timing and ideology of one revolution on what may well be the unique pattern of another.

Some preliminaries must first be considered. What is the modern state? On what base does its stability rest? The sovereign state, as I define it here, is a political organization exercising, or able to exercise, a monopoly of armed force, justice and administration over a given area and population. It is true that this state monopoly is merely a tendency which may never be completely fulfilled and which does not preclude the delegation of military, judicial and administrative functions to subordinate bodies, provided the latter recognize their subordination and act accordingly. The national government of a federal state such as the United States or Switzerland may be circumscribed in its inner dynamic by a constitutional separation of powers; yet this constitutes at most a difference in degree rather than in kind from centralized states. While this expansive tendency, this inner dynamic of the state, undoubtedly varies, the variations seem to have little to do with the ideological coloring of the government. I am aware that where the influence of Rousseau or Hegel has prevailed, the definition of the state as a moral or metaphysical being has been widely accepted. The rationale of my definition is not metaphysical: it is rather, in its way, empirical. Most political historians appear in practice to accept a postulate of the state in terms of power, a postulate which I am here stating explicitly.

In addition to this definition of the state as an incipient power monopoly, I wish to submit a further working hypothesis which seems verified by experience. I maintain that the power monopoly of the state depends largely, not on the consent of the governed, but on their habit of obedience, whatever its motive. It is the habit of obedience that, extended to institutions like the army and the bureaucracy, makes it possible for the state to delegate vital functions without jeopardizing its own effective monopoly of military, judicial and administrative power.

To summarize: the ensuing argument will rest on a definition of the state as a monopoly of power and on the crucial importance of the habit of obedience in assuring the stability of the state. We find, therefore, that the political historian's usual assumption of an identity of politics and government makes sense just so long as such a government enjoys a power monopoly resting in turn on an undisturbed habit of obedience. From the point of view of historical method, revolution may be said to be a breakdown, momentary or prolonged, of the state's monopoly of power, usually accompanied by a lessening of the habit of obedience. The sequence of this breakdown varies: in the Russian March Revolution the withdrawal of obedience preceded the appearance of any organized blocs that challenged the power of the state and led to the creation of such para-governments. By contrast, however sullen the popular attitude toward the Batista administration may have been, most Cubans transferred their habit of obedience to the Castro regime only after its seizure of power.

In a coup d'état or in a revolution not directly involving large sections of the population, the transfer of the habit of obedience from the old to the new government may be virtually automatic. If this is the case, the traditional methods of the political historian are adequate. From this specific point of view, once the transfer of power is effected the revolution is over—even though drastic social changes may yet follow the consolidation of the new regime. Once again the case of the Cuban revolution may be cited. As long as Batista's power was effectively unchallenged, Cuban politics could be studied in terms of his administration. As soon as Castro established himself as a para-governmental power in Oriente province, Cuban politics became, by my definition, revolutionary—that is, the historian was faced with more than one power center. Until Castro had succeeded Batista, only the study of *both* power centers, in their internal development as well as in their interaction, could reveal the history of Cuban politics. Once Castro's government had gained the monopoly of power formerly enjoyed by the Batista administration, Cuban politics ceased to be revolutionary, that is, they could once again be adequately documented in terms of the activities of the central government.

What emerges from this discussion is a new definition of revolution which serves a clearer function for the historian than the "common sense" one, being more precise, comprehensive and relatively independent of ideological value judgments. As I define it, revolution prevails when the state's monopoly of power is effectively challenged and persists until a monopoly of power is re-established. Such a definition avoids a number of traditional problems: the fine distinction between a coup d'état and a revolution; the degree of social change necessary before a movement may be called revolutionary; the possibility of a conservative revolution; the uncertain differentiation between wars of independence, civil wars and revolutions. By this definition the Algerian crisis is clearly revolutionary, since the French monopoly of armed force, justice and administration has been breached.

The definition also recognizes what might be called a suspended revolution: the prolonged co-existence of two or more antagonistic governmental power centers which are unable or unwilling to eliminate each other. This situation has, for instance, prevailed in Argentina since the ouster of the Perón dictatorship: the army has exercised a veto power over the Frondizi regime without displacing it. The relationship between government and army in the Weimar Republic of the late 1920s might also be cited as such an example of suspended revolution. This is not to assert that this definition of revolution makes it automatically possible to pinpoint a revolutionary situation. It would, for instance, be difficult at the present time to determine whether the French army has regained its habit of obedience to the state or whether it continues to exercise para-governmental powers, thus creating a revolutionary situation. In this respect the task of the historian with access to all available sources is considerably lighter than that of the student of contemporary politics hemmed in by a curtain of secrecy.

As we have already seen, in a revolutionary change carried out with little popular participation, the population may shift its habit of obedience without much disruption. If an established government is overthrown by a massive popular uprising, the chances of a revolutionary situation prevailing long after the actual overthrow of the established government are much greater. If a broadly based insurrection succeeds in capturing power, the prior involvement of a substantial segment of the people is likely to extend the time span of revolution, that is, the length of time during which state power is dispersed among several centers. The very act of insurrection is the most drastic break possible in the habit of obedience; hence the greater the number of combatants and active sympathizers engaged in insurrection, the greater the number of people who have decisively cast off their habit of obedience. The new government, which may crown the successful efforts of the insurgents, may well command their immediate loyalty, yet the fact that this government is their own personal creation deprives it of the *mystique* of impersonal power in which an established government is clothed. Obedience based on loyalty independent of habit or fear is, as Machiavelli saw, an insecure basis of state power. Loyalty freely given may be freely withdrawn.

It may be argued that the messianic expectations aroused by most revolutions are likely to lead some disappointed supporters to challenge sooner or later the government which they had helped to establish. At the very least the insurrectionists who remain outside the new "establishment" are likely to keep in abeyance some of their power in order to make their influence felt should the new government betray their ideals. In this sense the rising of the Kronstadt sailors against the Bolshevik regime is no historical accident; the bitterness of the insurgents was directed not against government in general, but against a government of their own creation which had, they felt, betrayed their aspirations.

Mass insurrection shatters the habit of obedience on a large scale and therefore tends to perpetuate revolution even after it is "officially" over. The rebel military build-up that made seizure of power possible also has the paradoxical effect of prolonging the revolutionary conditions after rebel victory. Lenin was quite right, though for the wrong reasons, in asserting that "the revolution" (as defined in Marxist terms) cannot take over the pre-revolutionary state as a going concern but can only destroy it to make room for its own. The new insurrectionary state cannot simply inherit what it has destroyed. While it inherits the still functioning parts of the administration—the judiciary, the armed forces—it must also bring under control its own armed adherents, a task made more difficult by the wide dispersion of weapons which a successful mass insurrection may require. Other things remaining equal, the larger the number of armed supporters the greater the likelihood of future armed opponents.

The number of insurgents is not by itself the sole criterion of the magnitude of the task confronting the successful insurrectionary government. Much depends on the state of organization or organizability of the insurgents and the degree of control exercised by an insurrectional leadership. If, as was true during the March Revolution in St. Petersburg, certain military units defected to the rebellious rioters, this was no assurance of automatic future support. The Parisian National Guard legions, which in February, 1848, refused to disperse the barricade builders, did not surrender their future freedom of action or blindly pledge themselves thereby to a successful insurrectionary government. Very clearly this collective withdrawal of the habit of obedience from an established government, while it may prove decisive in bringing victory to the insurrection, may also pose an explicit threat to the future authority of the new government.

Autonomous support is dangerous support, for the future of an insurrectionary government depends heavily on the disciplined unity of the rebels prior to their success and on the extent to which they have been conditioned to accept the decisions of a recognized leadership. It is possible that in the mid-twentieth century, the totalitarian party has succeeded in solving the dilemma of power seizure by controlling the revolutionary impetus from its very inception. The technique has involved not merely the creation of a highly centralized elite party but of a full-fledged state within a state in the very process of carrying on insurrection against the established regime. The examples of the Chinese Communists and the Viet Minh in Indochina come to mind—westernizing movements in an Oriental setting—though in both cases the accidents of prolonged conflict rather than deliberate policy may account for the blossoming of a full-fledged insurrectionary state with its own military, judicial and administrative powers long before final victory. In such a case the insurrection replaces the political power of the recognized state by its own within the area which it controls, thus conditioning a new habit of obedience both among its supporters and among the mass of the indifferent, the cautious and the hostile.

It may be objected that the foregoing discussion is no more than an elaborate semantic game, which, after conjuring up an artificial definition of political revolution, tests its suitability in a variety of historical settings. This new definition is not meant as a quixotic attempt to change common usage, even the common usage of historians. Just as professional economists will casually speak of capital and labor in connection with an industrial dispute, yet employ the term "capital" in a technical and much more specific meaning as well, historians may still use "revolution" in its undefinable sense, yet recognize the usefulness of a narrow and technical meaning of the word. The utility is two-fold: (1) revolution defined in terms of a dispersion of political power can be ascertained fairly readily and with reasonable objectivity; (2) once the historian has defined a situation as revolutionary, he is forewarned that he may have to shift his attention from the study of one power monopoly, the sovereign state, to two or more competing power blocs. This admonition will not, however, be very meaningful unless he has also defined a power bloc and has some idea where to look for one.

By a power bloc I refer to a group, too strong to be suppressed by ordinary police action, which has usurped military, administrative or judicial power traditionally held by the state. Such a group, defined in terms of its dynamics rather than its organization, may be a highly cohesive para-military formation such as the Nazi S. A. after 1930, an inspired improvisation like the workers' councils in the Russian Revolution of 1905 or a completely spontaneous jacquerie. It may be a cluster of state governments emerging as a Confederacy against a Federal Government;

it may be a bureaucracy systematically sabotaging the policies of its government or a national army that has escaped civilian tutelage. Since the power traditionally held by the central government varies according to country and period, what may be a revolutionary power bloc in one instance may not be recognized as such in another. While in the context of French centralization the Paris Commune of 1871 constituted a revolutionary power bloc, similar actions on the part of a Netherlands province of the seventeenth century would have been viewed as part and parcel of the established order.

Although this definition does not eliminate all ambiguities, the historian is able to identify readily the main power blocs where power has been dispersed by insurrection. Such a situation is most likely to occur, as our earlier discussion brought out, where the violent seizure of power has been accomplished by a loosely organized mass movement. Since insurrection substitutes armed force for the gentler art of political compromise, the major power blocs emerging before or after a successful uprising are likely also to rely on force or the threat of force. The exercise of military force by a substantial group unresponsive to state influence is the most obvious hallmark of a revolutionary power bloc. To identify such blocs the historian may well begin with the traditional agencies of governmental power—army, national guard, police, administration, judiciary—to determine whether any of these agencies have departed from their customary role of executors of state policy and become autonomous power centers. He must also survey new or revived organizations which have emerged from the insurrectional turmoil—political clubs, labor organizations, armed leagues—to assess the power at their disposal and the authority by which they exercise it.

Once several power blocs have been identified, the historian can construct a meaningful framework for studying revolutionary politics, whatever their ideological content. He should trace the internal structure and policies of each of these blocs as well as their interaction. Although among these the insurrectionary state is only one of several power centers, we may expect the state, regardless of ideology, to bend every effort toward reimposing obedience on its para-governmental competitors. In short, if an insurrection has been successful in toppling an established government, yet is unable to assume the traditional monopoly of power peculiar to the state, the very dynamic of the state qua state will prolong the contest. While stability under such circumstances is unlikely, the direction of change is by no means determined. What the historian will witness may be either the reconquest of power by the state, or the displacement of the state by one of the competing power blocs, or the disintegration of the country into smaller political units or into political chaos. The instability of revolution in the common sense meaning of the word and the tendency of most insurrectional governments to rely heavily on force even after they have come to power may thus be explained without recourse to some special revolutionary mentality or the implicit dialectic of a particular ideology. In the face of barriers to its power erected by Left or Right, the insurrectional state, regardless of program or ideology, will seek to surmount them by force if necessary.

The test of such a conceptual framework should be pragmatic: does it work? Does the use of such a device facilitate the historian's grasp of the politics of upheaval, or is this no more than a spelling out of what the historian does with or without conscious methodology? In the case of a revolution which has engaged the undivided attention of an army of historians over many decades, it may well be that such an approach may not provide any startling new insights. Even in the case of the French Revolution, however, it should be noted that not until very recent years has one of the decisive power blocs, the Parisian sansculottes, been seriously examined despite a wealth of surviving documentary evidence. The type of attack which I have suggested would not have relegated such analysis to the haphazard inducements of Marxist piety. Where revolutions have been studied less exhaustively, an analysis in terms of power blocs may be more fruitful, if only in uncovering significant gaps in our knowledge. . . .

By viewing revolution as a contest for state power in which all the contestants are on show, we may succeed in keeping the great simplifiers in check. We may at the same time become aware of how little is known about significant revolutionary movements. . . .We may also wish to take a second look at ideology as the motor of an insurrectionary government once we accept its drive for power as literally "natural," that is, in the nature of the state. Yet of itself this way of looking at revolution provides no answers. Though the framework may be new and even an improvement over the old, this is no guarantee that the completed structure for which we bear responsibility will be sound. What I offer is a tool, not a nostrum.

Samuel P. Huntington

3 REVOLUTION AND POLITICAL CHANGE

A revolution is a rapid, fundamental, and violent domestic change in the dominant values and myths of a society, in its political institutions, social structure, leadership, and government activity and policies. Revolutions are thus to be distinguished from insurrections, rebellions, revolts, coups, and wars of independence. A coup d'état in itself changes only leadership and perhaps policies; a rebellion or insurrection may change policies, leadership, and political institutions, but not social structure and values; a war of independence is a struggle of one community against rule by an alien community and does not necessarily involve changes in the social structure of either community. What is here called simply "revolution" is what others have called great revolutions, grand revolutions, or social revolutions. Notable examples are the French, Chinese, Mexican, Russian, and Cuban revolutions.

Revolutions are rare. Most societies have never experienced revolutions, and most ages until modern times did not know revolutions. Revolutions, in the grand sense, are, as Friedrich says, "a peculiarity of Western culture." The great civilizations of the past—Egypt, Babylon, Persia, the Incas, Greece, Rome, China, India, the Arab world—experienced revolts, insurrections, and dynastic changes, but these did not "constitute anything resembling the 'great' revolutions of the West."[1] The rise and fall of dynasties in the ancient empires and the changes back and forth from oligarchy and democracy in the Greek city-states were instances of political violence but not of social revolution. More precisely, revolution is characteristic of modernization. It is one way of modernizing a traditional society, and it was, of course, as unknown to traditional society in the

West as it was unknown to traditional societies elsewhere. Revolution is the ultimate expression of the modernizing outlook, the belief that it is within the power of man to control and to change his environment and that he has not only the ability but the right to do so. For this reason, as Hannah Arendt observes, "Violence is no more adequate to describe the phenomenon of revolution than change; only where change occurs in the sense of a new beginning, where violence is used to constitute an altogether different form of government, to bring about the formation of a new body politic . . . can we speak of revolution."[2]

The forerunner of the modern revolution was the English Revolution of the seventeenth century, whose leaders believed they had "great works to do, the planting of a new heaven and a new earth among us, and great works have great enemies."[3] Their semantics were religious but their purpose and effect were radically modern. By legislative action men would remake society. In the eighteenth century the image was secularized. The French Revolution created the awareness of revolution. It "cracked the modern consciousness and made men realize that revolution is a fact, that a great revolution may occur in a modern, progressive society. . . . after the French Revolution we find a conscious development of revolutionary doctrines in anticipation of revolutions to come, and the spread of a more active attitude toward conscious control over institutions in general."[4]

Revolution is thus an aspect of modernization. It is not something which can occur in any type of society at any period in its history. It is not a universal category but rather an historically limited phenomenon. It will not occur in highly traditional societies with very low levels of social and economic complexity. Nor will it occur in highly modern societies. Like other forms of violence and instability, it is most likely to occur in societies which have experienced some social and economic development and where the processes of political modernization and political development have lagged behind the processes of social and economic change.

Political modernization involves the extension of political consciousness to new social groups and the mobilization of these groups into politics. Political development involves the creation of political institutions sufficiently adaptable, complex, autonomous, and coherent to absorb and to order the participation of these new groups and to promote social and economic change in the society. The political essence of revolution is the rapid expansion of political consciousness and the rapid mobilization of new groups into politics at a speed which makes it impossible for existing political institutions to assimilate them. Revolution is the extreme case of the explosion of political participation. Without this explosion there is no revolution. A complete revolution, however, also involves a second phase: the creation and institutionalization of a new political order. The successful revolution combines rapid political mobilization and rapid political institutionalization. Not all revolutions produce a new political order. The measure of how revolutionary a revolution is is the rapidity and the scope of the expansion of political participation. The measure of how successful a revolution is is the authority and stability of the institutions to which it gives birth.

A full-scale revolution thus involves the rapid and violent destruction of existing political institutions, the mobilization of new groups into politics, and the creation of new political institutions. The sequence and the relations among these three aspects may vary from one revolution to another. Two general patterns can be identified. In the "Western" pattern, the political institutions of the old regime collapse; this is followed by the mobilization of new groups into politics and then by the creation of new political institutions. The "Eastern" revolution, in contrast, begins with the mobilization of new groups into politics and the creation of new political institutions and ends with the violent overthrow of the political institutions of the old order. The French, Russian, Mexican, and, in the first phases, Chinese revolutions approximate the Western model; the latter phases of the Chinese Revolution, the Vietnamese Revolution, and other colonial struggles against imperialist power approximate the Eastern model. In general, the sequence of movement from one phase to the next is much more clearly demarcated in the Western revolution than in the Eastern type. In the latter all three phases tend to occur more or less simultaneously. One fundamental difference in sequence, however, does exist between the two. In the Western revolution, political mobilization is the consequence of the collapse of the old regime; in the Eastern revolution it is the cause of the destruction of the old regime.

The first step in a Western revolution is the collapse of the old regime. Consequently, scholarly analysis of the causes of revolution usually focuses on the political, social, and economic conditions which existed under the old regime. Implicitly, such analyses assume that once the authority of the old regime has disintegrated, the revolutionary process is irreversibly underway. In fact, however, the collapse of many old regimes is not followed by full-scale revolution. The causes of collapse of the old regime are not necessarily sufficient to trigger off a major revolution. The events of 1789 in France led to a major social upheaval; those of 1830 and 1848 did not. The fall of the Manchu and Romanov dynasties was followed by great revolutions; the fall of the Hapsburg, Hohenzollern, Ottoman, and Qajar dynasties was not. The overthrow of traditional dictatorships in Bolivia in 1952 and in Cuba in 1958 set loose major revolutionary forces; the overthrow of traditional monarchies in Egypt in 1952 and in Iraq in 1958 brought new elites to power but did not completely destroy the structure of society. The downfall of the Syngman Rhee regime in Korea in 1960 might have marked the beginning of a great revolution, but it did not. In virtually all these instances, the same social, economic, and political conditions existed under the old regimes whose demise was not followed by revolution as existed under the old regimes whose demise was followed by revolution. Old regimes—traditional monarchies and traditional dictatorships with concentrated but little power—are continually collapsing but only rarely is this collapse followed by a major revolution. The factors giving rise to revolution, consequently, are as likely to be found in the conditions which exist after the collapse of the old regime as in those which exist before its downfall.

In the "Western" revolution very little overt action by rebellious groups is needed to overthrow the old regime. "The revolution," as Pettee says, "does not begin with the attack of a powerful new force upon the state. It begins simply with a sudden recognition by almost all the passive and active membership that the state no longer exists." The collapse is followed by an absence of authority. "Revolutionists enter the limelight, not like men on horseback, as victorious conspirators appearing in the forum, but like fearful children, exploring an empty house, not sure that it is empty."[5] Whether or not a revolution develops depends upon the number and the character of the groups entering the house. If there is a marked discrepancy in power among the remaining social forces after the old regime disappears, the strongest social force or combination of forces may be able to fill the vacuum and to reestablish authority, with relatively little expansion of political participation. The collapse of every old regime is followed by some rioting, demonstrations, and the projection into the political sphere of previously quiescent or suppressed groups. If a new social force (as in Egypt in 1952) or combination of social forces (as in Germany in 1918-19) can quickly secure control of the state machinery and particularly the instruments of coercion left behind by the old regime, it may well be able to suppress more revolutionary elements intent on mobilizing new forces into politics (the Moslem Brotherhood, the Spartacists) and thus forestall the emergence of a truly revolutionary situation. The crucial factor is the concentration or dispersion of power which follows the collapse of the old regime. The less traditional the society in which the old regime has collapsed and the more groups which are available and able and inclined to participate in politics, the more likely is revolution to take place.

If no group is ready and able to establish effective rule following the collapse of the old regime, many cliques and social forces struggle for power. This struggle gives rise to the competitive mobilization of new groups into politics and makes the revolution revolutionary. Each group of political leaders attempts to establish its authority and in the process either develops a broader base of popular support than its competitors or falls victim to them. Following the collapse of the old regime, three social types play major roles in the process of political mobilization. Initially, as Brinton and others have pointed out, the moderates (Kerensky, Madero, Sun Yat-sen) tend to assume authority. Typically, they attempt to establish some sort of liberal, democratic, constitutional state. Typically, also, they describe this as the restoration of an earlier constitutional order: Madero wanted to restore the constitution of 1856; the liberal Young Turks the constitution of 1876; and even Castro in his initial moderate phase held that his goal was the restoration of the constitution of 1940. In rare cases, these leaders may adapt to the subsequent intensification of the revolutionary process: Castro was the Kerensky and the Lenin of the Cuban Revolution. More frequently, however, the moderates remain moderate and are swept from power. Their failure stems precisely from their inability to deal with the problem of political mobilization. On the one hand, they lack the drive and the ruthlessness to stop the mobilization of new groups into politics; on the other, they lack the radicalism to lead it. The first alternative requires the concentration of power, the second its expansion. Unable and unwilling to perform either function, the liberals are brushed away either by counterrevolutionaries who perform the first or by more extreme revolutionaries who perform the second.

In virtually all revolutionary situations, counterrevolutionaries, often with foreign assistance, attempt to stop the expansion of political participation and to reestablish a political order in which there is little but concentrated power. Kornilov, Yuan Shih-kai, Huerta, and, in a sense, Reza Shah and Mustafa Kemal all played these roles in the aftermath of the downfall of the Porfirian regime and the Romanov, Ch'ing, Qajar, and Ottoman dynasties. As these examples suggest, the counterrevolutionaries are almost invariably military men. Force is a source of power, but it can have longer range effectiveness only when it is linked to a principle of legitimacy. Huerta and Kornilov had nothing but force and failed in the face of the radicalization of the revolution and the mobilization of more social groups into politics. Yuan Shih-kai and Reza Shah both attempted to establish new, more vigorous traditional systems of rule on the ruins of the previous dynasty. Many similarities existed between the two countries; the old dynasty had decayed and collapsed; foreign powers were openly and competitively intervening and preparing themselves for the possible dismemberment of the country; warlordism and anarchy were rampant; the principal hope for stability seemed to lie in the commanders of the new military forces which had been brought into existence in the last years of the decaying dynasty.

That Yuan Shih-kai failed to establish a new dynasty while Reza Shah Pahlevi succeeded is due primarily to the fact that political mobilization had gone much further in China than it had in Persia. The middle class in the Chinese cities was sufficiently well developed to have supported a nationalist movement since the 1890s. Students and intellectuals played a crucial role in Chinese politics while they were almost absent from the Persian scene. The lower level of social mobilization in Persia made it possible to give new vigor to traditional forms of rule. Indeed, in a sense, Reza Shah had no alternative: reportedly he was anxious to establish a Kemalist style republic in Iran but the opposition to abandonment of the traditional forms of legitimacy was so strong that he dropped the idea. In part because of this lower level of social mobilization, Reza Shah was able to identify himself with Persian nationalism. He became a symbol of Persian independence from Russian and British influence. In China, on the other hand, Yuan Shih-kai notably failed to respond vigorously to the Twenty-One Demands from Japan in 1915. This failure completed his isolation from the middle-class nationalist groups and deprived him of the authority necessary to counter-balance the disintegrative forces of warlordism.

The radical revolutionaries are the third major political group in a revolutionary situation. For ideological and tactical reasons, their goal is to expand political participation, to bring new masses into politics, and thereby to increase their own power. With the breakdown of the established institutions and procedures for co-opting groups into power and socializing them into the political order, the extremists have a natural advantage over their rivals. They are more willing to mobilize more groups into politics. Hence the revolution becomes more radical as larger and larger masses of the population are brought into the political scales. Since in most modernizing countries the peasants are the largest social force, the most revolutionary leaders are those who mobilize and organize the peasants for political action. In some instances, the appeals to the peasants and other lower class groups may be social and economic; in most instances, however, these will be supplemented by nationalist appeals. This process leads to the redefinition of the political community and creates the foundations for a new political order.

In Western revolutions the symbolic or actual fall of the old regime can be given a fairly precise date: July 14, 1789; October 19, 1911; May 25, 1911; March 15, 1917. These dates mark the beginning of the revolutionary process and the mobilization of new groups into politics as the competition among the new elites struggling for power leads them to appeal to broader and broader masses of the people. Out of this competition one group eventually establishes its dominance and re-establishes order either through force or the development of new political institutions. In Eastern revolutions, in contrast, the old regime is modern, it has more power and legitimacy, and hence it does not simply collapse and leave a vacuum of authority. Instead it must be overthrown. The distinguishing characteristic of the Western revolution is the period of anarchy or statelessness after the fall of the old regime while moderates, counterrevolutionaries, and radicals are struggling for power. The distinguishing characteristic of the Eastern revolution is a prolonged period of "dual power" in which the revolutionaries are expanding political participation and the scope and authority of their institutions of rule at the same time that the government is, in other geographical areas and at other times, continuing to exercise its rule. In the Western revolution the principal struggles are between revolutionary groups; in the Eastern revolution they are between one revolutionary group and the established order.

In terms of our twin concerns of institutions and participation, the Western revolution moves through the collapse of the established political institutions, the expansion of participation, the creation of new institutions. More elaborately, in Brinton's terms, it evolves from the fall of the old order, through the revolutionary honeymoon, the rule of the moderates, the efforts at counterrevolution, the rise of the radicals, the reign of terror and of virtue, and eventually, the thermidor.[6] The pattern of the Eastern revolution is quite different. The expansion of political participation and the creation of new political institutions are carried on simultaneously and gradually by the revolutionary counterelite and the collapse of the political institutions of the old regime marks the end rather than the beginning of the revolutionary struggle. In the Western revolution the revolutionaries come to power in the capital first and then gradually expand their control over the countryside. In the Eastern revolution they withdraw from central, urban areas of the country, establish a base area of control in a remote section, struggle to win the support of the peasants through terror and propaganda, slowly expand the scope of their authority, and gradually escalate the level of their military operations from individual terroristic attacks to guerrilla warfare to mobile warfare and regular warfare. Eventually they are able to defeat the government troops in battle. The last phase of the revolutionary struggle is the occupation of the capital.

In the Western revolution the fall of the old regime which marks the beginning of the revolutionary struggle can be given a precise date, but the end of the struggle is virtually impossible to identify; the revolution, in a sense, peters out as one group gradually establishes its preeminence and restores order. In the Eastern revolution, in contrast, it is impossible to date precisely the beginning of the revolution in the local attacks by small bands of insurrectionaries on village chiefs, governmental officials, and police patrols. The origins of the revolt are lost in the obscurity of jungle and mountain. The end of the revolutionary process, on the other hand, can be precisely dated symbolically or actually by the final conquest of power by the revolutionaries in the capital of the regime: January 31, 1949, January 1, 1959.

In the Western revolution, the revolutionaries fight their way out of the capital to capture control of the countryside. In the Eastern revolution they fight their way in from the remote areas of the countryside and eventually capture control of the capital. Hence, in the Western revolution the bloodiest fighting comes after the revolutionaries have seized power in the capital; in the Eastern revolution it comes before they capture the capital. In a Western revolution the capture of the central institutions and symbols of power is usually very rapid. In January, 1917, the Bolsheviks were a small, illegal, conspiratorial group, most of whose leaders were either in Siberia or in exile. Less than a year later they were the principal, although far from undisputed, political rulers of Russia. "You know," Lenin observed to Trotsky, "from persecution and a life underground, to come so suddenly into power. . . . *Es schwindelt!*"[7] The Chinese Communist leaders, in contrast, experienced no such exhilarating and dramatic change in circumstances. Instead they had to fight their way gradually and slowly to power over a 22-year period from their retreat into the countryside in 1927, through the fearsome battles of Kiangsi, the exhaustion of the Long March, the struggles against the Japanese, the civil war with the Kuomintang, until finally they made their triumphal entry into Peking. There was nothing "dizzying" about this process. During most of these years the Communist Party exercised effective political authority over substantial amounts of territory and numbers of people. It was a government attempting to expand its authority at the expense of another government rather than a band of conspirators attempting to overthrow a government. The acquisition of national power for the Bolsheviks was a dramatic change; for the Chinese Communists it was simply the culmination of a long drawn-out process.

One major factor responsible for the differing patterns of the Western and Eastern revolutions is the nature of the prerevolutionary regime. The Western revolution is usually directed against a highly traditional regime headed by an absolute monarch or dominated by a land-owning aristocracy. The revolution typically occurs when this regime comes into severe financial straits, when it fails to assimilate the intelligentsia and other urban elite elements, and when the ruling class from which its leaders are drawn has lost its moral self-confidence and will to rule. The Western revolution, in a sense, telescopes the initial "urban breakthrough" of the middle class and the "green uprising" of the peasantry into a single convulsive, revolutionary process. Eastern revolutions, in contrast, are directed against at least partially modernized regimes. These may be indigenous governments that have absorbed some modern and vigorous middle-class elements and that are led by new men with the ruthlessness, if not the political skill, to hang on to power, or they may be colonial regimes in which the wealth and power of a metropolitan country gives the local government a seemingly overwhelming superiority in all the conventional manifestations of political authority and military force. In such circumstances no quick victory is possible and the urban revolutionaries have to fight their way to power through a prolonged rural insurrectionary process. Western revolutions are thus precipitated by weak traditional regimes; Eastern revolutions by narrow modernizing ones.

In the Western revolution the principal struggle is usually between the moderates and the radicals; in the Eastern revolution it is between the revolutionaries and the government. In the Western revolution the moderates hold power briefly and insecurely between the fall of the old regime and the expansion of participation and conquest of power by the radicals. In the Eastern pattern, the moderates are much weaker; they do not occupy positions of authority; and as the revolution gets underway, they are crushed by the government or the revolutionaries or they are forced by the polarization process to join one side or the other. In the Western revolution, terror occurs in the latter phases of the revolution and is employed by the radicals after they come to power primarily against the moderates and other revolutionary groups with whom they have struggled. In the Eastern revolution, in contrast, terror marks the first phase of the revolutionary struggle. It is used by the revolutionaries when they are weak and far removed from power to persuade or to coerce support from peasants and to intimidate the lower reaches of officialdom. In the Eastern pattern, the stronger the revolutionary movement becomes the less it tends to rely on terrorism. In the Western pattern the loss of the will and the ability to rule by the old elite is the first phase in the revolution; in the Eastern model it is the last phase and is a product of the revolutionary war waged by the counterelite against the regime. Emigration, consequently, reaches its peak at the beginning of the revolutionary struggle in the Western model but at the end of the struggle in the Eastern pattern.

INSTITUTIONAL AND SOCIAL CIRCUMSTANCES OF REVOLUTION

Revolution, as we have said, is the broad, rapid, and violent expansion of political participation outside the existing structure of political institutions. Its causes thus lie in the interaction between political institutions and social forces. Presumably revolutions occur when there is the coincidence of certain conditions in political institutions and certain circumstances among social forces. In these terms, the two prerequisites for revolution are, first, political institutions incapable of providing channels for the participation of new social forces in politics and of new elites in government, and secondly, the desire of social forces, currently excluded from politics, to participate therein, this desire normally arising from the group's feeling that it needs certain symbolic or material gains which it can achieve only by pressing its demands in the political sphere. Ascending or aspiring groups and rigid or inflexible institutions are the stuff of which revolutions are made.[8]

The many recent efforts to identify the causes of revolution have given primary emphasis to its social and psychological roots. They have thus tended to overlook the political and institutional factors which affect the probability of revolution. Revolutions are unlikely in political systems which have the capacity to expand their power and to broaden participation within the system. It is precisely this fact that makes revolutions unlikely in highly institutionalized modern political systems—constitutional or communist—which are what they are simply because they have developed the procedures for assimilating new social groups and elites desiring to participate in politics. The great revolutions of history have taken place either in highly centralized traditional monarchies (France, China, Russia), or in narrowly based military dictatorships (Mexico, Bolivia, Guatemala, Cuba), or in colonial regimes (Vietnam, Algeria). All these political systems demonstrated little if any capacity to expand their power and to provide channels for the participation of new groups in politics.

Perhaps the most important and obvious but also most neglected fact about successful great revolutions is that they do not occur in democratic political systems. This is not to argue that formally democratic governments are immune to revolution. This is surely not the case, and a narrowly based, oligarchical democracy may be as incapable of providing for expanded political participation as a narrowly based oligarchical dictatorship. Nonetheless, the absence of successful revolutions in democratic countries remains a striking fact, and suggests that, on the average, democracies have more capacity for absorbing new groups into their political systems than do political systems where power is equally small but more concentrated. The absence of successful revolutions against communist dictatorships suggests that the crucial distinction between them and the more traditional autocracies may be precisely this capacity to absorb new social groups.

If a democracy acts in an "undemocratic" manner by obstructing the expansion of political participation, it may well encourage revolution. In the Philippines, for instance, the Hukbalahap movement of the tenant farmers of Luzon first attempted to achieve its goals by exploiting the opportunities for participation offered by a democratic political system. The Huks participated in the elections and elected several members of the Philippine legislature. The legislature, however, refused to seat these representatives, and, as a result, the Huk leaders returned to the countryside to precipitate revolt. The revolution was subdued only when the Philippine government under the leadership of Magsaysay undercut the Huk appeal by providing symbolic and actual opportunities for the peasantry to identify themselves with and to participate in the existing political institutions.

Revolution requires not only political institutions which resist the expansion of participation but also social groups which demand that expansion. In theory, every social class which has not been incorporated into the political system is potentially revolutionary. Virtually every group does go through a phase, brief or prolonged, when its revolutionary propensity is high. At some point, the group begins to develop aspirations which lead it to make symbolic or material demands on the political system. To achieve its goals, the group's leaders soon realize that they must find avenues of access to the political leaders and means of participation in the political system. If these do not exist and are not forthcoming, the group and its leaders become frustrated and alienated. Conceivably this condition can exist for an indefinite period of time; or the original needs which led the group to seek access to the system may disappear; or the group may attempt to enforce its demands on the system through violence, force, or other means illegitimate to the system. In the latter instance, either the system adapts itself to accord some legitimacy to these means and thus to accept the necessity of meeting the demands which they were used to support, or the political elite attempts to suppress the group and to end the use of these methods. No inherent reason exists why such action should not be successful, provided the groups within the political system are sufficiently strong and united in their opposition to admitting the aspiring group to political participation.

Frustration of its demands and denial of the opportunity to participate in the political system may make a group revolutionary. But it takes more than one revolutionary group to make a revolution. A revolution necessarily involves the alienation of many groups from the existing order. It is the product of "multiple dysfunction" in society.[9] One social group can be responsible for a coup, a riot, or a revolt, but only a combination of groups can produce a revolution. Conceivably this combination might take the form of any number of possible group coalitions. In actuality, however, the revolutionary alliance must include some urban and some rural groups. The opposition of urban groups to the government can produce the continued instability characteristic of a praetorian state. But only the combination of urban opposition with rural opposition can produce a revolution. In 1789, Palmer observes, "Peasant and bourgeois were at war with the same enemy, and this is what made possible the French Revolution."[10] In a broader sense, this is what makes possible every revolution. To be more precise, the probability of revolution in a modernizing country depends upon: (a) the extent to which the urban middle class—intellectuals, professionals, bourgeoisie—are alienated from the existing order; (b) the extent to which the peasants are alienated from the existing order; and (c) the extent to which the urban middle class and peasants join together not only in fighting against "the same enemy" but also in fighting for the same cause. This cause is usually nationalism.

Revolutions are thus unlikely to occur if the period of the frustration of the urban middle class does not coincide with that of the peasantry. Conceivably, one group might be highly alienated from the political system at one time and the other group at another time; in such circumstances revolution is improbable. Hence a slower general process of social change in a society is likely to reduce the possibility that these two groups will be simultaneously alienated from the existing system. To the extent that social-economic modernization has become more rapid over time, consequently, the probability of revolution has increased. For a major revolution to occur, however, not only must the urban middle class and the peasantry be alienated from the existing order, but they must also have the capacity and the incentive to act along parallel, if not cooperative, lines. If the proper stimulus to joint action is missing, then again revolution may be avoided.

Claude Welch, Jr., and Mavis B. Taintor

4 WHAT IS POLITICAL REVOLUTION?

Nothing could have been further from the minds of the French court of mid-1789 than sweeping and violent political upheaval. Some signs of danger could be glimpsed. But the nobles clustered around the king paid little heed. Why should they alter their ways? Was France, as they knew it, really endangered by the attitudes of scattered peasants and pedants? Was not the country experiencing relatively steady economic growth?

When Parisian mobs sacked the Bastille, shock ran through the court. What did this spontaneous action portend? Upon hearing the news, Louis XVI murmured, "It is a revolt." "No Sire," replied the Duke de Rouchefoucauld-Liancourt, "It is a revolution." The Duke was correct, for in the next decade France experienced tumultuous change—the execution of the king and several thousand others, civil insurrection, international war, several coups d'état, an attempt to change basic philosophical foundations of the state, and finally the emergence of Napoleon Bonaparte. The French Revolution—not the "revolt" Louis XVI imagined—ran its violent course.

Since 1789, revolution has become a popular word. It is used loosely to mean any major change, and is frequently confused with other words that refer to sudden shifts in government institutions or personnel, such as revolt, rebellion, coup, putsch, jacquerie, insurrection or civil war. Two examples of imprecise use recently appeared in the daily press, when President Nixon described a proposed federal administrative restructuring as "the new American Revolution," while Yippie leader Abbie Hoffman entitled his sardonic book *Revolution for the Hell of It.* Certainly Richard Nixon and Abbie Hoffman use revolution in widely different ways!

Speaking broadly, a revolution involves profound change—in lifestyle, in institutions, in social relationships. The sweeping alterations involved in the shifts from agricultural to industrial society were aptly deemed the "Industrial Revolution." Looking at the rapid spread of communications to the developing countries, many scholars and diplomats have commented upon the "Revolution of rising aspirations" and its counterpart, the "Revolution of rising frustrations." Karl Marx considered shifts in the "mode of production" to be revolutionary transformations. Peasant discontent and militancy have been viewed (by Mao Tse-tung and Frantz Fanon, for example) as the essence of revolution. In short, any serious student of revolution confronts confusion about its definition, its causes, its pathways, its results.

This [work] will attempt to clear up some of the ambiguities surrounding the word revolution by focusing upon political revolution. We will thus leave the study of social and economic transformation to others, although we recognize that political revolution is heavily influenced by economic and social factors. Political revolution as used in this work, exhibits four aspects:

1. a change in the means of selecting political leaders, and the creation of new political elites, usually by extra-constitutional or non-systemic means;
2. new and expanded channels for access to positions of political power;
3. expanded political participation, possibly temporarily; and
4. the creation and solidification of a new political order on a different basis of political legitimacy.

To clarify this definition, we shall, in these opening pages, sketch contrasts among various types of extra-constitutional means of political change, then turn to "revolution" as a concept employed by political philosophers. The third section . . . will examine the factors that apparently precipitate political revolution. In the final part, we shall suggest the attributes of the new order to which political revolution gives birth.

VARIETIES OF POLITICAL CHANGE

Political change takes many forms. Revolution is perhaps the least common form. Most political systems change through gradual reform, as by change of elites or government institutions through electoral means. Revolution, on the other hand, involves rapid tearing down of existing political institutions and building them anew on different foundations.

Some types of political change closer in form to revolution than reform such as coup d'état, revolt or civil war, can easily be confused with revolution. Political change of these types generally is accompanied by violence and bloodshed, as revolution may be. However, these similarities are superficial, at best. Violence is *not* the distinguishing mark of political revolution. Nor is change of leadership the essence of political revolution. Coups, revolts or civil wars all involve the change of leadership of the central government, or of a certain geographical area within a state. What distinguishes political revolution from these other quick and violent forms of political change is the institutionalization and consolidation of a new political order. A coup involves an illegal or extra-constitutional change of leadership at the upper levels of government; a revolt or a civil war is an organized politico-military challenge to the established central government. These forms do not create new political institutions based on a different source of legitimacy. A revolution, unlike a coup or revolt, brings political change that penetrates all levels of society and encompasses the entire state. To be certain, a coup, a civil war, or revolt could preface a revolution, as the triggering event for a complete overthrow of existing political institutions. Without new political institutions, and without the mobilization of new groups into politics, however, a change in leadership or a challenge to the existing political order stops short of political revolution.

Political revolution should also be distinguished from what Ted Gurr has termed "turmoil" and "conspiracy." Turmoil, according to Gurr, is characterized by "mass participation, usually rather spontaneous, disorganized, and with low intensity of violence."[1] It reflects widespread, but relatively unfocused, discontent. Turmoil may be found in either urban or rural settings. Examples of turmoil drawn from American history might include Nat Turner's rebellion, the 1863 New York City conscription riots, or the Watts uprising of 1965. Conspiracy, by contrast, lacks a mass basis. It is a creation of, by, and for an elite. Conspiracy (especially in its most prevalent form, the coup d'état) aims at replacing government personnel, usually with the plotters themselves. Thus, the target is highly specific, in contrast to the more scattered, diffuse targets of turmoil. Conspiracy typically is limited to the capital city; turmoil may arise as easily in teeming urban quarters as in relatively open rural settings.

Political revolution differs qualitatively from both turmoil and conspiracy—even though turmoil and conspiracy figure in the history of "Great Revolutions," such as in France or the Soviet Union. For example, both included urban turmoil (the capture of the Bastille and the invasion of the Tuileries; the march on the Winter Palace); rural uprisings (the Vendee); and attempted coup d'état (the displacement of the Girondins by the Jacobins or the coups of the Directory period; the Kornilov putsch or Lenin's conspiracy against the Kerensky government). Yet the whole became greater than the sum of the parts. Participation was not confined to limited groups; it became widespread. Discontent with the existing political system was reflected in both alienation and willingness to resort to violence to effect change; discontent led to the establishment of new political institutions and bases of legitimacy, thereby succeeding as political revolutions.

REVOLUTION AS A CONCEPT IN POLITICAL PHILOSOPHY

The origin of the word revolution comes from astronomy. The Latin term from which the English word is derived designated the regular cyclical motion of the stars in the heavens in accordance with immutable law, and gained increasing importance from Copernicus's famous *De Revolutionibus Orbium Coelestrium*. Revolution first was applied to politics as a metaphor in the seventeenth century, to describe a political movement that returned to some previous point. It carried the connotation of a swing back, through some irresistible and preordained plan, to the point of departure. A revolution was out of the hands of man and guided by the forces of nature. As should be obvious, any elements of novelty (intimately connected with the contemporary meaning of the word) were conspicuously absent from the original meaning. In its seventeenth century political usage, revolution meant that the few forms of government known to man recurred on earth with the same regularity and irresistible force that made the stars follow their prescribed paths in the heavens.

Certainly the concepts of revolt and rebellion were well known in the ancient and medieval eras. However, these concepts were not synonymous with the contemporary concept of political revolution, for three reasons. First, political theorists prior to the eighteenth century considered rebellion against established authority legitimate under certain conditions, such as against the rule of an unjust monarch. Such "legitimate" rebellion would not challenge the foundations of the political order, but could replace a person or modify the type of regime. Until the appearance of Calvinist spokesmen in the seventeenth century, political philosophers remained silent on the right of a people to be their own rulers or to appoint people from their own ranks to govern. There were words and phrases in all languages that described subjects rising against rulers, but there were none that could describe a change so fundamental that subjects became rulers. The vast majority of mankind—the low and the poor and all those who had always lived in subjection to others—had never risen up to become the sovereigns of the land. The very thought of such an action was impossible.

Secondly, political change before the Calvinist movement was inextricably associated with divine authority or with a non-human force. To the ancient Greeks, the course of human events and of political change was guided by divine forces beyond the reach of man. These forces were commonly referred to as "fortune" or "divine machinery." Later, the idea of non-human forces deciding the course of human events became bound up in Christian conceptions of God's omnipotence. It was not until the Calvinists had brought about what Michael Walzer calls the "revolution of the saints"[2] that men, independent of the established government, thought that they could play a creative role in the political world and could significantly affect the political order.

Men involved in political revolution must be conscious that a new political beginning is possible, though they may not initially be aware that fundamental political change can or will occur. Political revolution may start as an attempt to make limited governmental reforms. For reform to become political revolution, it is necessary that those involved sense that the course of history will begin anew, that an entirely new story never told before is about to unfold, perhaps in accord with a specific program.

A shared faith in the common man, or in "the people" in general, forms an integral part of political revolution, in its contemporary sense. The notion that men are born free and equal and that all mankind has a right to participate in government affairs did not exist in the ancient world, the third reason political revolution is a creation primarily of the past two centuries.

The equality that became the byword of the American and French revolutions was a totally new and different notion from the ancient concept of equality. Equality between men existed, according to the ancients, only under the authority of the polis or city-state, and only within prescribed social gradations. Men were born unequal, and remained unequal. Rights of citizenship were confined to a fraction of those living within each political unit. Fundamental differences thus exist between this ancient concept of inequality based upon birth and the modern notion of men being born free and equal. Among the most revolutionary of documents is that intoning "We hold these truths to be self-evident, that all men are created equal." This idea of all mankind being born free, equal and capable of worldly success was new to the eighteenth century, and it fired the imagination of the revolutionary leaders in both America and Europe. Today the involvement of the people—the great mass of the lowly and poor—in political revolution is considered to be both natural and necessary; it has become enshrined in revolutionary tradition; it has been confirmed by twentieth century revolutionary writings. Political revolution thus reflects the observation of Samuel P. Huntington: "Revolution is the ultimate expression of the modernizing outlook, the belief that it is within the power of man to control and to change his environment. . . ."[3] A far cry, indeed, from the eternally recurring motions of heavenly bodies!

WHAT PRECIPITATES POLITICAL REVOLUTION?

Explanations of "why" particular political revolutions break out abound in university libraries. Finding the harbingers or causes common to all political revolutions becomes a complex task. For example, analysts of the French Revolution have cited a wide variety of factors: the critical writings of Rousseau and other philosophes, barriers within the French aristocracy to upward mobility, sharp contrasts between overall rising prosperity and the economic degradation of peasants, the imminent bankruptcy and fiscal mismanagement of the state, and confusion within the governing structure. A similar variety arises in the literature dealing with the Russian Revolution: the exhaustion of World War 1, awakened political consciousness manifested in political strikes, the conspiratorial genius of Lenin, the vacillation of the Kerensky government, and its continued prosecution of the war.

At the risk of over-simplification, we suggest four preconditions of political revolution:

1. a widespread sense of disappointment with the conditions of life, usually characterized as a feeling of relative deprivation;
2. a focusing of this feeling of disappointment upon political institutions, reflected in growing alienation from them, and enhanced by such factors as increased nationalist sentiment, military defeat, or sudden economic setbacks;
3. vacillation, incompetence, and incoherence of political leadership, particularly through unyielding resistance to reform or through injudicious use of force;
4. a combination of economic and political feelings of deprivation with the acceptance of a myth or ideology of change, through which alternative political institutions develop their own bases of legitimacy.

Popular Discontent and Relative Deprivation. No political system exists without some degree of popular discontent. In many political systems, discontent may be extensive—and resources insufficient to meet demands. The translation of discontent into sweeping political change requires politicization of discontent; the delegitimization of political institutions; divisions and incompetence among the political elite; and the development of a revolutionary ideology that gains its own legitimacy.

Revolution seems to require a sense of discontent suffused throughout the entire population, leadership strata and ordinarily politically quiescent citizens. As Alexander Groth has suggested, numerous political systems have suffered from "mass alienation, discontent and even serious sporadic outbursts of popular violence without succumbing to 'revolutions' or even substantial modifications of regime for very long periods of time."[4] Two earlier analysts of revolution have spoken of "general restlessness"[5] and of a sense of "cramp"[6] as harbingers of revolution. Restlessness and concern can be found in any political system. However, the *extent* and *nature* of discontent become significant in this context. Politically-directed discontent, if confined to the elite, leads to conspiracy; discontent within the populace at large results in turmoil. Conspiracy may change personnel, turmoil certain government policies; neither by itself constitutes political revolution. Political revolution requires a coalescence of the discontents that, under other circumstances, might lead either to turmoil or to conspiracy. "Only organization elites with a measure of expertise and resources at their command have been able to translate riot into revolution, and effectuate a transition from a mere negation of an existent political order into the establishment of a new one," Groth has written.[7]

Especially marked in the French and Russian revolutions was the alienation of intellectuals. Their disenchantment forms only part of the story, however. Such alienation might not have been transformed into political action: after all, grumbling about "the system" on the pages of obscure journals has satisfied the creative urges of many intellectuals in many settings. The likelihood of political revolution depends upon the alienation of both the usually voiceless masses and the intellectuals.

Several social scientists have suggested ways of assessing alienation. As symptoms of restlessness, Lyford Edwards pointed to increases in foreign travel, crime rates or urbanization, and emigration.[8] Widespread discouragement about the possiblity for change (to use Edwards' term, "balked disposition") indicates restlessness and the inability of the political system to cope with change. More recently, scholars have emphasized relative deprivation as a way of assessing popular discontent or restlessness. Gurr, whose article on psychological factors in civil violence is [an important article], defines relative deprivation as discrepancies perceived by individuals between the goods and conditions of life to which they feel justly entitled and the goods and conditions of life actually within reach. By measuring the magnitude, intensity, and scope of such discrepancies over time, social scientists might predict the likelihood of civil violence, and whether it will take the form of conspiracy, turmoil, or revolution.

Relative deprivation, we suggest, may arise from the breakdown of traditional mores and the emergence of a desire to raise individuals' standards of life. In Bagehot's expressive phrase, breaking the "cake of custom" may bring widespread alienation.

Alienation from Political Institutions. No political revolution has ever sprung directly and solely from a sense of relative deprivation, however, no matter how widespread. Discontent must become politicized—that is, directed against political institutions—to bring about the second pre-condition. When a substantial portion of the population withdraws allegiance to these institutions, political revolution becomes likely.

All political systems seek ways of enhancing and rewarding compliance. In the well-known words of Hobbes, might must be transformed into right. Stability in political systems depends upon two factors, the apathy toward politics that usually characterizes a large majority of citizens, and the legitimacy which systems enjoy. Acquiescence appears to be a more usual response to politics than activity. Individuals may be prompted to political activity only if they believe their action will have beneficial effect. Required, in Walzer's words, are individuals who can carry out a detached appraisal of existing political systems, express their discontents and aspirations in terms of specific programs, and organize persons for sustained political activity.[9] They must share the belief that what the government does affects them—and, conversely, that what they do affects the government.

Should the government enjoy widespread support and legitimacy, political activity likely will follow "normal" pathways. Reform, not political revolution, will result. Under conditions of widespread popular discontent, however, individuals may be tempted toward extra-constitutional channels to press for change. A government experiencing relatively low legitimacy finds alterations pushed upon it, rather than through it; the political system becomes a target for pressure, not an instrument. The outbreak of political revolution symbolizes the near-total collapse of the government as a legitimate form of governance, in the eyes of the populace.

One of the most salient factors in political revolution and the loss of legitimacy by governments has been nationalism, notably in colonial territories. Evoked by awareness that the government is controlled by a foreign minority, political revolution in the twentieth century has become largely a nationalist phenomenon. The breakdown of colonial empires after both World Wars (the Ottoman and Austro-Hungarian empires after World War 1, on the basis of self-determination; the British, French, Belgian, and Dutch empires after World War 2, on the basis of anti-colonialism) bears witness to the importance of group awareness and differentiation from the ruling personnel in facilitating major political change. An alien government was not a legitimate government. The governed, who had not chosen to be governed from abroad, demanded the opportunity to select their own rulers.

Defeat in war may also reduce the legitimacy of the government. Military setback dissolves, or at least diminishes, the ability of the officer corps to support the governing elite. No revolution can be won against a modern army when the army puts its full strength against the insurrection, Katharine Chorley noted in 1943. Should an army be dispirited by defeat, however, it may actually abet insurrection. Lady Chorley's observations seem to have been confirmed by the triumph of the Chinese Communist Party in the face of the Kuomintang's defeat by the Japanese, and by the ouster of King Farouk by the Free Officers following Egypt's defeat by Israel in 1948.

Sharp, sudden economic downturns likewise have the effect of turning popular discontent or relative deprivation toward political institutions. James Davies deemed political revolution most likely to occur "when a prolonged period of objective economic and social development is followed by a short period of sharp reversal."[10] Individuals do not lightly participate in insurrection—unless they seek, as Eric Hoffer suggests . . . , a new, close-knit collective body with which they can feel pride and confidence.

Nationalism under conditions of foreign rule, defeat in war, and the "J-curve" of sudden economic deprivation, in combination or singly, substantially diminish the legitimacy a government enjoys. Should this diminution be accompanied by inconsistent and possibly self-defeating policies, as we shall now discuss, the legitimacy of political institutions will be seriously jeopardized.

Inconsistent Government Policies. The historian of revolution generally works with a profoundly incomplete set of sources: he is usually limited to "successful" revolutions, which have widened political participation and developed new institutions atop the ruins of the old. Since history is written—at least initially—by the victors, the chronicles of revolution have emphasized the malfeasance of the ancien régime, whose blunderings made political upheaval unavoidable. Many an apologist of revolution has documented his case by almost exclusive reference to the venality of the Kuomintang, the court of Louis XVI, or the Czarist autocracy. This explanation is insufficient, and possibly misleading.

As Alexis de Tocqueville emphasized, revolution occurred *not* in extremely poorly administered states, but in countries experiencing major efforts at administrative reform. The fiscal changes of Necker on the eve of the French Revolution, or the Stolypin reforms of post-

1905 Russia, come readily to mind. The key point is not elite incompetence, as glimpsed with the clarity of hindsight, but the gap between the capacities of governmental institutions and the burdens and expectations placed upon them. Where there is high expectation for improvement without a corresponding capability to carry it through, the sense of relative deprivation becomes all the greater, and all the more focused upon the political institutions that had promised change.

There are several partial explanations of the gap. An unresponsive elite, unwilling to carry out reform effectively or to incorporate new ideas, may nonetheless increase the expectation of change, and so overburden the institutions of government as to debilitate them further. Unwilling to make major changes in "the system," political leaders can become intransigent, entrenched, apparently paralysed from significant action. Reforms that enhance expectations remain on the books, unimplemented; old ways linger, despite a rhetoric of alteration. Channels for peaceful protest or constitutional alteration may be blocked; the political elite may lose effective contact with the populace. Above all, if reform of any sort is obstinately blocked by those who hold power, the possibility for peaceful change may be lost and the likelihood of explosive change enhanced. "What is ultimately fatal," Lawrence Stone has noted, "is the compounding of [the elite's] errors by intransigence. If it fails to anticipate the needs for reform, if it blocks all peaceful, constitutional means of social adjustment, then it unites the various deprived elements in singleminded opposition to it, and drives them down the narrow road to violence."[11]

The extensive use of violence by the state itself may enhance the likelihood of political revolution. It was noted earlier that political systems derive their authority from a sense their decisions are legitimate. Force remains an ultimate sanction, employed relatively rarely—at least in a "healthy" system. Individual citizens have the opportunity to express their discontents within the system, without major risk of incarceration or similar restraints. However, should a government ham-handedly resort to coercion, it may find its legitimacy seriously weakened, through a process Talcott Parsons has deemed "power deflation":

Essentially, a constitutional regime is marked, on the one hand, by restraints in the expectation of fulfillment of various demands and, on the other, by restraint in the coercion of the opposition by those in power. In particular, the leadership refrain from abridging the freedom to displace the incumbents from power, not only by maintaining the electoral rules, but by upholding the other normal components of political freedom like freedoms of the press, of assembly, and so forth. The opposition must be free to influence the voters, although neither they nor the incumbents should coerce or bribe them.

It is when, in the vicious circle of power deflation, these restraints are broken in the interaction between incumbents and opposition that the makings of a revolutionary situation are present.[12]

Inconsistent use of coercion can both speedily alienate individuals and focus their discontent upon political institutions. "Power deflation"— a resort to force because the usual channels of peaceful change are clogged—testifies to the inadequacies of political institutions prior to revolution. "Power deflation" signifies loss of legitimacy.

Are there ways of assessing this diminution of legitimacy? Greater resort by the government to the use of force; diminished levels of political trust; withdrawal of support in such direct ways as refusal to pay taxes; development of new symbols, particularly nationalistic symbols; and indications of alienation noted earlier: such can be suggested as tentative, impressionistic measures of the delegitimization of political institutions. If they no longer seem capable of resolving major problems, political institutions have lost their legitimacy, their raison d'être. When coupled with leadership errors and the growth of a myth or ideology of a new society, political revolution looms even closer.

Motivating Ideals of Political Revolution. The shortcomings of the incumbent elite help enhance the appeal of an ideology of profound political transformation, the fourth precondition of political revolution. Legitimacy, to be transferred from existing institutions to the "new order" embodied in the revolution, requires a rationalization—be it called an ideology, a myth, a motivating ideal, or some other term. Whatever title may be used, revolution depends fourthly upon the presence of a vision of a better future, whose advent is portrayed as inevitable, which will improve the economic, political and social status of the participants, and which will establish broadened forms of political participation. It is the hope for a better future that unites the "have-nots" and the "have-to-have mores" into a broad basis of popular support.

"The emotion which furnishes the driving power to revolution is hope, not despair," Edwards has written.[13] Three major sets of ideas that provide a hope for the future and a vision of equality—Christianity, nationalism, and Marxism—have helped motivate political revolution. Christianity preached the equality of all before God. Nationalism promised the equality of all citizens as members of an independent political unit. Marxism furnished its followers with a vision of a better future, a society of classless harmony. Let us briefly examine all three.

Christianity is by no means unique in its promise of a transcendent future for its adherents. What is of particular note—and which gained political significance in the German peasant wars of 1525 and a little over a century later in the English Revolution—was the notion of the equality of all members, irrespective of their social status. Emphasis upon the individual marked Christianity especially in Protestantism—far more than other major world religions, such as Islam, Hinduism, or Buddhism, which spoke in terms of the "community of the faithful" or an ethic of subordination. It should not be assumed that Christianity is the only religion propitious for political revolution. Sweeping political transformations have been carried out in the name of indigenous religion (for example, the role of Shinto in the Meiji transformation of Japan), and in the name of Islam (for example, the separation of Pakistan from India). However, in the Western world, Albert Camus has written, "the history of rebellion is inseparable from the history of Christianity."[14]

Nationalism as a foundation for revolution took root in the American Revolution, and animated the French Revolution as it spread to the "natural frontiers" of France. However, in the twentieth century nationalism has become one of the two primary ideologies for political revolution. It extends the promise of participation and involvement in the workings of the state and society. In its anticolonial guise, nationalism suggests that a far better life might be achieved by ending foreign control. Its scope extends beyond the political sphere. To take India as an example, Gandhi pressed for *swaraj*, normally translated as "self-rule." Gandi intended more than political independence, on the other hand. *Swaraj* embraced moral, economic, and political self-sufficiency from Great Britain; reform of the caste system, the wearing of home-spun cloth rather than imported fabrics, and pressure for the transfer of power all entered into Gandhi's objectives.

A word of caution is in order here. The acquisition of self-government by a previously dependent colony should not be viewed, in and of itself, as a political revolution; this is a transfer of control, and may not have involved a basic shift in the social and economic contours of the particular state. A writer such as Frantz Fanon, for example, has castigated independence as a hand-over to so-called nationalist political parties, who distrust what Fanon considered to be the revolutionary proclivities of the peasantry. Fanon believed that violence would be necessary to complete what the acquisition of political independence had only started: the transition of individuals from "colonized persons" to self-governing citizens of independent nations. He favored, in other words, a major psychological reorientation beyond the hoisting of a new flag and admission to the United Nations. Nationalism, to Fanon, found its fruition in the development of an aware, responsible citizenry free of the constraints of external models.

The third set of ideas, and the other primary contemporary ideology for political revolution, is Marxism, as reinterpreted and applied by

Lenin and Mao Tse-tung in particular. Marxism, as a set of beliefs, mingled the historically "inevitable," the economically determined, and the better life that would follow changes in the mode of production. It offered panaceas to a society disoriented by industrialization and agrarian reform. States in the early stages of industrial development may find Marxism and its variants a compelling explanation for their condition.

We must distinguish, however, between Marxism and techniques of seizing power suggested by Lenin in (for example) *State and Revolution*. The "historical inevitability" argument seems to have carried most weight when combined with peasant grievances, especially over land. Marx had envisaged revolution in the most industrialized societies—yet his beliefs had their greatest political impact in relatively backward societies, notably the Soviet Union and China. This impact resulted, in substantial measure, from the opportunity for rural inhabitants to join their land grievances with the belief of urban dwellers (especially the relatively better-educated) in the inevitability of revolutionary transformation. Leon Trotsky, one of the prime architects of the Russian Revolution, recognized this union as highly significant, [but] the . . . standard Marxist conception of revolution emanating from change in the mode of production may obscure rather than clarify the "causes" of contemporary political revolutions.

To recapitulate, the likelihood of political revolution appears to depend upon a host of factors. Feelings of frustration and discontent, widespread in society, must be focused upon political institutions. These institutions, in turn, must be viewed as rigid and unyielding, as inaccessible and unconcerned. Inconsistent use of force by the political elite may deepen the grievances harbored against political institutions. The growth of a myth of economic, social and political betterment provides an opportunity for the full transfer of allegiance and legitimacy to new institutions. It is with the emergence of alternative political institutions that revolution comes to public attention. The absence of any of the above factors makes revolution unlikely; the alternatives seem to be reform spread over time, maintenance of the status quo, or possible political disintegration.

REVOLUTION AND THE CONSOLIDATION OF A NEW POLITICAL ORDER

A "successful" revolution not only overthrows the ancien régime; it carries through political mobilization of new groups, creates new and stronger political institutions, and leads to the acceptance of new political values and concepts of legitimacy. Most studies of revolution stop short of the creation of new political institutions. Such analyses tend to emphasize preconditions, precipitants, and the seizure of control, rather than the consolidation of power and the implantation of new political values.

For example, both Lyford Edwards (*The Natural History of Revolution*) and Crane Brinton (*The Anatomy of Revolution*) conclude with "the return to normality" or "Thermidor." Revolutions end, these authors hint, not with a bang, but with a sigh of relief. However, it should be obvious that what is "normal" after the upheavals of political revolution is not the "normal" of the ancien régime. From political revolution issues a new political order, marked by changed values, institutions, and attitudes toward politics.

In her fascinating book *On Revolution*, Hannah Arendt pointed out a basic contradiction in the aims of political revolutionaries. On the one hand, they seek destruction of a beleaguered and sclerosed ancien régime, of instruments of government apparently inadequate to retain the necessary support of the populace. On the other hand, political revolutionaries seek construction, as well as destruction: the building of institutions that create a "more perfect union," that more effectively promote the common welfare.

Such institution-building lacks the excitement and immediacy of the outbreak of political revolution. Yet the "success" of political revolution depends not upon a dramatic seizure of control, but upon the conscious and inspired development of legitimized political institutions as the tumult of insurrection ebbs. Changes of this sort rarely attract attention. They occur in an atmosphere not charged with the excitement and tension of the outbreak of revolution. The prevalent aura is rather one of retreat and disinterest. After a period of major political and social upheaval, a population becomes both physically and psychologically exhausted. Thus crisis is followed by fatigue; after the reign of terror comes Thermidor. However, it is the final stage of a revolution that determines its success or failure.

Much more must go on during this last phase of the revolution than the mere quieting down or cooling off of society in general. During this period, the new political order as envisioned by the revolutionary leaders and as suggested in the motivating ideals or ideology must become authoritative and legitimate heir to the old social and political society, become modified, or be lost altogether. In the latter case, no new political order has been established. The revolution has failed. The violence and upheaval experienced by society have not been followed by fundamental and sweeping political change. For political revolution to succeed, a new order must be institutionalized, made legitimate, and stabilized. Only then can fundamental change permeate all levels and aspects of society.

The consolidation of the new order is brought about through legal and constitutional steps, through elite support, and through mass support. The legal foundation of the revolutionary political order begins by issuing a new constitution. A constitution has become a sine qua non for any nation state in the modern world. For a new government, a constitution symbolizes the authority and legitimacy of its order, and also provides an outline of political institutions. Through the constitution, the revolutionary government can legalize new political institutions, the new leadership, and popular involvement in the political process. However, the importance of such documents can be over-emphasized. The constitution of a contemporary post-revolutionary state such as China may serve only as a symbol of nationhood, not as an important source of legitimacy or authority.

A more important source of legitimacy in the contemporary world is expanded political mobilization, so that individuals become participants. In order to be stable, the new regime must build political institutions, such as parties, that can accept and channel this large and rapid expansion of political participation. Without such institutions, popular support for the new political order may be difficult to maintain.

It is not happenstance that the French Revolution gave birth to both political parties and popular councils, through which individuals can participate in politics.[15] As Arendt noted, both party and council systems were unknown prior to the eighteenth century, inasmuch as both sprang from the modern, revolutionary tenet that all inhabitants of a given territory are entitled to be admitted to the public political realm.[16] Political participation and popular support require avenues that are known, utilized, and regarded as legitimate, by the citizens.

Political revolution also affects the composition and outlooks of government personnel. In order to implement revolutionary programs and plans, the elites who staff government bureaucracies must co-operate with the political leaders who rose to the top as the old order disintegrated. Without such support, the new political leadership is powerless and isolated, although it can continue to appeal to the spirit of the revolution to forestall . . . its apparent suffocation.

There are two ways that the political leaders can assure bureaucratic elites so necessary to the daily running of a government. Revolutionary leaders may either utilize the old elite structure, thereby creating a situation of dual power, or they may create new elites, in the process possibly losing much efficiency and expertise. Neither method is problem-free. Relying on the elites of a former regime creates a potential challenge to the leaders' power and authority; building new elites is both costly and time-consuming. . . .

The institutionalization of mass participation and the development of elite support are both necessary aspects of the consolidation of the new political order brought through revolution. While the legal foundations of the new regime are useful for symbolic purposes in the modern world, they are less important than mass participation and elite support in ensuring a stable and firm future for the revolution.

To conclude, political revolution is not a short-run, sudden phenomenon. Before political revolution can occur, individuals must enjoy opportunities for political participation without the fetters (at least theoretically!) of presumed inability to influence the structures, not simply the activities of political institutions. Only in the "modern" age—generally speaking, in the past two centuries—have individuals sensed the opportunity for major political restructuring. Since revolutions are born of hope, an aspiration for political transformation logically precedes the building of the new order. Rebelliousness, not acquiescence, lies at the root of political revolution.

The focusing of discontent upon political institutions stretches over many years. No political revolution, in the judgment of Lyford Edwards, spanned less than three generations. Though the "events" that capture popular imagination may occupy a brief span of time, both the preparation for the revolution and the consolidation of the new political order take up many decades. Political revolution is not made in a moment. It is a rare, protracted, complex, and intermeshing set of events that, if successful in the clear hindsight that history offers, brings the effective establishment of new political institutions and the popular attitudes necessary for their support. Of such is political revolution made.

Hannah Arendt

5   THE MEANING OF REVOLUTION

The modern concept of revolution, inextricably bound up with the notion that the course of history suddenly begins anew, that an entirely new story, a story never known or told before, is about to unfold, was unknown prior to the two great revolutions at the end of the eighteenth century. Before they were engaged in what then turned out to be a revolution, none of the actors had the slightest premonition of what the plot of the new drama was going to be. However, once the revolutions had begun to run their course, and long before those who were involved in them could know whether their enterprise would end in victory or disaster, the novelty of the story and the innermost meaning of its plot became manifest to actors and spectators alike. As to the plot, it was unmistakably the emergence of freedom: in 1793, four years after the outbreak of the French Revolution, at a time when Robespierre could define his rule as the "despotism of liberty" without fear of being accused of speaking in paradoxes, Condorcet summed up what everybody knew: "The word 'revolutionary' can be applied only to revolutions whose aim is freedom."[1] That revolutions were about to usher in an entirely new era had been attested even earlier with the establishment of the revolutionary calendar in which the year of the execution of the king and the proclamation of the republic was counted as the year one.

Crucial, then, to any understanding of revolutions in the modern age is that the idea of freedom and the experience of a new beginning should coincide. And since the current notion of the Free World is that freedom, and neither justice nor greatness, is the highest criterion for judging the constitutions of political bodies, it is not only our understanding of revolution but our conception of freedom, clearly revolutionary in origin, on which may hinge the extent to which we are prepared to accept or reject this coincidence. Even at this point, where we still talk historically, it may therefore be wise to pause and reflect on one of the aspects under which freedom than appeared—if only to avoid the more common misunderstandings and to catch a first glance at the very modernity of revolution as such.

It may be a truism to say that liberation and freedom are not the same; that liberation may be the condition of freedom but by no means leads automatically to it; that the notion of liberty implied in liberation can only be negative, and hence, that even the intention of liberating is not identical with the desire for freedom. Yet if these truisms are frequently forgotten, it is because liberation has always loomed large and the foundation of freedom has always been uncertain, if not altogether futile. Freedom, moreover, has played a large and rather controversial role in the history of both philosophic and religious thought, and thus throughout those centuries—from the decline of the ancient to the birth of the modern world—when political freedom was non-existent, and when, for reasons which do not interest us here, men were not concerned with it. Thus it has become almost axiomatic even in political theory to understand by political freedom not a political phenomenon, but, on the contrary, the more or less free range of non-political activities which a given body politic will permit and guarantee to those who constitute it.

Freedom as a political phenomenon was coeval with the rise of the Greek city-states. Since Herodotus, it was understood as a form of political organization in which the citizens lived together under conditions of no-rule, without a division between rulers and ruled. This notion of no-rule was expressed by the word "isonomy," whose outstanding characteristic among the forms of government, as the ancients had enumerated them, was that the notion of rule (the "archy" from *archein* in monarchy and oligarchy, or the "-cracy" from *Kratein* in democracy) was entirely absent from it. The polis was supposed to be an isonomy, not a democracy. The word "democracy," expressing even then majority rule, the rule of the many, was originally coined by those who were opposed to isonomy and who meant to say: What you say is "no-rule" is in fact only another kind of rulership; it is the worst form of government, rule by the demos.

Hence, equality, which we, following Tocqueville's insights, frequently see as a danger to freedom, was originally almost identical with it. But this equality within the range of the law, which the word isonomy suggested, was not equality of condition—though this equality, to an extent, was the condition for all political activity in the ancient world, where the political realm itself was open only to those who owned property and slaves—but the equality of those who form a body of peers. Isonomy guaranteed *isotes*, equality but not because all men were born or created equal, but, on the contrary, because men were by nature *(phusei)* not equal, and needed an artificial institution, the polis, which by virtue of its *nomos* would make them equal. Equality existed only in this specifically political realm, where men met one another as citizens and not as private persons. The difference between this ancient concept of equality and our notion that men are born or created equal and become unequal by virtue of social and political, that is man-made institutions, can hardly be over-emphasized. The equality of the Greek polis, its isonomy, was an attribute of the polis and not of men, who received their equality by virtue of citizenship, not by virtue of birth. Neither equality nor freedom was understood as a quality inherent in human nature, they were both not *phusei*, given by nature and growing out by themselves; they were *nomō*, that is, conventional and artificial, the products of human effort and qualities of the man-made world.

The Greeks held that no one can be free except among his peers, that therefore neither the tyrant nor the despot nor the master of a household—even though he was fully liberated and was not forced by others—was free. The point of Herodotus's equation of freedom with no-rule was that the ruler himself was not free; by assuming the rule over others, he had deprived himself of those peers in whose company he could have been free. In other words, he had destroyed the political space itself, with the result that there was no freedom extant any longer, either for himself or for those over whom he ruled. The reason for this insistence on the interconnection of freedom and equality in Greek political thought was that freedom was understood as being manifest in certain, by no means all, human activities, and that these activities could appear and be real only when others saw them, judged them, remembered them. The life of a free man needed the presence of others. Freedom itself needed therefore a place where people could come together—the agora, the marketplace, or the polis, the political space proper.

If we think of this political freedom in modern terms, trying to understand what Condorcet and the men of the revolutions had in mind when they claimed that revolution aimed at freedom and that the birth of freedom spelled the beginning of an entirely new story, we must first notice the rather obvious fact that they could not possibly have had in mind merely those liberties which we today associate with constitutional government and which are properly called civil rights. For none of these rights, not even the right to participate in government because taxation demands representation, was in theory or practice the result of revolution. They were the outcome of the "three great and primary rights": life, liberty, property, with respect to which all other rights were "subordinate rights [that is] the remedies or means which must often be employed in order to fully obtain and enjoy the real and substantial liberties" (Blackstone). Not "life, liberty, and property" as such, but their being inalienable rights of man, was the result of revolution. But even in the new revolutionary extension of these rights to all men, liberty meant no more than freedom from unjustified restraint, and as such was fundamentally identical with freedom of movement—"the power of locomotion . . . without imprisonment or restraint, unless by due course of law"—which Blackstone, in full agreement with ancient political thought, held to be the most important of all civil rights. Even the right of assembly, which has come to be the most important positive political freedom, appears still in the American Bill of Rights as "the right of people peacefully to assemble, and to petition the government for a redress of grievances" (First Amendment) whereby "historically the right to petition is the primary right" and the historically correct interpretation must read: the right to assemble in order to petition. All these liberties, to which we might add our own claims to be free from want and fear, are of course essentially negative; they are the results of liberation but they are by no means the actual content of freedom, which, as we shall see later, is participation in public affairs, or admission to the public realm. If revolution had aimed only at the guarantee of civil rights, then it would not have aimed at freedom but at liberation from governments which had overstepped their powers and infringed upon old and well-established rights.

The difficulty here is that revolution as we know it in the modern age has always been concerned with both liberation and freedom. And since liberation, whose fruits are absence of restraint and possession of "the power of locomotion," is indeed a condition of freedom—nobody would ever be able to arrive at a place where freedom rules if he could not move without restraint—it is frequently very difficult to say where the mere desire for liberation, to be free from oppression, ends, and the desire for freedom as the political way of life begins. The point of the matter is that while the former, the desire to be free from oppression, could have been fulfilled under monarchical—though not under tyrannical, let alone despotic—rulership, the latter necessitated the formation of a new, or rather rediscovered form of government; it demanded the constitution of a republic. Nothing, indeed, is truer, more clearly borne out by facts which, alas, have been almost totally neglected by the historians of revolutions, than "that the contests of that day were contests of principle, between the advocates of republican, and those of kingly government.[2]

But this difficulty in drawing the line between liberation and freedom in any set of historical circumstances does not mean that liberation and freedom are the same, or that those liberties which are won as the result of liberation tell the whole story of freedom, even though those who tried their hand at both liberation and the foundation of freedom more often than not did not distinguish between these matters very clearly either. The men of the eighteenth-century revolutions had a perfect right to this lack of clarity; it was in the very nature of their enterprise that they discovered their own capacity and desire for the "charms of liberty," as John Jay once called them, only in the very act of liberation. For the acts and deeds which liberation demanded from them threw them into public business, where, intentionally or more often unexpectedly, they began to constitute that space of appearances where freedom can unfold its charms and become a visible, tangible reality. Since they were not in the least prepared for these charms, they could hardly be expected to be fully aware of the new phenomenon. It was nothing less than the weight of the entire Christian tradition which prevented them from owning up to the rather obvious fact that they were enjoying what they were doing far beyond the call of duty.

Whatever the merits of the opening claim of the American Revolution—no taxation without representation—it certainly could not appeal by virtue of its charms. It was altogether different with the speech-making and decision-taking, the oratory and the business, the thinking and the persuading, and the actual doing which proved necessary to drive this claim to its logical conclusion: independent government and the foundation of a new body politic. It was through these experiences that those who, in the words of John Adams, had been "called without expectation and compelled without previous inclination" discovered that "it is action, not rest, that constitutes our pleasure."[3]

What the revolutions brought to the fore was this experience of being free, and this was a new experience, not, to be sure, in the history of Western mankind—it was common enough in both Greek and Roman antiquity—but with regard to the centuries which separate the downfall of the Roman Empire from the rise of the modern age. And this relatively new experience, new to those at any rate who made it, was at the same time the experience of man's faculty to begin something new. These two things together—a new experience which revealed man's capacity for novelty—are at the root of the enormous pathos which we find in both the American and the French revolutions, this ever-repeated insistence that nothing comparable in grandeur and significance had ever happened in the whole recorded history of mankind, and which, if we had to account for it in terms of successful reclamation of civil rights, would sound entirely out of place.

Only where this pathos of novelty is present and where novelty is connected with the idea of freedom are we entitled to speak of revolution. This means of course that revolutions are more than successful insurrections and that we are not justified in calling every coup d'état a revolution or even in detecting one in each civil war. Oppressed people have often risen in rebellion, and much of ancient legislation can be understood only as safeguards against the ever-feared, though rarely occurring, uprising of the slave population. Civil war and factional strife, moreover, seemed to the ancients the greatest dangers to every body politic, and Aristotle's *philia*, that curious friendship he demanded for the relationships between the citizens, was conceived as the most reliable safeguard against them. Coups d'état and palace revolutions, where power changes hands from one man to another, from one clique to another, depending on the form of government in which the coup d'état occurs, have been less feared because the change they bring about is circumscribed to the sphere of government and carries a minimum of unquiet to the people at large, but they have been equally well known and described.

All these phenomena have in common with revolution that they are brought about by violence, and this is the reason why they are so frequently identified with it. But violence is no more adequate to describe the phenomenon of revolution than change; only where change occurs in the sense of a new beginning, where violence is used to constitute an altogether different form of government, to bring about the formation of a new body politic, where the liberation from oppression aims at least at the constitution of freedom can we speak of revolution. And the fact is that although history has always known those, who like Alcibiades, wanted power for themselves or those who, like Catiline, were *rerum novarum cupidi*, eager for new things, the revolutionary spirit of the last centuries, that is, the eagerness to liberate *and* to build a new house where freedom can dwell, is unprecedented and unequaled in all prior history.

Ever since the French Revolution, it has been common to interpret every violent upheaval, be it revolutionary or counterrevolutionary, in terms of a continuation of the movement originally started in 1789, as though the times of quiet and restoration were only the pauses in which the current had gone underground to gather force to break up to the surface again—in 1830 and 1832, in 1848 and 1851, in 1871, to mention only the more important nineteenth-century dates. Each time adherents and opponents of these revolutions understood the events as immediate consequences of 1789. And if it is true, as Marx said, that the French Revolution had been played in Roman clothes, it is equally true that each of the following revolutions, up to and including the October Revolution, was enacted according to the rules and events that led from the fourteenth of July to the ninth of Thermidor and the eighteenth of Brumaire—dates which so impressed themselves on the memory of the French people that even today they are immediately identified by everybody with the fall of the Bastille, the death of Robespierre, and the rise of Napoleon Bonaparte. It was not in our time but in the middle of the nineteenth century that the term "permanent revolution" or even more tellingly *révolution en permanence,* was coined (by Proudhon) and, with it, the notion that "there never has been such a thing as several revolutions, that there is only one revolution, selfsame and perpetual."[4]

If the new metaphorical content of the word "revolution" sprang directly from the experiences of those who first made and then enacted the revolution in France, it obviously carried an even greater plausibility for those who watched its course, as if it were a spectacle, from the outside. What appeared to be most manifest in this spectacle was that none of its actors could control the course of events, that this course took a direction which had little if anything to do with the willful aims and purposes of men, who, on the contrary, must subject their will and purpose to the anonymous force of the revolution if they wanted to survive at all. This sounds commonplace to us today, and we probably find it hard to understand that anything but banalities could have been derived from it. Yet we need only remember the course of the American Revolution, where the exact opposite took place, and recall how strongly the sentiment that man is master of his destiny, at least with respect to political government, permeated all its actors, to realize the impact which the spectacle of the impotence of man with regard to the course of his own action must have made. The well-known shock of disillusion suffered by the generation in Europe which lived through the fatal events from 1789 to the restoration of the Bourbons transformed itself almost immediately into a feeling of awe and wonder at the power of history itself. Where yesterday, that is in the happy days of Enlightenment, only the despotic power of the monarch had seemed to stand between man and his freedom to act, a much more powerful force had suddenly arisen which compelled men at will, and from which there was no release, neither rebellion nor escape, the force of history and historical necessity.

Theoretically, the most far-reaching consequence of the French Revolution was the birth of the modern concept of history in Hegel's philosophy. Hegel's truly revolutionary idea was that the old absolute of the philosophers revealed itself in the realm of human affairs, that is, in precisely that domain of human experiences which the philosophers unanimously had ruled out as the source or birthplace of absolute standards. The model for this new revelation by means of a historical process was clearly the

French Revolution, and the reason why German post-Kantian philosophy came to exert its enormous influence on European thought in the twentieth century, especially in countries exposed to revolutionary unrest—Russia, Germany, France—was not its so-called idealism but, on the contrary, the fact that it had left the sphere of mere speculation and attempted to formulate a philosophy which would correspond to and comprehend conceptually the newest and most real experiences of the time. However, this comprehension itself was theoretical in the old, original sense of the word "theory"; Hegel's philosophy, though concerned with action and the realm of human affairs, consisted in contemplation. Before the backward-directed glance of thought, everything that had been political—acts, and words, and events—became historical, with the result that the new world which was ushered in by the eighteenth-century revolutions did not receive, as Tocqueville still claimed, a "new science of politics," but a philosophy of history—quite apart from the perhaps even more momentous transformation of philosophy into philosophy of history, which does not concern us here.

Politically, the fallacy of this new and typically modern philosophy is relatively simple. It consists in describing and understanding the whole realm of human action, not in terms of the actor and the agent, but from the standpoint of the spectator who watches a spectacle. But this fallacy is relatively difficult to detect because of the truth inherent in it, which is that all stories begun and enacted by men unfold their true meaning only when they have come to their end, so that it may indeed appear as though only the spectator, and not the agent, can hope to understand what actually happened in any given chain of deeds and events. It was to the spectator even more forcefully than to the actor that the lesson of the French Revolution appeared to spell out historical necessity or that Napoleon Bonaparte became a "destiny." Yet the point of the matter is that all those who, throughout the nineteenth century and deep into the twentieth, followed in the footsteps of the French Revolution, saw themselves not merely as successors of the men of the French Revolution but as agents of history and historical necessity, with the obvious and yet paradoxical result that instead of freedom necessity became the chief category of political and revolutionary thought.

Still, without the French Revolution it may be doubted that philosophy would ever have attempted to concern itself with the realm of human affairs, that is, to discover absolute truth in a domain which is ruled by men's relations and relationships with one another and hence is relative by definition. Truth, even though it was conceived "historically," that is, was understood to unfold in time and therefore did not necessarily need to be valid for all times, still had to be valid for all men, regardless of where they happened to dwell and of which country they happened to be citizens. Truth, in other words, was supposed to relate and to correspond not to citizens, in whose midst there could exist only a multitude of opinions, and not to nationals, whose sense for truth was limited by their own history and national experience. Truth had to relate to man qua man, who as a worldly, tangible reality, of course, existed no-where. History, therefore, if it was to become a medium of the revelation of truth, had to be world history, and the truth which revealed itself had to be a "world spirit." Yet while the notion of history could attain phi-losophic dignity only under the assumption that it covered the whole world and the destinies of all men, the idea of world history itself is clearly political in origin; it was preceded by the French and the American Revolution, both of which prided themselves on having ushered in a new era for all mankind, on being events which would concern all men qua men, no matter where they lived, what their circumstances were, or what nationality they possessed. The very notion of world history was born from the first attempt at world politics, and although both the American and the French enthusiasm for the "rights of man" quickly subsided with the birth of the nation-state, which short-lived as this form of govern-ment has proved to be, was the only relatively lasting result of revolution in Europe, the fact is that in one form or another world politics has been an adjunct to politics ever since.

Another aspect of Hegel's teaching which no less obviously derives from the experiences of the French Revolution is even more important in our context, since it had an even more immediate influence on the revolu-tionists of the nineteenth and twentieth centuries—all of whom, even if they did not learn their lessons from Marx (still the greatest pupil Hegel ever had) and never bothered to read Hegel, looked upon revolution through Hegelian categories. This aspect concerns the character of his-torical motion, which, according to Hegel as well as all his followers, is at once dialectical and driven by necessity: out of the revolution and counterrevolution, from the fourteenth of July to the eighteenth of Brumaire and the restoration of the monarchy, was born the dialectical movement and counter movement of history which bears men on its irre-sistible flow, like a powerful undercurrent, to which they must surrender the very moment they attempt to establish freedom on earth. This is the meaning of the famous dialectics of freedom and necessity in which both eventually coincide—perhaps the most terrible and, humanly speaking, the least bearable paradox in the whole body of modern thought. And yet, Hegel, who once had seen in the year 1789 the moment when the earth and the heavens had become reconciled, might still have thought in terms of the original metaphorical content of the word "revolution," as though in the course of the French Revolution the lawfully irresistible movement of the heavenly bodies had descended upon the earth and the affairs of men, bestowing upon them a "necessity" and regularity which had seemed beyond the "melancholy haphazardness" (Kant), the sad "mixture of violence and meaninglessness" (Goethe) which up to then had seemed to be the outstanding quality of history and of the course of the world. Hence, the paradox that freedom is the fruit of necessity, in Hegel's own understanding, was hardly more paradoxical than the reconciliation of heaven and earth. Moreover, there was nothing facetious in Hegel's theory and no empty witticism in his dialectics of freedom and necessity. On the contrary, they must even then have forcefully appealed to those who still stood under the impact of political reality; the unabated strength of their plausibility has resided ever since much less on theoretical evidence than on an experience repeated time and again in the centuries of war and revolution. The modern concept of history, with its unparalleled emphasis on history as a process, has many origins and among them especially the earlier modern concept of nature as a process. As long as men took their cue from the natural sciences and thought of this process as a primarily cyclical rotating, ever-recurring movement—and even Vico still thought of historical movement in these terms—it was unavoidable that necessity should be inherent in historical as it is in astronomical motion. Every cyclical movement is a necessary movement by definition. But the fact that necessity as an inherent characteristic of history should survive the modern break in the cycle of eternal recurrences and make its reappearance in a movement that was essentially rectilinear and hence did not revolve back to what was known before but stretched out into an unknown future, this fact owes its existence not to theoretical speculation but to political experience and the course of real events.

It was the French and not the American Revolution that set the world on fire, and it was consequently from the course of the French Revolution, and not from the course of events in America or from the acts of the Founding Fathers, that our present use of the word "revolution" received its connotations and overtones everywhere, this country not excluded. The colonization of North America and the republican government of the United States constitute perhaps the greatest, certainly the boldest, enterprises of European mankind; yet this country has been hardly more than a hundred years in its history truly on its own, in splendid or not so splendid isolation from the mother continent. Since the end of the last century, it has been subject to the threefold onslaught of urbanization, industrialization, and, perhaps most important of all, mass immigration. Since then, theories and concepts, though unfortunately not always their underlying experiences, have migrated once more from the old to the new world, and the word "revolution," with its associations, is no exception to this rule. It is odd indeed to see that twentieth-century American even more than European learned opinion is often inclined to interpret the American Revolution in the light of the French Revolution, or to criticize it because it so obviously did not conform to lessons learned from the latter. The sad truth of the matter is that the French Revolution, which ended in disaster, has made world history, while the American Revolution, so triumphantly successful, has remained an event of little more than local importance.

For whenever in our own century revolutions appeared on the scene of politics, they were seen in images drawn from the course of the French Revolution, comprehended in concepts coined by spectators, and understood in terms of historical necessity. Conspicuous by its absence in the minds of those who made the revolutions as well as those who watched and tried to come to terms with them, was the deep concern with forms of government so characteristic of the American Revolution, but also very important in the initial stages of the French Revolution. It was the men of the French Revolution who, overawed by the spectacle of the multitude, exclaimed with Robespierre, "La République? La Monarchie? Je ne connais que la question sociale"; and they lost, together with the institutions and constitutions which are "the soul of the Republic" (Saint-Just), the revolution itself. Since then, men swept willy nilly by revolutionary stormwinds into an uncertain future have taken the place of the proud architects who intended to build their new houses by drawing upon an accumulated wisdom of all past ages as they understood it; and with these architects went the reassuring confidence that a *novus ordo saeclorum* could be built on ideas, according to a conceptual blueprint whose very age vouchsafed its truth. Not thought, only the practice, only the application would be new. The time, in the words of Washington, was "auspicious" because it had "laid open for use . . . the treasures of knowledge acquired through a long succession of years"; with their help, the men of the American Revolution felt, they could begin to act after circumstances and English policy had left them no other alternative than to found an entirely new body politic. And since they had been given the chance to act, history and circumstances could no longer be blamed: if the citizens of the United States "should not be completely free and happy, the fault will be entirely their own."[5] It would never have occurred to them that only a few decades later the keenest and most thoughtful observer of what they had done would conclude: "I go back from age to age up to the remotest antiquity, but I find no parallel to what is occurring before my eyes; as the past has ceased to throw its light upon the future, the mind of man wanders in obscurity."[6]

The magic spell which historical necessity has cast over the minds of men since the beginning of the nineteenth century gained in potency by the October Revolution, which for our century has had the same profound meaningfulness of first crystallizing the best of men's hopes and then realizing the full measure of their despair that the French Revolution had for its contemporaries. Only this time it was not unexpected experiences which hammered the lesson home, but a conscious modeling of a course of action upon the experiences of a bygone age and event. To be sure, only the two-edged compulsion of ideology and terror, one compelling men from within and the other compelling them from without, can fully explain the meekness with which revolutionists in all countries which fell under the influence of the Bolshevik Revolution have gone to their doom; but there the lesson presumably learned from the French Revolution has become an integral part of the self-imposed compulsion of ideological thinking today. The trouble has always been the same: those who went into the school of revolution learned and knew beforehand the course a revolution must take. It was the course of events, not the men of the revolution, which they imitated. Had they taken the men of the revolution as their models, they would have protested their innocence to their last breath. But they could not do this because they knew that a revolution must devour its own children, just as they knew that a revolution would take its course in a sequence of revolutions, or that the open enemy was followed by the hidden enemy under the mask of the "suspects," or that a revolution would split into two extreme factions—the *indulgents* and the *enragés*—that actually or "objectively" worked together in order to undermine the revolutionary government, and that the revolution was "saved" by the man in the middle, who, far from being more moderate, liquidated the right and left as Robespierre had liquidated Danton and Hebert. What the men of the Russian Revolution had learned from the French Revolution—and this learning constituted almost their entire preparation—was history and not action. They had acquired the skill to play whatever part the great drama of history was going to assign them, and if no other role was available but that of the villain, they were more than willing to accept their part rather than remain outside the play.

There is some grandiose ludicrousness in the spectacle of these men— who had dared to defy all powers that be and to challenge all authorities on earth, whose courage was beyond the shadow of a doubt—submitting, often from one day to the other, humbly and without so much as a cry of outrage, to the call of historical necessity, no matter how foolish and incongruous the outward appearance of this necessity must have appeared to them. They were fooled, not because the words of Danton and Vergniaud, of Robespierre and Saint-Just, and of all the others still rang in their ears; they were fooled by history, and they have become the fools of history.

Part Two

HISTORICAL PERSPECTIVES ON THE AMERICAN REVOLUTION

Historians from the very beginning have interpreted variously the cause-effect relationships within the American "Revolution." Arguments have raged fundamentally between those claiming primarily internal causes versus those blaming England alone; those giving an economic interpretation versus those concentrating on the events as exclusively a political-constitutional crisis. Contemporary scholarship has contrasted those arguing that the revolution was a constitutional crisis between colonies and the imperial center—broadly classified as the neo-Whigs—with those who persist in seeing internal social conflicts leading to a dual revolution, one that brought the break with England and that transformed the underlying internal society of America—the Progressives.

Since evidence seems to exist for both these views, historians are synthesizing them, bringing an increased sophistication to our understanding of the so-called American Revolution.

Robert Brown represents the neo-Whigs (chapter 6). It seems unfair to contrast his undocumented article, a reprinted speech, with other almost overdocumented views; yet it projects the neo-Whigs' overall position and, even more, their confidence: it was widely felt that they destroyed the foundations of the economic determinists of the 1930s and 1940s (e.g., Charles Beard). Jack Greene, on the other hand, while basically sympathetic with the Progressive interpretation of "social origins," argues in the end that though socioeconomic strain was not a primal cause of the revolution, social "malintegration" and "strain" did affect individual colonies' responses.

If the neo-Whigs reacted to the early Progressive excesses, Gordon Wood blunts the overacceptance of neo-Whig views (chapter 8). If ideas were fundamental to the constitutional issues of the neo-Whigs, then Wood argues that the severe rhetoric that accompanied the march toward revolution must have come from severe social strain. This assumption allows the Progressives' behaviorism to be incorporated into the history of the Revolution. Wood, then, is a neo-Whig synthesist.

According to Marc Egnal and Joseph Ernst (chapter 9), fundamental economic changes in the eighteenth-century Atlantic economy provided a platform for revolution. Their synthesis thus has Progressive roots and is based on the economic environment of the prerevolutionary period.

It should be noted that all these historians, including those in part 3, assume that a revolution has taken place without defining what type of revolution the American experience represented. Some appear to define "revolution" loosely while applying strict criteria to the events (e.g., Bailyn, chapter 13).

Robert Brown

6 REINTERPRETATION OF THE REVOLUTION AND CONSTITUTION

I am making this discussion general rather than technical. I would like to deal briefly with three widely-accepted interpretations of the American Revolution and the formation of the Constitution. Before beginning my discussion, however, I should like to give a brief history of my own interest in these particular interpretations. As an undergraduate, I was introduced to the views generally accepted in the 1930s concerning the why of the Revolution and Constitution. I was well grounded in the works of such scholars as Carl Becker, Vernon Louis Parrington, Arthur M. Schlesinger, Sr., James Truslow Adams, George Louis Beer, Charles McLean Andrews, J. Allen Smith, and Charles A. Beard. At that time, I thought that I had a pretty good idea as to why the Revolution had occurred and how the Constitution was adopted.

But when I started to do graduate work, and began to look into the source material, I suffered a rather rude awakening. The evidence that I found did not support the interpretations which I had accepted as true. Something seemed to be wrong. There was a sharp discrepancy between evidence and interpretation, and it is with this discrepancy that I wish to deal today.

The first interpretation, and one you are doubtless familiar with, is what has been called the Dual Revolution or the Internal Revolution. According to this view, there were two revolutions occurring simultaneously. One was a war between England and her colonies which resulted ultimately in American independence. The other revolution, and perhaps the most important, was an internal clash between classes in this country. This second revolution rests on the assumption that colonial society was undemocratic, and that because of property qualifications for voting and office holding, only a limited number of men were enfranchised. Hence there arose a colonial aristocracy composed of wealthy merchants in the North and wealthy planters in the South, who dominated the lower classes or common people politically, economically, and socially. Resentful of this domination, the lower classes used the trouble with England as an excuse for gaining more political, economic, and social democracy. The late Carl Becker stated the problem of the Dual Revolution about as succinctly as anyone when he said that the issues at stake were not merely home rule but who should rule at home. Furthermore, historians have generally accepted the view that both revolutions were successful in some measure, and that Americans not only won their independence from England but that the lower classes also won a measure of democracy from the upper classes.

The question then is this: How valid is this interpretation of the Dual or Internal Revolution? There is no quarrel with the first part involving colonial independence, for obviously there was a war between the British and the Americans, and the Americans did win their independence. But how valid is our concept of the Revolution as an integral class conflict? This, of course, is merely part of the larger question of the importance of class conflict throughout history.

My own researches led me to the conclusion that there are many misconceptions about our early history. Because there were property qualifications for voting, and perhaps because of other influences also, historians have assumed a sharply-divided society in colonial times in which only the few had political privileges. This is merely an assumption, not a generalization based on adequate evidence. The extent of democracy is absolutely essential to an interpretation of the Revolution as a class conflict, yet very little has been done on this problem. Before we can make such an interpretation, we must first find out how property was distributed, how many men owned property, and how many could therefore meet the property qualifications for voting.

My initial venture in research was on early Massachusetts, where the evidence produced some interesting generalizations. Instead of a society of the few rich and the many poor, I discovered that Massachusetts was what we would call middle class. Evidence from the probate, tax, and deeds records indicated that there were a few men who might be considered wealthy and a few who were poor, but that the great mass of men were middle-class property owners. Contemporaries referred to them as the "middling" sort.[1]

Furthermore, most of these men had sufficient property to qualify as voters. The forty shilling freehold or the 40 required for voting in

Massachusetts represented a very small amount of property. A man could not have made a living on a farm too small to give him the vote. Usually any kind of a house and five or six acres sufficed. In the towns, a house or small amount of personal property were sufficient. Governor Thomas Hutchinson once pointed out that although there were property qualifications for voting, the people counted all their property to qualify, and, he said, the result was that anything that looked like a man was a voter.

I should hasten to point out, of course, that then, as now, not all men exercised their voting rights. But that is another story, and if they had the right to vote, their failure to exercise it, as Tom Paine once said, was no one's fault but their own.

In addition to revealing a wide electorate in Massachusetts, my researches also disclosed that representation was not a major problem. Most historians have stressed in the Dual Revolution the ability of a conservative seaboard aristocracy to control politics because of inequitable representation of the backcountry. In Massachusetts, just the reverse was true. The agricultural backcountry was represented much better than the towns were, and could dominate the seaports at any time by at least ten or more to one. So here again the concept of a dominant seaboard aristocracy does not hold.

If the Revolution in Massachusetts was not an internal class conflict, was it anything more than just a war for independence from England? The answer is yes. British measures after 1760 were a very definite threat to colonial democracy; in fact the British decided that they would have to curtail colonial democracy if they expected to recover their authority in the colonies. So the war did involve democracy, but it was a war to *preserve* the democracy that was already present, not a war to democratize an aristocratic American society.

Additional evidence which I have seen pertaining to all the colonies seems to indicate that the other colonies were not radically different from Massachusetts. I shall present some of this in a few moments in my discussion of the Constitution. At the present time Mrs. Brown and I are spending the year in Virginia working on this problem of colonial democracy. It is too early to draw definite conclusions, but indications now are that our findings there will materially change current concepts about Virginia democracy.

If what was true in Massachusetts proves to be true in the other colonies—as the evidence now indicates—what becomes of our concept of a Dual or Internal Revolution based on class conflict? It will obviously have to be discarded or greatly modified. Instead of an internal revolution of rich against poor, enfranchised against unenfranchised, and upper against lower classes, perhaps we must eventually interpret the American

Revolution from the standpoint of a middle-class society in which most men were voters, most men owned or hoped to own property, and most men believed that one of the important functions of government was the protection of property.

Another indication of the nature of the Revolution can be found in the changes that came as a result of that upheaval. Historians who stress the Dual Revolution contend that the common man made significant gains as a result of the conflict. But somehow or other these gains seem to vanish after the Revolution, for these same historians almost invariably point out that the new state constitutions were not very radical and that except for the elimination of the British there were very few changes made. That is quite true. Samuel Adams once remarked that there never had been a revolution in the world's history in which there had been so little change. If conditions were not such as to produce sharp class conflict before the Revolution, and if the colonists were fighting to preserve rather than to gain democracy, we would not expect much of an internal social upheaval as a result of the war.

The absence of internal social revolution becomes even more pronounced when we eliminate the social changes which the Americans effected after the Revolution started but which they had tried to adopt under the British. I am thinking here of such items as taxing the importation of slaves and lowering the property qualifications for voting from 100 acres to 50 acres in Virginia.

Before we leave the subject of the Dual Revolution, a word needs to be said about the terms, democracy and liberalism, and especially about the confusion in the use of these terms. From the questions which I have received about my own work, I have the impression that many people equate the terms of democracy and liberalism. To such people, democracy is not really democracy unless it leads to liberal results. This, of course, is erroneous. Throughout our history, democracy has never been a guarantee of liberal action. The elections of McKinley, Taft, Harding, Coolidge, and Hoover should be ample evidence that giving the people the vote does not insure the election of liberal candidates. When all women received the right to vote in 1920, their first act was to elect Warren G. Harding, and at least some historians do not regard Harding as a great liberal. During the period of the Revolution and Constitution, the people were equally capable of electing conservatives, but such action does not signify that the society of the time was undemocratic.

The second interpretation of concern to us today is what is referred to as the imperial or pro-British interpretation. This interpretation gained stature through the writings of George Louis Beer, Charles McLean Andres, and James Truslow Adams, and in recent years its chief exponent has been Lawrence Henry Gipson. According to these authors, the British were usually in the right and the Americans were usually in the wrong in the controversies between the mother country and the colonies. They justify British taxation and other restrictive measures on the ground that the colonies did not carry their share of the imperial burden, that the colonial wars were fought primarily for the protection of the colonists, and that Britain accumulated a tremendous national debt as a result of these colonial wars.

There are many criticisms of the imperial interpretations. In order to substantiate this view, it seems to me that one must accept at face value the British side of the story and discount almost completely the American side. As the sources so well demonstrate, there were American denials or answers to every contention or accusation put forth by the British. Americans contended that they had always defended themselves before 1754 without British armies, that armies were sent here for British, not American, interests, that the colonists paid more than their share in fighting the French and Indian War as testified by the fact that Britain indemnified the colonies for their expenditures.

Eventually we may come to see the American Revolution as primarily the result of imperialism, as the historian, George Bancroft, saw it a hundred years ago. Certain it is that there had long been a smouldering discontent on the part of the colonists against the Navigation Acts, a discontent which might have flared into a rebellion sooner had the British attempted earlier to enforce their colonial system. Certain it is also that the restrictions and regulations about which the colonists complained were of such a nature that we today would consider them grievances. There are lessons on imperialism to be learned from the American Revolution— lessons which we ignore at our peril in our dealings with colonial people of the world today.

The third interpretation which I want to discuss today is the widely-accepted thesis of the late Charles A. Beard concerning the Constitution. Beard's work is based on the concept of the Dual Revolution, and hence it follows logically that if the Dual Revolution is open to question, Beard's interpretation of the Constitution is also open to question.[2]

There are two parts to the Beard thesis as he presented it in *An Economic Interpretation of the Constitution.* These two aspects are not always clearly explained, and one of them is usually presented erroneously.

First there is the assumption by Beard that because of property restrictions for the franchise, the Constitution was the product of an undemocratic society. If most men had property and were voters, however, this half of the Beard thesis can be disposed of very quickly. In fact, Beard himself actually disposed of it without realizing that he did so, for the evidence which he presented, in contrast with his conclusions, pointed to a democratic society. Furthermore, no one can read the debates in the Constitutional Convention without coming to the conclusion that American society in 1787 was democratic, and I might add that this evidence includes all the states, not just Massachusetts. It is quite true that some of the delegates at Philadelphia did not favor democracy, and in fact, would have done everything possible to restrict it. But this does not elminate the fact that American society at the time was democratic and that the men who drew up the Constitution had to keep in mind constantly what the people would or would not accept. There was scarcely a provision in the Constitution that was not attacked or defended on the ground that the people would oppose or approve it. Time and again the delegates stated that the trouble with the country was too much democracy, but at the same time they recognized that the Constitution which they constructed would have to meet the approval of a democratic society.

The second part of the Beard thesis, and the one most often misinterpreted, is his account of the economic interests of the men who put over the Constitution. This part of Beard's work stems from the assumption that the lower classes won out over the upper classes in the Revolution and proceeded to democratize American society under the Articles of Confederation and under new state constitutions. The lower classes were thus enabled to pass debtor legislation at the expense of other economic groups in the country. Unable to amend the Articles of Confederation in their own interests, these upperclass economic groups proceeded to overthrow the Articles by a virtual coup d'état and to establish a conservative counterrevolutionary government under the Constitution.

Actually Beard did not define his conservative counterrevolutionaries as merely the upper-economic group. They were the holders of personal property as opposed to the holders of real estate—not just the owners of property in general. This personality group included merchants, shippers, manufacturers, money-lenders, speculators, and particularly the security holders, the men who owned the public debt. At one point, in fact, Beard virtually eliminated all others but the security holders. These were the men who wanted a strong government that would force debtors to pay their debts, collect taxes to pay off the security holders, and protect the kind of property that these men held.

What is wrong with the Beardian interpretation of the Constitution? Time precludes a detailed analysis, which is available in print, so a few observations will have to suffice. I have already pointed out the fallacies in the assumption that American society was undemocratic. I should only add that if the lower classes won the Revolution, if they controlled state governments in their own interests, and if men in the Constitutional Convention were interested in checking democracy, all these things indicate a democratic society in 1787.

Beard's view that personal property was responsible for the Constitution does not hold up any better than his view of an undemocratic society in 1787. In the first place, Beard stated time after time that the evidence for an economic interpretation of the Constitution did not exist when he wrote his book, or at least that the evidence had not been assembled. Beard said that he, himself, did not have time to collect the evidence. So the old adage—no evidence, no history—would seem to apply here. If Beard did not have the evidence to support the thesis that personalty put over the Constitution, he did not have a thesis.

Furthermore, what source material Beard did use refutes his thesis. Time after time he produces convincing proof that the important economic interest in the country was really, not personalty. By his own figures, the preponderance in favor of realty was about 96 percent to 4 percent. So he who explains the Constitution on economic grounds must certainly consider this dominant agricultural interest. Unfortunately Beard did not follow the dictates of his own evidence.

Beard's clinching argument on the influence of personalty has often been considered his famous Chapter 5 in which he presumably analyzes the property of the men in the Convention to show that they were holders of personalty. But what does the evidence he uses in this chapter really show? If we simply analyze the material Beard presents, only six of the delegates were definitely holders of personalty. Eighteen were predominantly holders of real estate, including Washington, undoubtedly the most influential man in the Convention. Of the remaining 30 men, we cannot tell from Beard's evidence what kind of property they held, or, in some instances, whether they held any property.

If the Beard thesis were correct, we would expect to find some correlation between personalty or realty on the one hand, and the ease or quickness of ratification of the Constitution on the other. States with the most personalty should have ratified the quickest and by the largest majorities, and opposition should have been greatest where agriculture predominated. What actually happened? Agricultural states such as Georgia, Delaware, and New Jersey ratified unanimously, while South Carolina, Maryland, Pennsylvania, and Connecticut accepted the Constitution by substantial majorities. Only in agricultural North Carolina, Virginia, and New Hampshire was there a close struggle. On the other hand, some of the sharpest fights took place in Massachusetts and New York, the states with the largest personalty interests, and commercial Rhode Island refused to ratify at all.

The fact is, of course, that all of the states were agricultural by at least ten or more to one, and that the farmers could have defeated the Constitution if they had so desired. . . . It is also a fact that the 11 states which had ratified when the Constitution went into effect did so by a vote of 64.37 percent to 35.63 percent, a larger margin than Franklin D. Roosevelt enjoyed in 1936, or that Eisenhower obtained in 1956.

And so in conclusion, as far as my research now tells me, I think we must explain the American Revolution and the Constitution in terms of a democratic, middle-class, agricultural society, not a society in which democracy was restricted and class divisions were sharp. Only then will we understand the actions and ideals of the American people—both in the past and in the present.

Jack P. Greene

7 THE SOCIAL ORIGINS OF THE AMERICAN REVOLUTION

Given the rich theoretical literature on revolution that has been published over the last decade with its heavy emphasis on the relationship
between revolutions and the social systems in which they occur, it is
hardly surprising that historians of modern political revolutions have
increasingly turned their attention to the wider social context in their
search for an explanation for those events or that their discussions of
the causal pattern of revolutions now give as much attention to social
strain as to political and ideological conflict; to social dysfunction,
frustration, anomie, and their indices as to weaknesses and tensions
within the political system. This enlarged frame of inquiry has yielded a
much more comprehensive understanding of several specific revolutions.
The question of whether it will prove equally fruitful for all varieties
of great modern political revolutions is raised by several recent efforts
to apply it to the American Revolution.

The idea that the American Revolution may have had a social content—
that is, social origins and social consequences—is hardly a new one. It
has existed in a crude form ever since the Revolution, and between 1900
and 1930 a number of individual scholars—especially Charles H. Lincoln,
Carl L. Becker, Arthur M. Schlesinger, Sr., Charles A. Beard, and J. Franklin
Jameson—formulated an elaborate social interpretation of the Revolution.
Investigating various aspects of the internal political life of the American
colonies between 1760 and 1790, they discovered what they took to be
serious economic and social antagonisms underlying the major events of the
American Revolution at virtually every stage of its development. Far from

having been simply a war for independence from Great Britain, the American Revolution—as these men came to see it—was a *social* struggle by underprivileged groups against the special privileges and political dominance of the old colonial aristocracy.

The details of this interpretation are too well known to require lengthy discussion here. Colonial society by the middle decades of the eighteenth century was everywhere fraught with severe class conflict arising out of an ever greater concentration of wealth into the hands of the privileged few and an ever more rigid social structure, an increasingly aristocratic political system, and severe resentment among the masses who were more and more being deprived of any opportunity to realize their own economic and political ambitions. Not surprisingly, the resulting tensions among these antagonistic social groups came surging to the surface during the revolutionary controversy between 1765 and 1776 and, as Merrill Jensen later argued, converted the Revolution from a simple movement for independence from Great Britain into a "war against the colonial aristocracy."[1] Assessing the results of this "internal revolution," Jameson explicitly argued that the American Revolution profoundly altered many features of colonial social and economic life and represented a significant advance toward a "levelling democracy" in the revolutionary era.[2]

In origins as well as in results, the American Revolution thus came to be thought of as the product not merely of a quarrel between Britain and the colonies but also of deep fissures within colonial society and as a social upheaval equal to the French, if not the Russian, Revolution. Because of its obvious indebtedness to the liberal concept of American public life during the era from which it emerged, this view of the Revolution has subsequently been labeled the Progressive interpretation. But it was elaborated by still other scholars during the 1930s and 1940s. So widespread was its acceptance that it continued well into the 1950s to be the orthodox interpretation of the Revolution.

As is well known, this whole interpretation was shattered and deeply discredited by the research of a wide range of scholars between 1945 and 1965. A number of detailed studies of segments and aspects of the political life in virtually every colony as well as many of the concrete social changes emphasized by Jameson seemed to indicate that, far from being similar to the French Revolution, the American Revolution was a peculiarly American event in which there had been remarkably little social discontent expressed, no real social upheaval, and relatively few changes in the existing American social structure. Thus, in the decades after the Second World War, the American Revolution came to be interpreted as an event that had been almost entirely political with little specific social content and that could be understood, therefore, almost exclusively in political terms. Where the Progressive historians had gone wrong was, first, in reading the fundamental social conflicts of their own day back into the Revolution and, second, in using a conceptual framework derived from the French Revolution and later European revolutions to identify the questions they brought to the American Revolution—questions, the data seemed to indicate, that were obviously irrelevant to the American experience.

Predictably, and happily, we had just begun to feel comfortable with this view of the origins and nature of the American Revolution when the new analysis itself came under assault. The most compelling call for a revival of interest in the social content of the Revolution came from Gordon S. Wood in 1966 in an extended analysis of Bernard Bailyn's book-length introduction to *Pamphlets of the American Revolution 1750-1776*.[3] Commenting on Bailyn's heavy emphasis upon the role of ideas in the coming of the Revolution, Wood argues that it is "precisely the remarkable revolutionary character of the Americans' ideas now being revealed by historians [such as Bailyn] that best indicates that something profoundly unsettling was going on in society." The "very nature" of the colonists' rhetoric, "its obsession with corruption and disorder, its hostile and conspiratorial outlook, and its millennial vision of a regenerated society," Wood argues, reveals "as nothing else apparently can the American Revolution as a *true revolution* with its sources lying deep within the social structure. For this kind of frenzied rhetoric," he contends, "could spring only from the most severe sorts of social strain."[4]

As yet, Wood's call for "a new look at the social sources of the Revolution"[5] has not been answered by any systematic or comprehensive assault upon this problem. But there has been a wide assortment of specialized studies of various aspects of American social life between 1725 and 1775. Most of them have been, at the most, only implicitly concerned with explaining the American Revolution. But the data and conclusions they have provided may be used to construct and to evaluate some hypotheses about the possible relationship between social strain and the origins of the Revolution. The findings of these studies seem to lend themselves to one or the other of two central hypotheses. The first, which has never been explicitly formulated but has been gradually taking shape over the past fifteen years, is that colonial society underwent a dramatic erosion of internal social cohesion over the period from 1690 to 1760. The second, an updated and more sophisticated variant of the old Progressive thesis, is that over the same period, the social structure of the colonies was becoming more and more rigid and social strain correspondingly more intense.

The most impressive support for the first of these hypotheses is found in Richard L. Bushman's penetrating *From Puritan to Yankee: Character and the Social Order in Connecticut, 1690-1765*, a case study of the various strains created by the rapid economic and demographic growth of that colony. But many other studies can also be used for its elaboration. According to this hypothesis, a great variety of developments combined to keep colonial society in a state of perpetual and disorienting ferment, a state that was both rapidly accelerating and increasing in intensity and extent in the decades just prior to the Revolution. Chief among these developments were, first, the rapid territorial and demographic expansion, including the influx of many previously unrepresented religious and ethnic groups, and, second, the extraordinary acceleration of the economy with an attendant increase in economic opportunity and abundance. But there were many other developments that contributed to the ferment: (1) the shattering of religious uniformity by that great spiritual upheaval known as the Great Awakening; (2) the rise of towns and small cities with life styles and social dynamics that pointedly distinguished them from the traditional rural communities of colonial America; (3) a quickening of the pace of social differentiation marked by the appearance of an increasingly more complex institutional and social structure and greater extremes in wealth; (4) the intensification of the seemingly endemic factionalism of colonial politics as men competed vigorously and ruthlessly with one another in their quest for land, wealth, status, and supremacy.

Some of the potentially corrosive effects of this ferment have been noted by a number of scholars. The movement of people from older communities to newly opened regions greatly weakened the ties of authority or community. Extremely high rates of upward social mobility threatened the standing of traditional elites by devaluing their status and confronting them with a seemingly endless series of challenges to their monopoly of social and political power. At the same time, their reluctance to share authority with new men created severe status inconsistencies in which the new men had wealth—the main attribute of elite status in the colonies—minus the political power and social position to go with it. To the traditional elite, the movement toward a more inclusive leadership structure appeared to be too rapid, while to the new men it seemed to be too slow. Moreover, as new men challenged traditional leaders or as elites splintered in their bitter contests for political supremacy, the political and social standing of the elite as a whole as well as its internal cohesion was seriously undermined. In addition, the settlement of new areas put severe strains upon existing political structures at both the local and provincial levels, as older centers of power sought to extend their authority over distant areas with economic interests, social and political orientations, and ethnic and religious compositions that diverged sharply from those of the older centers. Those strains sometimes—in North Carolina, New Hampshire, and New Jersey in the late 1740s and early 1750s; in Pennsylvania from the late 1740s through the mid-1760s; and in both Carolinas in the late 1760s and early 1770s—resulted in the breakdown of government or even in open sectional conflict.

Nor are these by any means all of the examples of the severe destabilizing effects of the rapid changes taking place in the colonies during the middle of the eighteenth century. The Great Awakening unleashed and mobilized widespread discontent with existing religious establishments from New England to Virginia. From this discontent emerged a militant evangelicalism that rejected many aspects of the traditional social as well as religious order of the colonies and demanded sweeping changes in the relationship between church and state. Rapid urbanization also produced some unsettling effects. For one thing, it led to the appearance of an urban-rural dichotomy in many colonies. More important, by crowding together in a small area large numbers of not fully assimilated and sometimes impoverished people, it created for the first time in the colonies a potential for the emergence of intraurban class and group antagonisms within the cities themselves. It might also be argued that the process of institutional differentiation that was taking place within medium-sized and large urban communities contributed to the attenuation of the traditional highly personal pattern of social relations by establishing institutional barriers between groups and thereby helping to bring about a significant depersonalization of the social system. Finally, by whetting the social and economic appetites and increasing the material aspirations of men at all levels of society, the "profuse abundance" of the American environment seemed to have produced, in direct violation of inherited norms, a disturbing rise in several forms of hedonistic and anomic behavior and a corresponding decline in moral standards and devotion to the public good. What was even worse, at least in some quarters, such forms of behavior seemed to be gaining public acceptance, thus endangering the normative cohesion of colonial society.

If the first hypothesis emphasizes the unsettled and chaotic state of colonial society during the mid-eighteenth century, the second argues that it was becoming too settled. Several case studies of communities as diverse in size and character as Boston and Chester County, Pennsylvania, strongly suggest that during the decades just prior to the Revolution, opportunity was declining and the social structure becoming less open in the older settled communities as a result of overcrowding brought on by a shortage of land, increasing social stratification, a greater concentration of wealth in the hands of the upper classes, rising numbers of poor, and a pronounced tendency toward political elitism. All of these developments, the argument runs, created deep frustrations for those who found opportunity constricting and their life prospects growing correspondingly dimmer. The supposed result was the creation of severe underlying tensions between the privileged and the unprivileged, landed and landless, masters and servants, even fathers and sons. These studies are still too few to know whether the phenomena they describe were widespread. But Jackson Turner Main in his more comprehensive investigation *The Social Structure of Revolutionary America* has speculated about the existence of a general "long-term tendency . . . toward greater inequality, with more marked class distinctions throughout the colonies on the eve of the pre-Revolutionary disturbances."[6]

Obviously, an enormous amount of further research will be required before we will know with some degree of certainty to what extent either or both of these two general hypotheses—the one emphasizing the destabilizing effects of rapid change and the other the frustrations created by a closing society—accurately represent some of the realities of mid-eighteenth-century colonial social development. On the basis of present knowledge, however, it is clear that at least three major questions need to be confronted.

The first is simply how to resolve a number of important ambiguities about the meaning and operation of several of these specific components of social strain we have just described. For one thing, there is an apparent contradiction between the two general hypotheses. How could colonial society have been becoming less coherent and more rigid at the same time? This contradiction might of course be explained in one of three ways. First, it is possible that there were significant spatial variations, that there was a tendency toward less coherence in some rapidly developing areas and more rigidity in other older and more stable areas. A less likely possibility is that a generalized long-term linear process was at work with a period of intense social and economic upheaval being followed just before the Revolution by a time of declining opportunity and greater stratification. Finally, it is possible, as P. M. G. Harris has recently suggested,[7] that this process was cyclical, with colonial society becoming more or less flexible according to population change, community growth, institutional development, and various contingency factors, though the cycles may not have been quite so regular as Harris has posited. My own suspicion is that some combination of the first and third possibilities will probably turn out to provide the most plausible resolution to the problem.

But there are many other more specific problems with each of these hypotheses, especially with the first. Like many of the works which can be cited in its support, this hypothesis rests upon an obvious, though unstated, and relatively crude application of an equilibrium theory of society. As critics of such theories have pointed out, to the extent that equilibrium theories, first, assess the health or sickness of society in terms of whether or not the elements within it are in a condition of homeostasis and, second, view change as an essentially disequilibrating force, such theories are potentially distorting, for it is not at all clear that the invariable price of rapid change is social instability. Obviously, change can be so well institutionalized and so widely accepted as to produce stabilizing effects. Indeed, in the specific situation at hand, it can be argued that change—and increasingly rapid change at that—was at the heart of the colonial life experience and that the colonists had been forced almost from the beginning to come to terms with it. Moreover, the second hypothesis suggests that the slowing down of change rather than its acceleration created a potential for serious social disruption.

More particularly, it is not yet at all clear that the cost of rapid economic and demographic growth in combination with increasing social differentiation was always a loss of social cohesion; certainly, although there was everywhere an acceleration of the economy and the population, it does not appear that there was a movement from more to less social coherence in most of the colonies during the first three-quarters of the eighteenth century. In New England, where the early settlers were reasonably homogeneous and for most of the seventeenth century at least generally devoted to an explicit religious and "social synthesis" that had been worked out by the leaders of the first settlements, this thesis seems to work fairly well, and it is significant that most of the evidence for it comes from New England. But the colonies to the south, the provinces from New York to Georgia, had been settled by disparate groups and individuals with widely divergent backgrounds, goals, interests, and orientations; and the direction of social development there during the eighteenth century was clearly toward more rather than less coherence and homogeneity as the settlers fashioned out of diverse materials a social synthesis where none had been before. Even with regard to the New England colonies, it may be argued that the breakdown of the old Puritan synthesis early in the eighteenth century was accompanied by the emergence of a new one that, while retaining a distinctly Puritan flavor, was not so dissimilar in form and character from those achieved at the same time by the colonies father south.

And there are still other problems. One arises out of the uncertainty that the rapid upward social mobility, the accelerated movement toward political inclusion, or the Great Awakening functioned as destabilizing rather than stabilizing forces or that the kinds of conflict they engendered did not relieve as much social strain as they created. In addition, it is also possible that the widespread expression of concern about rising standards of consumption in the colonies was less an indication of fundamental discontent with existing modes of behaviour than an appropriate—and necessary—device through which the colonists could fulfill an apparent need to preserve the *ideal* of a more static, coherent, goal-oriented, and instrumental social order without requiring them to alter their actual behaviour.

There are far fewer obvious problems with the second hypothesis. But it is entirely possible that, in terms of opportunity and career chances for individuals throughout colonial society, the shortage of land in older communities may have been more than offset not only by the opening up of new areas but also by new opportunities in nonfarm occupations created by the ongoing process of social differentiation and institutional development. Moreover, from the evidence so far adduced, it is by no means certain that the decline in opportunity and the concentration of wealth were sufficiently general or intense to create serious social conflict, even in older settled areas.

A second major question raised by these two hypotheses is the extent to which there were significant variations in the nature of social development, not only from colony to colony, but also from region to region within the colonies and even from one segment of society to another within a given community. From what we already know, it is clear that the differences were enormous, and the extent of these differences suggests that it is improbable that either or both of these hypotheses can subsume all of them.

Finally, the third, and for the present discussion much the most important and pressing, question posed by these hypotheses is the precise relationship between the many manifestations of social strain they have described and the American Revolution. Several scholars, especially Wood and Lockridge, have asserted the existence of direct causal links. But these assertions have been accompanied by what Clifford Geertz has called "a studied vagueness" that conceals the fact that as yet no one has succeeded either in establishing the existence of such links or in specifying exactly what they may have been and how they may have functioned in the overall causal pattern of the Revolution.[8] To a large extent, this failure accounts for the perpetuation of the widespread conviction among students of the Revolution that no such links were present or that, if they were, they could not have been very important.

This conviction has been reinforced by the obvious fact that the American Revolution failed to generate a *societal revolution*. Note that I purposely use the term *societal revolution*, which connotes a "discontinuous process of structural innovation," rather than *social revolution*, which implies no more than some "quantitative increments" or qualitative changes within an existing structure.[9] Though the Revolution obviously helped to accelerate some long-standing tendencies within colonial society toward greater political and social inclusion and more individual autonomy and although incremental changes in patterns of social organization, institutional arrangements, and values may be observed in many sectors of American life during the Revolution, there do not seem to be any sharp discontinuities that cannot be traced primarily to exigencies created by the separation from Britain. In other words we do not need to look for strain, frustration, and dysfunction within colonial society, but we must look to the political conflict between Britain and the colonies to find a plausible explanation for these discontinuities.

But the limited character of the internal social changes produced by the Revolution obviously cannot be taken to mean that these various components of strain had no causal relationship to the Revolution. That social context has an important bearing upon political events is a truism, and because these components were all present to one degree or another in colonial society at the time the Revolution occurred, it may be safely assumed that they had some effect upon the Revolution. The main question, then, is not whether a causal relationship existed but what kind of a relationship it may have been.

At least four possibilities immediately present themselves. First, from the evidence offered in support of the first hypothesis discussed above, we may surmise that the severity of social strain was so great—the anomie, disorientation, frustration, and friction so intensive and extensive—within colonial society as to make it exceptionally prone toward revolution by creating either a single social crisis of such magnitude that it cut across and through most segments and areas of colonial life or a complex multitude of interlocking local, group, and personal crises that converged to produce severe disruption in many strategic sectors of colonial society. Something of this sort seems to be what Wood is implying. Second, a corollary of this argument, suggested by Heimert and others, is that the Great Awakening and presumably the many other changes that contributed to the social ferment of the mid-eighteenth century prepared the colonists intellectually and emotionally for the rejection of British authority after 1763 by calling into question or otherwise undermining confidence in the authority of traditional religious, social, and political institutions and leaders. On the other hand, the findings on which the second hypothesis rests can be marshaled in support of still a third argument which is a variant of the old formula of the Progressive historians:

that declining opportunity and a rigidifying social structure created fierce resentments among the middle and lower classes against the elite that came surging to the surface of public life during the pre-revolutionary years and these resentments merged with the protest against Britain to generate an internal revolution. Still a fourth alternative is suggested by combining the two hypotheses: that, however upsetting it may have been to older members of the elite, the economic and demographic expansion and social ferment throughout the first five decades of the eighteenth century created rising economic and social expectations among the rest of society which were subsequently frustrated by a decline in opportunity beginning about midcentury. According to this formulation, which is merely an application of James C. Davies's general theory of revolution to the American Revolution, the most critical element in turning American society toward revolution was not the erosion of social coherence or even the decline of opportunity but the frustrated expectations of a large segment of the population as a result of a general closing of society after a prolonged period of apparently becoming increasingly more open.

Some or all of these theories may turn out to be appropriate vehicles for relating to the Revolution the various components of social strain in mid-eighteenth-century America. So far, we have been offered little more than a kind of superficial historicism that suggests that the behavior of the generation of the Revolution somehow emerged from or was conditioned by the social environment, a suggestion that is obviously "so general as to be truistic."[10] Before we will know which, if any, of these four theories are appropriate, we will have to be able to specify much more precisely than we can at present the ways in which those manifestations of strain impinged upon and affected the actual behavior of particular groups and individuals during the 1760s and 1770s; how, when, where, why, and to what extent the uncoordinated individual and group dissatisfactions that may have been produced by those strains merged into the collective opposition to Britain; and whether, in what sense, and by what sorts of psychological mechanisms those social strains actually did find "mitigation through revolution and republicanism," as Wood has contended.[11]

In the meantime, two different categories of existing studies provide some—but only some—help in this regard. By revealing, if in many cases only implicitly, the connection between political factionalism and particular sorts of social, economic, and religious strain, the rather extensive literature on political divisions within individual colonies between 1750 and 1776 and their relationship to the Revolution provides some general indications of what the answers to at least some of these questions may be for several colonies. In particular, this literature makes it clear that there were enormous variations from one colony to another and that virtually every colony had its own specific forms of social strain. Recent studies of the many symbolic representations of internal social strains in revolutionary rhetoric have confronted more directly the general question of the connection between such strains and the Revolution. They have shown how the colonists' fears about moral decline and the increase in self-oriented behavior in their own societies merged with the opposition to Britain to turn the Revolution into a "norm-oriented movement" that looked forward to the regeneration of American society and the restoration of traditional social norms. There can be no doubt that this projection of American corruption upon Britain helped make it easier to reject the monarchy and the British connection and to accept revolution and republicanism. To what extent it also relieved Americans of the guilt produced by their own moral failures and thereby actually helped to mitigate an important source of social strain within the colonies is not so clear. Indeed, by turning them toward republicanism with its even higher and less attainable standards, it may actually have exacerbated such strains. Moreover, in the absence of any systematic attempt to assess the *relative* importance of these fears of moral decline in mobilizing widespread popular support for the Revolution, it is extremely difficult to know what causal weight they may have actually borne.

Whenever and however these crucial problems are resolved, it is doubtful that we will be able to assign to any or all of the components of social strain so far discussed a major causal role in the Revolution. To do so we would have to show that the extent of strain was infinitely greater and the degree to which they impinged themselves on individuals and groups was much more powerful than anyone has so far suggested or than our present knowledge seems to warrant. It is extremely doubtful that we will be able to say even that any or all of those components were a necessary cause of the Revolution, that is, that without them there would have been no Revolution. In all probability, we will be able to say only that these several components—for the most part, the regular concomitants of the normal processes of incremental change within colonial society—affected the Revolution in the same sense that they would have affected any other major political event that occurred in the context of which they were a part. Thus, they may be said to have "aggravated," perhaps in some cases even "intensely," "antagonism to the imperial system" and to have "fed into the revolutionary movement."[12] But they cannot be said either to have created the movement or to have been necessary for it to occur.

But this is not in any way to suggest that an understanding of the complex internal social, economic, political, and religious changes that were taking place within the colonies is not essential to a comprehension of many aspects of the Revolution or that it would be desirable either to relegate them to a residual role or to eliminate them from further discussions of the causes of the Revolution. On the contrary, existing knowledge suggests and future investigations will surely confirm that there was a direct relationship between the degree and special character of social malintegration and the particular configuration of the Revolution in each colony and that an understanding of the nature and intensity of internal strain within a given colony during the quarter-century prior to independence would enable us to predict what general shape the Revolution would assume in that state. If this suggestion is correct, then it is obvious that an analysis of the character and operation of various elements of social strain within the colonies is absolutely crucial to any comprehension of the many variations in the form and nature of the Revolution from one colony or one region to another.

For analytical and heuristic purposes, we might say, for instance, that only if every one of the components of strain so far identified and discussed as well as any that may subsequently be discovered impinged directly upon the Revolution in a given colony would we be likely to find the Revolution in its fullest and most extreme form. For simplicity, we can call this most extreme form of the Revolution R. It then follows that the absence of one or more of these components in another colony will result in something less than all of R. What we can finally say, then, about the causal importance of all of these strain-producing elements— perhaps all we can say—is that without any or all of them, we would not have all of R.

The larger point is that without the conflict between Britain and the colonies these components of social strain would not by themselves have produced a revolution. In any explanation of the causes of the Revolution, then, what one wants to know about such components is how they related to the Anglo-American conflict, how they may be used to illuminate the traditional and still central question of how and why the old structure of interests, institutions, and symbols—the sacred moral order—that had bound the colonies to Britain for the previous century broke down so rapidly during the third quarter of the eighteenth century. For that breakdown—as well as the frenzied rhetoric that accompanied it—can be explained largely by the anxieties deriving out of what the vast majority of both the colonial and British political nations took to be a series of fundamental violations of that sacred order by the other side, without invoking whatever frustrations or resentments may have arisen out of social strains within the colonies.

If these conclusions turn out to be correct, they raise serious doubts both about the argument—implicit in the theories of Chalmers Johnson, Neil J. Smelser, and other modern analysts of revolution—that "true revolutions," to quote Wood, must derive from "sources lying deep within the social structure"[13] and about the utility of such generalized themes of social change in explaining the origins of political revolutions. Certainly, the example of the American Revolution would seem to make it clear that social strain is a concept of limited value for explaining at least one variety of great modern political revolution. As James Rule and Charles Tilly suggest in a persuasive critique of these and other natural-history models of revolution, the central feature of any political revolution is "the seizure of power over a governmental apparatus by one group from another," and such a development can usually be explained largely as a result of some conflict between two or more contenders within the polity over one or more issues of great moment. These issues may have social or economic, religious or cultural content, but they are invariably political because they are fought out in a political arena and involve questions of basic concern to the polity. What we need to know, then, to understand what caused a particular revolution is what specific conditions—short-term, intermediate, or long-term—led to (1) the appearance of rival contenders for authority and legitimacy; (2) the acceptance of the claims of the revolutionaries by a significant or strategic segment of the politically relevant population; and (3) the unwillingness or incapacity of the old regime to suppress its opponents. Usually, there is no special need to search for the existence of "anomie, strain, dysfunction or frustration" to explain these events. Wherever such evidences of disequilibration are present, they may well feed into the revolutionary situation; but, because they will usually be found to exist both before and after the revolution and at any number of intervening periods when no revolution occurred, they "fail to characterize situations that are distinctly revolutionary, and thus lack [much] explanatory power."[14] Not only can they not in themselves provide a sufficient explanation for many modern revolutions but in cases like the American Revolution they cannot even be said to have been necessary for them to occur.

The limited causal importance of the many evidences of social strain we have been discussing in this essay does not imply that we should abandon their study; but it does suggest that they should be approached from a different and considerably broader perspective. Whatever their relationship to the American Revolution, they were obviously manifestations of fundamental, long-term social changes taking place within the colonies. To the very great extent that those changes were in the direction of more rational and less traditional patterns of social, economic, and political relations, institutional structures, and values that put ever higher premiums upon individual autonomy, self-fulfillment, pursuit of self interest, and that thus emphasized economic returns, accumulation, achievement rather than ascription, functional specificity of economic and social roles, and universalistic criteria for membership in the polity and society, these changes were part of what E. A. Wrigley has described as a "revolution of modernization,"[15] a sweeping social revolution that had been in progress in Western Europe since the middle of the fifteenth century and, by the time of the American Revolution, had been underway in the colonies for at least a century.

This broader social revolution, which in many respects is far more crucial to an understanding of the first two centuries of American life and far more worthy of scholarly attention than the American Revolution, would have been completed with or without the American Revolution, albeit perhaps at a different rate of speed and in a somewhat different form, and it would be unfortunate if this broader revolution continues to be confused with the American Revolution. For however interwoven it may have been with the American Revolution during the brief span of time between 1760 and 1790, there is always the danger that an excessive concentration upon discovering and specifying the links between the two will not only divert attention from and obscure the nature of the broader social revolution but will also contribute to prolonging the unfortunate American tendency to view social history as primarily interesting for what it can tell us about politics. As E. J. Hobsbawm has recently warned, the value of studies of "major transformation of society" may well be "in inverse proportion to our concentration on the brief moment of conflict." It is a commonplace, of course, that political revolutions, by bringing into the open and dramatizing "crucial aspects of social structure" that would remain hidden or obscure in normal times, provide a magnificent window into the societies in which they occur.[16] But the particular phenomena thereby observed will only appear in their fullest meaning when they are fitted into the wider context of the long-term tendencies of which they are a part. Only when such a context has been established will we finally be able to understand the precise relationship between America's late eighteenth-century political revolution and its peculiar variant of the wider social revolution of modernization that, by the end of the eighteenth century, was sweeping through much of the Western world.

Gordon S. Wood

8 RHETORIC AND REALITY IN THE AMERICAN REVOLUTION

If any catch phrase is to characterize the work being done on the American Revolution by this generation of historians, it will probably be "the American Revolution considered as an intellectual movement."[1] For we now seem to be fully involved in a phase of writing about the Revolution in which the thought of the revolutionaries, rather than their social and economic interests, has become the major focus of research and analysis. This recent emphasis on ideas is not of course new, and indeed right from the beginning it has characterized almost all our attempts to understand the Revolution. The ideas of a period which Samuel Eliot Morison and Harold Laski once described as, next to the English revolutionary decades of the seventeenth century, the most fruitful era in the history of Western political thought could never be completely ignored in any phase of our history writing.

It has not been simply the inherent importance of the revolutionary ideas, those "great principles of freedom,"[2] that has continually attracted the attention of historians. It has been rather the unusual nature of the Revolution and the constant need to explain what on the face of it seems inexplicable that has compelled almost all interpreters of the Revolution, including the participants themselves, to stress its predominantly intellectual character and hence its uniqueness among Western revolutions. Within the context of revolutionary historiography the one great effort to disparage the significance of ideas in the Revolution—an effort which dominated our history writing in the first half of the twentieth century—becomes something of an anomaly, a temporary aberration into a deterministic social and economic explanation from which we have been

123

retreating for the past two decades. Since roughly the end of World War 2 we have witnessed a resumed and increasingly heightened insistence on the primary significance of conscious beliefs, and particularly of constitutional principles, in explaining what once again has become the unique character of the American Revolution. In the hands of idealist-minded historians the thought and principles of the Americans have consequently come to repossess that explanative force which the previous generation of materialist-minded historians had tried to locate in the social structure.

Indeed, our renewed insistence on the importance of ideas in explaining the Revolution has now attained a level of fullness and sophistication never before achieved, with the consequence that the economic and social approach of the previous generation of behaviorist historians has never seemed more anomalous and irrelevant than it does at present. Yet paradoxically it may be that this preoccupation with the explanatory power of the revolutionary ideas has become so intensive and so refined, assumed such a character, that the apparently discredited social and economic approach of an earlier generation has at the same time never seemed more attractive and relevant. In other words, we may be approaching a crucial juncture in our writing about the Revolution where idealism and behaviorism meet.

It was the revolutionaries themselves who first described the peculiar character of what they had been involved in. The Revolution, as those who took stock at the end of three decades of revolutionary activity noted, was not "one of those events which strikes the public eye in the subversions of laws which have usually attended the revolutions of governments." Because it did not seem to have been a typical revolution, the sources of its force and its momentum appeared strangely unaccountable. "In other revolutions, the sword has been drawn by the arm of offended freedom, under an oppression that threatened the vital powers of society."[3] But this seemed hardly true of the American Revolution. There was none of the legendary tyranny that had so often driven desperate peoples into revolution. The Americans were not an oppressed people; they had no crushing imperial shackles to throw off. In fact, the Americans knew they were probably freer and less burdened with cumbersome feudal and monarchical restraints than any part of mankind in the eighteenth century. To its victims, the Tories, the Revolution was truly incomprehensible. Never in history, said Daniel Leonard, had there been so much rebellion with so "little real cause." It was, wrote Peter Oliver, "the most wanton and unnatural rebellion that ever existed."[4] The Americans' response was out of all proportion to the stimuli. The objective social reality scarcely seemed capable of explaining a revolution.

Yet no American doubted that there had been a revolution. How then was it to be justified and explained? If the American Revolution, lacking "those mad, tumultuous actions which disgraced many of the great revolutions of antiquity," was not a typical revolution, what kind of revolution was it? If the origin of the American Revolution lay not in the usual passions and interests of men, wherein did it lay? Those Americans who looked back at what they had been through could only marvel at the rationality and moderation, "supported by the energies of well weighed choice," involved in their separation from Britain, a revolution remarkably "without violence or convulsion."[5] It seemed to be peculiarly an affair of the mind. Even two such dissimilar sorts of Whigs as Thomas Paine and John Adams both came to see the Revolution they had done so much to bring about as especially involved with ideas, resulting from "a mental examination," a change in "the minds and hearts of the people."[6] The Americans were fortunate in being born at a time when the principles of government and freedom were better known than at any time in history. The Americans had learned "how to define the rights of nature, how to search into, to distinguish, and to comprehend, the principles of physical, moral, religious, and civil liberty," how, in short, to discover and resist the forces of tyranny before they could be applied. Never before in history had a people achieved "a revolution by reasoning" alone.[7]

The Americans, "born the heirs of freedom,"[8] revolted not to create but to maintain their freedom. American society had developed differently from that of the Old World. From the time of the first settlements in the seventeenth century, wrote Samuel Williams in 1794, "every thing tended to produce, and to establish the spirit of freedom." While the speculative philosophers of Europe were laboriously searching their minds in an effort to decide the first principles of liberty, the Americans had come to experience vividly that liberty in their everyday lives. The American Revolution, said Williams, joined together these enlightened ideas with America's experience. The Revolution was thus essentially intellectual and declaratory: it "explained the business to the world, and served to confirm what nature and society had before produced." "All was the result of reason. . . ."[9] The Revolution had taken place not in a succession of eruptions that had crumbled the existing social structure, but in a succession of new thoughts and new ideas that had vindicated that social structure.

The same logic that drove the participants to view the Revolution as peculiarly intellectual also compelled Moses Coit Tyler, writing at the end of the nineteenth century, to describe the American Revolution as "pre-eminently a revolution caused by ideas, and pivoted on ideas." That ideas played a part in all revolutions Tyler readily admitted. But in most revolutions, like that of the French, ideas had been perceived and acted upon only when the social reality had caught up with them, only when the ideas had been given meaning and force by long-experienced "real evils." The American Revolution, said Tyler, had been different: it was directed "not against tyranny inflicted, but only against tyranny anticipated." The Americans revolted not out of actual suffering but out of reasoned principle. "Hence, more than with most other epochs of revolutionary strife, our epoch of revolutionary strife was a strife of ideas: a long warfare of political logic; a succession of annual campaigns in which the marshalling of arguments not only preceded the marshalling of armies, but often exceeded them in impression upon the final result."[10]

It is in this historiographical context developed by the end of the nineteenth century, this constant and at times extravagant emphasis on the idealism of the Revolution, that the true radical quality of the Progressive generation's interpretation of the Revolution becomes so vividly apparent. For the work of these Progressive historians was grounded in a social and economic explanation of the revolutionary era that explicitly rejected the causal importance of ideas. These historians could scarcely have avoided the general intellectual climate of the first part of the twentieth century which regarded ideas as suspect. By absorbing the diffused thinking of Marx and Freud and the assumptions of behaviorist psychology, men had come to conceive of ideas as ideologies or rationalizations, as masks obscuring the underlying interests and drives that actually determined social behavior. For too long, it seemed, philosophers had reified thought, detaching ideas from the material conditions that produced them and investing them with an independent will that was somehow alone responsible for the determination of events. As Charles Beard pointed out in his introduction to the 1935 edition of *An Economic Interpretation of the Constitution*, previous historians of the Constitution had assumed that ideas were "entities, particulars, or forces, apparently independent of all earthly considerations coming under the head of 'economic.' " It was Beard's aim, as it was the aim of many of his contemporaries, to bring into historical consideration "those realistic features of economic conflict, stress, and strain" which previous interpreters of the Revolution had largely ignored.[11]

The product of this aim was a generation or more of historical writing about the revolutionary period (of which Beard's was but the most famous expression) that sought to explain the Revolution and the formation of the Constitution in terms of socio-economic relationships and interests rather than in terms of ideas.

Curiously, the consequence of this reversal of historical approaches

was not the destruction of the old-fashioned conception of the nature of ideas. As Marx had said, he intended only to put Hegel's head in its rightful place; he had no desire to cut it off. Ideas as rationalization, as ideology, remained—still distinct entities set in opposition to interests, now however lacking any deep causal significance, becoming merely a covering superstructure for the underlying and determinative social reality. Ideas therefore could still be the subject of historical investigation, as long as one kept them in their proper place, interesting no doubt in their own right but not actually counting for much in the movement of events.

Even someone as interested in ideas as Carl Becker never seriously considered them to be in any way determinants of what happened. Ideas fascinated Becker, but it was as superstructure that he enjoyed examining them, their consistency, their logic, their clarity, the way men formed and played with them. In his *Declaration of Independence: A Study in the History of Political Ideas* the political theory of the Americans takes on an unreal and even fatuous quality. It was as if ideas were merely refined tools to be used by the colonists in the most adroit manner possible. The entire Declaration of Independence, said Becker, was calculated for effect, designed primarily to "convince a candid world that the colonies had a moral and legal right to separate from Great Britain." The severe indictment of the King did not spring from unfathomable passions but was contrived, conjured up, to justify a rebellion whose sources lay elsewhere. Men to Becker were never the victims of their thought, always masters of it. Ideas were a kind of legal brief. "Thus step by step, from 1764 to 1776, the colonists modified their theory to suit their needs."[12] The assumptions behind Becker's 1909 behaviorist work on New York politics in the Revolution and his 1922 study of the political ideas in the Declaration of Independence were more alike than they at first might appear.

Bringing to their studies of the Revolution similar assumptions about the nature of ideas, some of Becker's contemporaries went on to expose starkly the implications of those assumptions. When the entire body of revolutionary thinking was examined, these historians could not avoid being struck by its generally bombastic and overwrought quality. The ideas expressed seemed so inflated, such obvious exaggerations of reality, that they could scarcely be taken seriously. The Tories were all "wretched hirelings, and execrable parricides"; George III, the "tyrant of the earth," a "monster in human form"; the British soldiers, "a mercenary, licentious rabble of banditti," intending to "tear the bowels and vitals of their brave but peaceable fellow subjects, and *to wash the ground with a profusion of innocent blood.*"[13] Such extravagant language, it seemed, could be nothing but calculated deception, at best an obvious distortion of fact, designed to incite and mold a revolutionary fervor. "The stigmatizing of British policy as 'tyranny,' 'oppression' and 'slavery,' " wrote Arthur M. Schlesinger, the dean of the Progressive historians, "had little or no objective reality, at least prior to the Intolerable Acts, but ceaseless repetition of the charge kept emotions at fever pitch."[14]

Indeed, so grandiose, so overdrawn it seemed, were the ideas that the historians were ncessarily led to ask not whether such ideas were valid but why men should have expressed them. It was not the content of such ideas but the function that was really interesting. The revolutionary rhetoric, the profusion of sermons, pamphlets, and articles in the patriotic cause, could best be examined as propaganda, that is, as a concerted and self-concious effort by agitators to manipulate and shape public opinion. Because of the Progressive historians' view of the Revolution as the movement of class minorities bent on promoting particular social and economic interests, the conception of propaganda was crucial to their explanation of what seemed to be a revolutionary consensus. Through the use of ideas in provoking hatred and influencing opinion and creating at least "an appearance of unity," the influence of a minority of agitators was out of all proportion to their number. The Revolution thus became a display of extraordinary skillfulness in the manipulation of public opinion. In fact, wrote Schlesinger, "no disaffected element in history has ever risen more splendidly to the occasion."[15]

Ideas thus became, as it were, parcels of thought to be distributed and used where they would do the most good. This propaganda was not of course necessarily false, but it was always capable of manipulation. "Whether the suggestions are to be true or false, whether the activities are to be open or concealed," wrote Philip Davidson, "are matters for the propagandist to decide." Apparently ideas could be turned on or off at will, and men controlled their rhetoric in a way they could not control their interests. Whatever the importance of propaganda, its connection with social reality was tenuous. Since ideas were so self-consciously manageable, the Whigs were not actually expressing anything meaningful about themselves but were rather feigning and exaggerating for effect. What the Americans said could not be taken at face value but must be considered as a rhetorical disguise for some hidden interest. The expression of even the classic and well-defined natural rights philosophy became, in Davidson's view, but "the propagandist's rationalization of his desire to protect his vested interests."[16]

With this conception of ideas as weapons shrewdly used by designing propagandists, it was inevitable that the thought of the revolutionaries should have been denigrated. The revolutionaries became by implication hypocritical demagogues, "adroitly tailoring their arguments to changing conditions." Their political thinking appeared to possess neither consistency nor significance. "At best," said Schlesinger in an early summary of his interpretation, "an exposition of the political theories of the anti-parliamentary party is an account of their retreat from one strategic position to another." So the Whigs moved, it was strongly suggested, easily if not frivolously from a defense of charter rights, to the rights of Englishmen, and finally to the rights of man, as each position was exposed and became untenable. In short, concluded Schlesinger, the Revolution could never be understood if it were regarded "as a great forensic controversy over abstract governmental rights."[17]

It is essentially on this point of intellectual consistency that Edmund S. Morgan has fastened for the past decade and a half in an attempt to bring down the entire interpretive framework of the socio-economic argument. If it could be shown that the thinking of the revolutionaries was not inconsistent after all, that the Whigs did not actually skip from one constitutional notion to the next, then the imputation of Whig frivolity and hypocrisy would lose its force. This was a central intention of Morgan's study of the political thought surrounding the Stamp Act. As Morgan himself has noted and others have repeated, "In the last analysis the significance of the Stamp Act crisis lies in the emergence, not of leaders and methods and organizations, but of well-defined constitutional principles." As early as 1765 the Whigs "laid down the line on which Americans stood until they cut their connections with England. Consistently from 1765 to 1776 they denied the authority of Parliament to tax them externally or internally; consistently they affirmed their willingness to submit to whatever legislation Parliament should enact for the supervision of the empire as a whole."[18] This consistency thus becomes, as one scholar's survey of the current interpretation puts it, "an indication of American devotion to principle."[19]

It seemed clear once again after Morgan's study that the Americans were more sincerely attached to constitutional principles than the behaviorist historians had supposed, and that their ideas could not be viewed as simply manipulated propaganda. Consequently the cogency of the Progressive historians' interpretation was weakened if not unhinged. And as the evidence against viewing the Revolution as rooted in internal class-conflict continued to mount from various directions, it appeared more and more comprehensible to accept the old-fashioned notion that the Revolution was after all the consequence of "a great forensic controversy over abstract governmental rights." There were, it seemed, no deprived and depressed populace yearning for a participation in politics that had long been denied; no coherent merchant class victimizing a mass of insolvent debtors; no seething discontent with the British mercantile system; no privileged aristocracy, protected by law, anxiously and insecurely holding power against a clamoring democracy. There was, in short, no internal class upheaval in the Revolution.

If the Revolution was not to become virtually incomprehensible, it must have been the result of what the American Whigs always contended it was—a dispute between Mother Country and colonies over constitutional liberties. By concentrating on the immediate events of the decade leading up to independence, the historians of the 1950s have necessarily fled from the economic and social determinism of the Progressive historians. And by emphasizing the consistency and devotion with which Americans held their constitutional beliefs they have once again focused on what seems to be the extraordinary intellectuality of the American Revolution and hence its uniqueness among Western revolutions. This interpretation, which, as Jack P. Greene notes, "may appropriately be styled neo-Whig," has turned the Revolution into a rationally conservative movement, involving mainly a constitutional defense of existing political liberties against the abrupt and unexpected provocations of the British government after 1760. "The issue then, according to the neo-Whigs, was no more and no less than separation from Britain and the preservation of American liberty." The Revolution has therefore become "more political, legalistic, and constitutional than social or economic." Indeed, some of the neo-Whig historians have implied not just that social and economic conditions were less important in bringing on the Revolution as we once thought, but rather that the social situation in the colonies had little or nothing to do with causing the Revolution. The Whig statements of principles iterated in numerous declarations appear to be the only causal residue after all the supposedly deeper social and economic causes have been washed away. As one scholar who has recently investigated and carefully dismissed the potential social and economic issues in pre-revolutionary Virginia has concluded, "What remains as the fundamental issue in the coming of the Revolution, then, is nothing more than the contest over constitutional rights."[20]

In a different way Bernard Bailyn in a recent article has clarified and reinforced this revived idealistic interpretation of the Revolution. The accumulative influence of much of the latest historical writing on the character of eighteenth-century American society has led Bailyn to the same insight expressed by Samuel Williams in 1794. What made the Revolution truly revolutionary was not the wholesale disruption of social groups and political institutions, for compared to other revolutions such disruption was slight; rather it was the fundamental alteration in the Americans' structure of values, the way they looked at themselves and their institutions. Bailyn has seized on this basic intellectual shift as a means of explaining the apparent contradiction between the seriousness with which the Americans took their revolutionary ideas and the absence of radical social and institutional change. The Revolution, argues Bailyn, was not so much the transformation as the realization of American society.

The Americans had been gradually and unwittingly preparing themselves for such a mental revolution since they first came to the New World in the seventeenth century. The substantive changes in American society had taken place in the course of the previous century, slowly, often imperceptibly, as a series of small piecemeal deviations from what was regarded by most Englishmen as the accepted orthodoxy in society, state, and religion. What the Revolution marked, so to speak, was the point when the Americans suddenly blinked and saw their society, its changes, its differences, in a new perspective. Their deviation from European standards, their lack of an established church and a titled aristocracy, their apparent rusticity and general equality, now became desirable, even necessary, elements in the maintenance of their society and politics. The comprehending and justifying, the endowing with high moral purpose, of these confusing and disturbing social and political divergences, Bailyn concludes, was the American Revolution.

Bailyn's more recent investigation of the rich pamphlet literature of the decades before independence has filled out and refined his idealist interpretation, confirming him in his "rather old-fashioned view that the American Revolution was above all else an ideological-constitutional struggle and not primarily a controversy between social groups undertaken to force changes in the organization of society." While Bailyn's book-length introduction to the first of a multivolumed edition of revolutionary pamphlets makes no effort to stress the conservative character of the Revolution and indeed emphasizes (in contrast to the earlier article) its radicalism and the dynamic and transforming rather than the rationalizing and declarative quality of Whig thought, it nevertheless represents the culmination of the idealist approach to the history of the Revolution. For "above all else," argues Bailyn, it was the Americans' world-view, the peculiar bundle of notions and beliefs they put together during the imperial debate, "that in the end propelled them into Revolution." Through his study of the Whig pamphlets Bailyn became convinced "that the fear of a comprehensive conspiracy against liberty throughout the English-speaking world—a conspiracy believed to have been nourished in corruption, and of which, it was felt, oppression in America was only the most immediately visible part—lay at the heart of the Revolutionary movement." No one of the various acts and measures of the British government after 1763 could by itself have provoked the extreme and violent response of the American Whigs. But when linked together they formed in the minds of the Americans, imbued with a particular historical understanding of what constituted tyranny, an extensive and frightening program designed to enslave the New World. The Revolution becomes comprehensible only when the mental framework, the Whig world-view into which the Americans fitted the events of the 1760s and 1770s, is known. "It is the development of this view to the point of overwhelming persuasiveness to the majority of American leaders and the meaning this view gave to the events of the time, and not simply an accumulation of grievances," writes Bailyn, "that explains the origins of the American Revolution."[21]

It now seems evident from Bailyn's analysis that it was the Americans' peculiar conception of reality more than anything else that convinced them that tyranny was afoot and that they must fight if their liberty was to survive. By an empathic understanding of a wide range of American thinking Bailyn has been able to offer us a most persuasive argument for the importance of ideas in bringing on the Revolution. Not since Tyler has the intellectual character of the Revolution received such emphasis and never before has it been set out so cogently and completely. It would seem that the idealist explanation of the Revolution has nowhere else to go.

Labeling the recent historical interpretations of the Revolution as "neo-Whig" is indeed appropriate, for, as Page Smith has pointed out, "After a century and a half of progress in historical scholarship, in research techniques, in tools and methods, we have found our way to the interpretation held, substantially, by those historians who themselves participated in or lived through the era of, the Revolution." By describing the Revolution as a conservative, principled defense of American freedom against the provocations of the English government, the neo-Whig historians have come full circle to the position of the revolutionaries themselves and to the interpretation of the first generation of historians.[22] Indeed, as a consequence of this historical atavism, praise for the contemporary or early historians has become increasingly common.

But to say "that the Whig interpretation of the American Revolution may not be as dead as some historians would have us believe" is perhaps less to commend the work of David Ramsay and George Bancroft than to indict the approach of recent historians.[23] However necessary and rewarding the neo-Whig histories have been, they present us with only a partial perspective on the Revolution. The neo-Whig interpretation is intrinsically polemical; however subtly presented, it aims to justify the Revolution. It therefore cannot accommodate a totally different, an opposing perspective, a Tory view of the Revolution. It is for this reason that the recent publication of Peter Oliver's "Origin and Progress of the American Rebellion" is of major significance, for it offers us—"by attacking the hallowed traditions of the revolution, challenging the motives of the founding fathers, and depicting revolution as passion, plotting, and violence"— an explanation of what happened quite different from what we have been recently accustomed to.[24] Oliver's vivid portrait of the revolutionaries with his accent on their vicious emotions and interests seriously disturbs the present Whiggish interpretation of the Revolution. It is not that Oliver's description of, say, John Adams as madly ambitious and consumingly resentful is any more correct than Adams's own description of himself as a virtuous and patriotic defender of liberty against tyranny. Both interpretations of Adams are in a sense right, but neither can comprehend the other because each is preoccupied with seemingly contradictory sets of motives. Indeed, it is really these two interpretations that have divided historians of the Revolution ever since.

Any intellectually satisfying explanation of the Revolution must encompass the Tory perspective as well as the Whig, for if we are compelled to take sides and choose between opposing motives—unconscious or avowed, passion or principle, greed or liberty—we will be endlessly caught up in the polemics of the participants themselves. We must, in other words, eventually dissolve the distinction between conscious and unconscious motives, between the revolutionaries' stated intentions and their supposedly hidden needs and desires, a dissolution that involves somehow relating beliefs and ideas to the social world in which they operate. If we are to understand the causes of the Revolution we must therefore ultimately transcend this problem of motivation. But this we can never do as long as we attempt to explain the Revolution mainly in terms of the intentions of the participants. It is not that men's motives are unimportant; they indeed make events, including revolutions. But the purposes of men, especially in a revolution, are so numerous, so varied, and so contradictory that their complex interaction produces results that no one intended or could even foresee. It is this interaction and these results that recent historians are referring to when they speak so disparagingly of those "underlying determinants" and "impersonal and inexorable forces" bringing on the Revolution. Historical explanation which does not account for these "forces," which, in other words, relies simply on understanding the conscious intentions of the actors, will thus be limited. This preoccupation with men's purposes was what restricted the perspectives of the contemporaneous Whig and Tory interpretations; and it is still the weakness of the neo-Whig histories, and indeed of any interpretation which attempts to explain the events of the Revolution by discovering the calculations from which individuals supposed themselves to have acted.

No explanation of the American Revolution in terms of the intentions and designs of particular individuals could have been more crudely put than that offered by the revolutionaries themselves. American Whigs, like men of the eighteenth century generally, were fascinated with what seemed to the age to be the newly appreciated problem of human motivation and causation in the affairs of the world. In the decade before independence the Americans sought endlessly to discover the supposed calculations and purposes of individuals or groups that lay behind the otherwise incomprehensible rush of events. More than anything else perhaps it was this obsession with motives that led to the prevalence in the eighteenth century of beliefs in conspiracies to account for the confusing happenings in which men found themselves caught up. Bailyn has suggested that this common fear of conspiracy was "deeply rooted in the political awareness of eighteenth-century Britons, involved in the very structure of their political life"; it "reflected so clearly the realities of life in an age in which monarchical autocracy flourished, [and] in which the stability and freedom of England's 'mixed' constitution was a recent and remarkable achievement."[25] Yet it might also be argued that the tendency to see conspiracy behind what happened reflected as well the very enlightenment of the age. To attribute events to the designs and purposes of human agents seemed after all to be an enlightened advance over older beliefs in blind chance, providence, or God's interventions. It was rational and scientific, a product of both the popularization of politics and the secularization of knowledge. It was obvious to Americans that the series of events in the years after 1763, those "unheard of intolerable calamities, spring not of the dust, come not causeless." "Ought not the PEOPLE therefore," asked John Dickinson, "to watch? to observe facts? to search into causes? to investigate designs?"[26] And these causes and designs could be traced to individuals in high places, to ministers, to royal governors, and their lackeys. The belief in conspiracy grew naturally out of the enlightened need to find the human purposes behind the multitude of phenomena, to find the causes for what happened in the social world just as the natural scientist was discovering the causes for what happened in the physical world. It was a necessary consequence of the search for connections and patterns in events. The various acts of the British government, the Americans knew, should not be "regarded according to the simple force of each, but as parts of a system of oppression."[27] The Whigs' intense search for the human purposes behind events was in fact an example of the beginnings of modern history.

In attempting to rebut those interpretations disparaging the colonists' cause, the present neo-Whig historians have been drawn into writing as partisans of the revolutionaries. And they have thus found themselves entangled in the same kind of explanation used by the original antagonists, an explanation, despite obvious refinements, still involved with the discovery of motives and its corollary, the assessing of a personal sort of responsibility for what happened. While most of the neo-Whig historians have not gone so far as to see conspiracy in British actions (although some have come close), they have tended to point up the blundering and stupidity of British officials in contrast to "the breadth of vision" that moved the Americans. If George III was in a position of central responsibility in the British government, as English historians have recently said, then, according to Edmund S. Morgan, "he must bear most of the praise or blame for the series of measures that alienated and lost the colonies, and it is hard to see how there can be much praise." By seeking "to define issues, fix responsibilities," and thereby to shift "the burden of proof" onto those who say the Americans were narrow and selfish and the empire was basically just and beneficent, the neo-Whigs have attempted to redress what they felt was an unfair neo-Tory bias of previous explanations of the Revolution;[28] they have not, however, challenged the terms of the argument. They are still obsessed with why men said they acted and with who was right and who was wrong. Viewing the history of the Revolution in this judicatory manner has therefore restricted the issues over which historians have disagreed to those of motivation and responsibility, the very issues with which the participants themselves were concerned.

The neo-Whig "conviction that the colonists' attachment to principle was genuine"[29] has undoubtedly been refreshing, and indeed necessary, given the Tory slant of earlier twentieth-century interpretations. It now seems clearer that the Progressive historians, with their naive and crude reflex conception of human behavior, had too long treated the ideas of the Revolution superficially if not superciliously. Psychologists and sociologists are now willing to grant a more determining role to beliefs, particularly in revolutionary situations. It is now accepted that men act not simply in response to some kind of objective reality but to the meaning they give to that reality. Since men's beliefs are as much a part of the given stimuli as the objective environment, the beliefs must be understood and taken seriously if men's behavior is to be fully explained. The American revolutionary ideas were more than cooked up pieces of thought served by an aggressive and interested minority to a gullible and unsuspecting populace. The concept of propaganda permitted the Progressive historians to account for the presence of ideas but it prevented them from recognizing ideas as an important determinant of the Americans' behavior. The weight attributed to ideas and constitutional principles by the neo-Whig historians was thus an essential to the propagandist studies.

Yet in its laudable effort to resurrect the importance of ideas in historical explanation much of the writing of the neo-Whigs has tended to return to the simple nineteenth-century intellectualist assumption that history is the consequence of a rational calculation of ends and means, that what happened was what was consciously desired and planned. By supposing "that individual actions and immediate issues are more important than underlying determinants in explaining particular events," by emphasizing conscious and articulated motives, the neo-Whig historians have selected and presented that evidence which is most directly and clearly expressive of the intentions of the Whigs, that is, the most well-defined, the most constitutional, the most reasonable of the Whig beliefs, those found in their public documents, their several declarations of grievances and causes. It is not surprising that for the neo-Whigs the history of the American Revolution should be more than anything else "this history of the Americans' search for principles."[30] Not only, then, did nothing in the Americans' economic and social structure really determine their behavior, but the colonists in fact acted from the most rational and calculated of motives: they fought, as they said they would, simply to defend their ancient liberties against British provocation.

By implying that certain declared rational purposes are by themselves an adequate explanation for the Americans' revolt, in other words that the Revolution was really nothing more than a contest over constitutional principles, the neo-Whig historians have not only threatened to deny what we have learned of human psychology in the twentieth century, but they have also in fact failed to exploit fully the terms of their own idealist approach by not taking into account all of what the Americans believed and said. Whatever the deficiencies and misunderstandings of the role of ideas in human behavior present in the propagandist studies of the 1930s, these studies did for the first time attempt to deal with the entirety and complexity of American revolutionary thought—to explain not only all the well-reasoned notions of law and liberty that were so familiar but, more important, all the irrational and hysterical beliefs that had been so long neglected. Indeed, it was the patent absurdity and implausibility of much of what the Americans said that lent credence and persuasiveness to their mistrustful approach to the ideas. Once this exaggerated and fanatical rhetoric was uncovered by the Progressive historians, it should not have subsequently been ignored—no matter how much it may have impugned the reasonableness of the American response. No widely expressed ideas can be dismissed out of hand by the historian.

In his recent analysis of revolutionary thinking Bernard Bailyn has avoided the neo-Whig tendency to distort the historical reconstruction of the American mind. By comprehending "the assumptions, beliefs, and ideas that lay behind the manifest events of the time," Bailyn has attempted to get inside the Whigs' mind, and to experience vicariously all of what they thought and felt, both their rational constitutional beliefs and their hysterical and emotional ideas as well. The inflammatory phrases, "slavery," "corruption," "conspiracy," that most historians had either ignored or readily dismissed as propaganda, took on a new significance for Bailyn. He came to "suspect that they meant something very real to both the writers and their readers: that there were real fears, real anxieties, a sense of real danger behind these phrases, and not merely the desire to influence by rhetoric and propaganda the inert minds of an otherwise passive populace."[31] No part of American thinking, Bailyn suggests—not the widespread belief in a ministerial conspiracy, not the hostile and vicious indictments of individuals, not the fear of corruption and the hope for regeneration, not any of the violent seemingly absurd distortions and falsifications of what we now believe to be true, in short, none of the frenzied rhetoric—can be safely ignored by the historian seeking to understand the causes of the Revolution.

Bailyn's study, however, represents something other than a more complete and uncorrupted version of the common idealist interpretations of the Revolution. By viewing from the "interior" the revolutionary pamphlets, which were "to an unusual degree, *explanatory*," revealing "not merely positions taken but the reasons why positions were taken," Bailyn like any idealist historian has sought to discover the motives the participants themselves gave for their actions, to re-enact their thinking at crucial moments, and thereby to recapture some of the "unpredictable reality" of the Revolution.[32] But for Bailyn the very unpredictability of the reality he has disclosed has undermined the idealist obsession with explaining why, in the participants' own estimation, they acted as they did. Ideas emerge as more than explanatory devices, as more than indicators of motives. They become as well objects for analysis in and for themselves, historical events in their own right to be treated as other historical events are treated. Although Bailyn has examined the revolutionary ideas subjectively from the inside, he has also analyzed them objectively from the outside. Thus, in addition to a contemporary Whig perspective, he presents us with a retrospective view of the ideas—their complexity, their development, and their consequences—that the actual participants did not have. In effect his essay represents what has been called "a Namierism of the history of ideas,"[33] a structural analysis of thought that suggests a conclusion about the movement of history not very different from Sir Lewis Namier's, where history becomes something "started in ridiculous beginnings, while small men did things both infinitely smaller and infinitely greater than they knew."[34]

In his *England in the Age of the American Revolution* Namier attacked the Whig tendency to overrate "the importance of the conscious will and purpose in individuals." Above all he urged us "to ascertain and recognize the deeper irrelevancies and incoherence of human actions which are not so much directed by reason, as invested by it ex post facto with the appearances of logic and rationality," to discover the unpredictable reality, where men's motives and intentions were lost in the accumulation and momentum of interacting events. The whole force of Namier's approach tended to squeeze the intellectual content out of what men did. Ideas setting forth principles and purposes for action, said Namier, did not count for much in the movement of history.[35]

In his study of the revolutionary ideas Bailyn has come to an opposite conclusion: ideas counted for a great deal, not only being responsible for the Revolution but also for transforming the character of American society. Yet in his hands ideas lose that static quality they have commonly had for the Whig historians, the simple statements of intention that so exasperated Namier. For Bailyn the ideas of the revolutionaries take on an elusive and unmanageable quality, a dynamic self-intensifying character that transcended the intentions and desires of any of the historical participants. By emphasizing how the thought of the colonists was "strangely reshaped, turned in unfamiliar directions," by describing how the Americans "indeliberately, half-knowingly" groped toward "conclusions they could not themselves clearly perceive," by demonstrating how new beliefs and hence new actions were the responses not to desire but to the logic of developing situations, Bailyn has wrested the explanation of the Revolution out of the realm of motivation in which the neo-Whig historians had confined it.

With this kind of approach to ideas, the degree of consistency and devotion to principles become less important, and indeed the major issues of motivation and responsibility over which historians have disagreed become largely irrelevant. Action becomes not the product of rational and conscious calculation but of dimly perceived and rapidly changing thoughts and situations, "where the familiar meaning of ideas and words faded away into confusion, and leaders felt themselves peering into a haze, seeking to bring shifting conceptions somehow into focus." Men become more the victims than the manipulators of their ideas, as their thought unfolds in ways few anticipated, "rapid, irreversible, and irresistible," creating new problems, new considerations, new ideas, which have their own unforeseen implications. In this kind of atmosphere the Revolution, not at first desired by the Americans, takes on something of an inevitable character, moving through a process of escalation into levels few had intended or perceived. It no longer makes sense to assign motives or responsibility to particular individuals for the totality of what happened.

Men were involved in a complicated web of phenomena, ideas, and situations, from which in retrospect escape seems impossible.[36]

By seeking to uncover the motives of the Americans expressed in the revolutionary pamphlets, Bailyn has ended by demonstrating the autonomy of ideas as phenomena, where the ideas operate, as it were, over the heads of the participants, taking them in directions no one could have foreseen. His discussion of revolutionary thought thus represents a move back to a deterministic approach to the Revolution, a determinism, however, which is different from that which the neo-Whig historians have so recently and self-consciously abandoned. Yet while the suggested determinism is thoroughly idealist—indeed never before has the force of ideas in bringing on the Revolution been so emphatically put—its implications are not. By helping to purge our writing about the Revolution of its concentration on constitutional principles and its stifling judicial-like preoccupation with motivation and responsibility, the study serves to open the way for new questions and new appraisals. In fact, it is out of the very completeness of his idealist interpretation, out of his exposition of the Americans' thought that we have the evidence for an entirely different, a behaviorist, perspective on the causes of the American Revolution. Bailyn's book-length introduction to his edition of revolutionary pamphlets is therefore not only a point of fulfillment for the idealist approach to the Revolution, it is also a point of departure for a new look at the social sources of the Revolution.

It seems clear that historians of eighteenth-century America and the Revolution cannot ignore the force of ideas in history to the extent that Namier and his students have done in their investigations of eighteenth-century English politics. This is not to say, however, that the Namier approach to English politics has been crucially limiting and distorting. Rather it may suggest that the Namier denigration of ideas and principles is inapplicable for American politics because the American social situation in which ideas operated was very different from that of eighteenth-century England. It may be that ideas are less meaningful to a people in a socially stable situation. Only when ideas have become stereotyped reflexes do evasion and hypocrisy and the Namier mistrust of what men believe become significant. Only in a relatively settled society does ideology become a kind of habit, a bundle of widely shared and instinctive conventions, offering ready-made explanations for men who are not being compelled to ask any serious questions. Conversely, it is perhaps only in a relatively unsettled, disordered society, where the questions come faster than men's answers, that ideas become truly vital and creative.

Paradoxically it may be the very vitality of the Americans' ideas, then, that suggests the need to examine the circumstances in which they flourished. Since ideas and beliefs are ways of perceiving and explaining the world, the nature of the ideas expressed is determined as much by the character of the world being confronted as by the internal development of inherited and borrowed conceptions. Out of the multitude of inherited and transmitted ideas available in the eighteenth century, Americans selected and emphasized those which seemed to make meaningful what was happening to them. In the colonists' use of classical literature, for example, "their detailed knowledge and engaged interest covered only one era and one small group of writers," Plutarch, Livy, Cicero, Sallust, and Tacitus—those who had hated and feared the trends of their own time, and in their writing had contrasted the present with a better past, which they endowed with qualities absent from their own, corrupt era."[37] There was always, in Max Weber's term, some sort of elective affinity between the Americans' interest and their beliefs, and without that affinity their ideas would not have possessed the peculiar character and persuasiveness they did. Only the most revolutionary social needs and circumstances could have sustained such revolutionary ideas.

When the ideas of the Americans are examined comprehensively, when all of the Whig rhetoric, irrational as well as rational, is taken into account, one cannot but be struck by the predominant characteristics of fear and frenzy, the exaggerations and the enthusiasm, the general sense of social corruption and disorder out of which would be born a new world of benevolence and harmony where Americans would become the "eminent examples of every divine and social virtue."[38] As Bailyn and the propaganda studies have amply shown, there is simply too much fanatical and millennial thinking even by the best minds that must be explained before we can characterize the Americans' ideas as peculiarly rational and legalistic and thus view the Revolution as merely a conservative defense of constitutional liberties. To isolate refined and nicely-reasoned arguments from the writings of John Adams and Jefferson is not only to disregard the more inflamed expressions of the rest of the Whigs but also to overlook the enthusiastic extravagance—the paranoiac obsession with a diabolical Crown conspiracy and the dream of a restored Saxon era—in the thinking of Adams and Jefferson themselves.

The ideas of the Americans seem, in fact, to form what can only be called a revolutionary syndrome. If we were to confine ourselves to examining the revolutionary rhetoric alone, apart from what happened politically or socially, it would be virtually impossible to distinguish the American Revolution from any other revolution in modern Western history. In the kinds of ideas expressed the American Revolution is remarkably similar to the seventeenth-century Puritan Revolution and to the eighteenth-century French Revolution: the same general disgust with a chaotic and corrupt world, the same anxious and angry bombast, the same excited fears of conspiracies by depraved men, the same utopian hopes for the constitution of a new and virtuous order. It was not that this syndrome of ideas was simply transmitted from one generation or from one people to another. It was rather perhaps that similar, though hardly identical, social situations called forth within the limitations of inherited and available conceptions similar modes of expression. Although we need to know much more about the sociology of revolutions and collective movements, it does seem possible that particular patterns of thought, particular forms of expression, correspond to certain basic social experiences. There may be, in other words, typical modes of expression, typical kinds of beliefs and values, characterizing a revolutionary situation, at least within roughly similar Western societies. Indeed, the types of ideas manifested may be the best way of identifying a collective movement as a revolution. As one student of revolution writes, "It is on the basis of a knowledge of men's beliefs that we can distinguish their behavior from riot, rebellion or insanity."[39]

It is thus the very nature of the Americans' rhetoric—its obsession with corruption and disorder, its hostile and conspiratorial outlook, and its millennial vision of a regenerated society—that reveals as nothing else apparently can the American Revolution as a true revolution with its sources lying deep in the social structure. For this kind of frenzied rhetoric could spring only from the most severe sorts of social strain. The grandiose and feverish language of the Americans was indeed the natural, even the inevitable, expression of a people caught up in a revolutionary situation, deeply alienated from the existing sources of authority and vehemently involved in a basic reconstruction of their political and social order. The hysteria of the Americans' thinking was but a measure of the intensity of their revolutionary passions. Undoubtedly the growing American alienation from British authority contributed greatly to this revolutionary situation. Yet the very weakness of the British imperial system and the accumulating ferocity of American antagonism to it suggests that other sources of social strain were being fed into the revolutionary movement. It may be that the Progressive historians in their preoccupation with internal social problems were more right than we have recently been willing to grant. It would be repeating their mistake, however, to expect this internal social strain necessarily to take the form of coherent class conflict or overt social disruption. The sources of revolutionary social stress may have been much more subtle but no less severe.

Of all of the colonies in the mid-eighteenth century, Virginia seems the most settled, the most lacking in obvious social tensions. Therefore, as it has been recently argued, since conspicuous social issues were nonexistent, the only plausible remaining explanation for the Virginians' energetic and almost unanimous commitment to the Revolution must have been their devotion to constitutional principles. Yet it may be that we have been looking for the wrong kind of social issues, for organized conflicts, for conscious divisions, within the society. It seems clear that Virginia's difficulties were not the consequence of any obvious sectional or class antagonism, Tidewater versus Piedmont, aristocratic planters versus yeoman farmers. There was apparently no discontent with the political system that went deep into the social structure. But there does seem to have been something of a social crisis within the ruling group itself, which intensely aggravated the Virginians' antagonism to the imperial system. Contrary to the impression of confidence and stability that the Virginia planters have historically acquired, they seemed to have been in very uneasy circumstances in the years before the Revolution. The signs of the eventual nineteenth-century decline of the Virginia gentry were, in other words, already felt if not readily apparent.

The planters' ability to command the acquiescence of the people seems extraordinary compared to the unstable politics of the other colonies. But in the years before independence there were signs of increasing anxiety among the gentry over their representative role. The ambiguities in the relationship between the Burgesses and their constituents erupted into open debate in the 1750s. And men began voicing more and more concern over the mounting costs of elections and growing corruption in the soliciting of votes, especially by "those who have neither natural nor acquired parts to recommend them."[40] By the late sixties and early seventies the newspapers were filled with warnings against electoral influence, bribery, and vote seeking. The freeholders were stridently urged to "strike at the Root of this growing Evil; be influenced by Merit alone," and avoid electing "obscure and inferior persons."[41] It was as if ignoble ambition and demagoguery, one bitter pamphlet remarked, were a "Daemon lately come among us to disturb the peace and harmony, which had so long subsisted in this place."[42] In this context Robert Munford's famous play, *The Candidates*, written in 1770, does not so much confirm the planters' confidence as it betrays their uneasiness with electoral developments in the colony, "when coxcombs and jockies can impose themselves upon it for men of learning." Although disinterested virtue eventually wins out, Munford's satire reveals the kinds of threats the established planters faced from ambitious knaves and blockheads who were turning representatives into slaves of the people.[43]

By the eve of the Revolution the planters were voicing a growing sense of impending ruin, whose sources seemed in the minds of many to be linked more and more with the corrupting British connection and the Scottish factors, but for others frighteningly rooted in "our Pride, our Luxury, and Idleness."[44] The public and private writings of Virginians became obsessed with "corruption," "virtue," and "luxury." The increasing defections from the Church of England, even among ministers and vestrymen, and the remarkable growth of dissent in the years before the Revolution, "so much complained of in many parts of the colony," further suggests some sort of social stress. The strange religious conversions of Robert Carter may represent only the most dramatic example of what was taking place less frenziedly elsewhere among the gentry.[45] By the middle of the eighteenth century it was evident that many of the planters were living on the edge of bankruptcy, seriously overextended and spending beyond their means in an almost frantic effort to fulfill the aristocratic image they had created of themselves. Perhaps the importance of the Robinson affair in the 1760s lies not in any constitutional changes that resulted but in the shattering effect the disclosures had on that virtuous image. Some of the planters expressed openly their fears for the future, seeing the products of their lives being destroyed in the reckless gambling and drinking of their heirs, who, as Landon Carter put it, "play away and play it all away."[46]

The Revolution in Virginia, "produced by the wantonness of the Gentleman," as one planter suggested,[47] undoubtedly gained much of its force from this social crisis within the gentry. Certainly more was expected from the Revolution than simply a break from British imperialism, and it was not any crude avoidance of British debts. The revolutionary reforms, like the abolition of entail and primogeniture, may have signified something other than mere symbolic legal adjustments to existing reality. In addition to being an attempt to make the older Tidewater plantations more economically competitive with lands farther west, the reforms may have represented a real effort to redirect what was believed to be a dangerous tendency in social and family development within the ruling gentry. The Virginians were not after all aristocrats who could afford having their entailed families' estates in the hands of weak or ineffectual eldest sons. Entail, as the preamble to the 1776 act abolishing it stated, had often done "injury to the morals of youth by rendering them independent of, and disobedient to, their parents."[48] There was too much likelihood, as the Nelson family sadly demonstrated, that a single wayward generation would virtually wipe out what had been so painstakingly built. George Mason bespoke the anxieties of many Virginians when he warned the Philadelphia Convention in 1787 that "our own Children will in a short time be among the general mass."[49]

Precisely how the strains within Virginia society contributed to the creation of a revolutionary situation and in what way the planters expected independence and republicanism to alleviate their problems, of course, need to be fully explored. It seems clear, however, from the very nature of the ideas expressed that the sources of the Revolution in Virginia were much more subtle and complicated than a simple antagonism to the British government. Constitutional principles alone do not explain the Virginians' almost unanimous determination to revolt. And if the Revolution in the seemingly stable colony of Virginia possessed internal social roots, it is to be expected that the other colonies were experiencing their own forms of social strain that in a like manner sought mitigation through revolution and republicanism.

It is through the Whigs' ideas, then, that we may be led back to take up where the Progressive historians left off in their investigation of the internal social sources of the Revolution. By working through the ideas— by reading them imaginatively and relating them to the objective social world they both reflected and confronted—we may be able to eliminate the unrewarding distinction between conscious and unconscious motives, and eventually thereby to combine a Whig with a Tory, an idealist with a behaviorist, interpretation. For the ideas, the rhetoric, of the Americans was never obscuring but remarkably revealing of their deepest interests and passions. What they expressed may not have been for the most part factually true, but it was always psychologically true. In this sense their rhetoric was never detached from the social and political reality; and indeed it becomes the best entry into an understanding of that reality. Their repeated overstatements of reality, their incessant talk of "tyranny" when there seems to have been no real oppression, their obsession with "virtue," "luxury," and "corruption," their devotion to "liberty" and "equality"—all these notions were neither manipulated propaganda nor borrowed empty abstractions, but ideas with real personal and social significance for those who used them. Propaganda could never move men to revolution. No popular leader, as John Adams put it, has ever been able "to persuade a large people, for any length of time together, to think themselves wronged, injured, and oppressed, unless they really were, and saw and felt it to be so."[50] The ideas had relevance; the sense of oppression and injury, although often displaced onto the imperial system, was nonetheless real. It was indeed the meaningfulness of the connection between what the Americans said and what they felt that gave the ideas their propulsive force and their overwhelming persuasiveness.

It is precisely the remarkable revolutionary character of the Americans' ideas now being revealed by historians that best indicates that something profoundly unsettling was going on in the society, that raises the question, as it did for the Progressive historians, why the Americans should have expressed such thoughts. With their crude conception of propaganda the Progressive historians at least attempted to grapple with the problem. Since we cannot regard the ideas of the revolutionaries as simply propaganda, the question still remains to be answered. "When 'ideas' in full cry drive past," wrote Arthur F. Bentley in his classic behavioral study, *The Process of Government*, "the thing to do with them is to accept them as an indication that something is happening; and then search carefully to find out what it really is they stand for, what the factors of the social life are that are expressing themselves through the ideas."[51] Precisely because they sought to understand both the revolutionary ideas and American society, the behaviorist historians of the Progressive generation, for all of their crude conceptualizations, their obsession with "class" and hidden economic interests, and their treatment of ideas as propaganda, have still offered us an explanation of the revolutionary era so powerful and so comprehensive that no purely intellectual interpretation will ever replace it.

Marc Egnal and Joseph A. Ernst

9 AN ECONOMIC INTERPRETATION OF THE AMERICAN REVOLUTION

The Atlantic economy in the half century before American Independence underwent deep, wrenching changes. As a result, English capital and English decisions increasingly dominated the colonial economy. The freedom of the wealthy colonists, merchants and planters alike, to conduct business as they chose was restricted. Profit margins were lessened and possibilities for local development sacrificed. These broad, structural changes, and the accompanying short-run economic crises, troubled the colonial elite at least as much as did the parliamentary enactments which followed the Seven Years' War. These new British measures remain one ostensible cause of revolt. But the colonial reaction to them was determined in large part by a growing concern for the economy and for economic sovereignty, a concern that only coincidentally reinforced the dictates of patriotic principle.

This transformation of the colonial business world is the framework for the following broad and tentative reinterpretation of the American Revolution. Our reinterpretation, however, does not argue a monocausal explanation for the colonies' struggle with Britain. Consequently, an examination of the strengths and weaknesses of earlier writers provides a necessary introduction to the presentation of a new hypothesis.

Modern historians of the American Revolution conveniently fall into two schools: the Progressive and the neo-Whig. In seeking to explain the colonists' break with the mother country, Progressive authors wrestled with two stubborn problems for which they never achieved a happy resolution. One was the question of the impact of the Navigation Acts. At the turn of the century, the architects of the so-called "Imperial

School" of British-American history, George Beer and Charles M. Andrews, pronounced the administration of the empire from Whitehall and Westminster remarkably evenhanded. Some Progressive historians, including Arthur Schlesinger and Carl Becker, went along with this interpretation. For these writers no fundamental conflict existed between English and American societies. There was only a series of unwise measures passed by Parliament after 1763.

Other Progressives found this analysis of colonial-metropolitan relations less than satisfactory. Charles A. Beard, and later Louis Hacker, saw the rending of empire in 1776 as the product of long-standing conflicts between Britian and America, conflicts embodied in the Acts of Trade. Their condemnation of the Navigation Acts sits uneasily, however, and seems a weak foundation for any "economic interpretation." Hacker, for instance, dwelt on the restrictions on manufacture and trade before 1763. Yet these regulations either were ignored by the colonists (as in the case of the Molasses Act of 1733) or touched only the periphery of trade. The ambivalence of these historians' explanation is best illustrated by Beard's comment:

Modern calculators have gone to some pains to show that on the whole American colonists derived benefits from English policy which greatly outweighed their losses from the restrains laid on them. For the sake of argument the case may be conceded; it is simply irrelevant to the uses of history. The origins of the legislation are clear; and the fact that it restricted American economic enterprise in many respects is indisputable.[1]

In addition to the difficulties raised by the Navigation Acts, the Progressives wrestled with a second problem: the complex nature of the revolutionary movement in the decade before Independence. Seeking to answer the "why" of the Revolution, men like Becker, Andrews, and Schlesinger came up with two hypotheses. First, while dismissing the idea of long-standing conflict between Britain and the colonies, these historians argued that the measures adopted by Britain after the end of the French and Indian War in 1763, coupled with the postwar colonial depression, caused the ruling classes, the merchants in the North, the planters in the South, to take the lead in opposing British policy. And in sharp distinction to what neo-Whig historians contend, this hostility to British measures stemmed not from Whiggish constitutional principles, but from economics. Restrictive commercial regulations were imposed by the British upon colonies whose merchants were suffering in the depths of depression and whose large land- and slaveholders were groaning under a burden of indebtedness. This "economic interpretation" of the Progressives was narrowly focused upon the years after 1763 and was based upon an analysis which went little beyond the depiction of "hard times." Questions of the structure of the economy, or of long-term developments within the merchant and planting communities, were foreign to the concerns of these historians. The conclusion that merchants and wealthy planters sought imperial reform but shunned rebellion seems almost dictated by the limits of the economic analysis.

Since economic concerns did not make the merchants or planters into full-fledged revolutionaries, a different dynamic must have carried the movement of protest to fruition. Accordingly, an examination of the behavior of the "lower orders" provided the Progressives with their second, complementary hypothesis. During the decade before Independence, the argument ran, the lower classes of the cities fought to gain greater rights for themselves in what was essentially an undemocratic society. These "lower orders" supposedly joined the revolutionary movement both because of a desire for greater power and because of a dedication to constitutional and democratic principles—the latter point strangely sounding more neo-Whiggish than Progressive. With their adherence to the cause, the revolutionary movement was transformed, in Carl Becker's famous phrase, into a two-fold contest: a struggle not only over "home rule" but also over "who shall rule at home." Furthermore in the course of the revolutionary struggle, these "radicals" (i.e., in the North, the "lower orders" of the cities and their leaders, and in the South, certain of the debt-ridden tobacco and rice planters) came to dominate the protests against Great Britain. The radicals were now opposed in their desire for imperial change by their natural enemies, the "conservatives"—wealthy merchants of northern cities and Charles Town and certain of the aristocratic planters. The two theses offered by Progressive historians were tied together by a transition in the nature of the protest movement during 1770. Pinpointing this change, Charles M. Andrews stated, "The non-importation movement [against the Townshend Acts] began as a merchant's device wherewith to obtain a redress of trade grievances; it ended as an instrument in the hands of political agitators and radicals for the enforcement of their claims of constitutional liberty and freedom."[2]

The Progressives did not however cut short their analysis with the break from England in 1776. Instead, led by the logic of their explanation, they mapped out a broad interpretation of events through the adoption of the Constitution in 1789. The Revolution (at least in the North) was of the lower classes against a plutocracy. This implied serious social change after Independence, a theory the Progressive scholar, J. Franklin Jameson, sought to defend.[3] The Constitution then became the quintessential counterrevolutionary document, a position ably presented in Beard's *Economic Interpretation*.[4] But such a tidy and sweeping account of the revolutionary era rested on weak grounds. Research into areas such as the confiscation of loyalist estates, the nature of the new state governments, and so on, has shown that there was no social overturn accompanying the American Revolution and that what change did come about in the nature of society was most moderate. It was just these preoccupations and weaknesses of the Progressive approach that helped determine much of the content of the neo-Whig scholarship that was to follow and that was to reshape the history of the Revolution.

Neo-Whig critics have explicitly denied the existence of those internal conflicts so central to the Progressive view. For these historians, an understanding of the American Revolution rests in the realm of ideas and principles as opposed to economics or social classes. Both in the North and South, their argument goes, American society was dominated by consensus and ruled in the interests of a property-holding middle class. It follows that only minor social change accompanied Independence. Most important, the revolutionary movement appeared to be conservative in the fullest sense of the word. A trend toward greater colonial sovereignty had been underway since the time of the first settlements. The colonists had indeed acquired more and more of the "rights of Englishmen" and a stronger dedication to these principles. After 1763, British measures threatened American liberty, leading colonists to react both to preserve their formal rights and to protect themselves against what they felt to be a genuine threat of British conspiracy, corruption, and enslavement. Declaring Independence merely confirmed trends dating back a century or more.

For the neo-Whigs, an examination of the colonial economy only strengthens their argument. The abundance of cheap land and the richness of the soil underscore a picture of contented, middle-class farmers. More recently, and with perhaps some contradiction, writers such as Bernard Bailyn and Gordon Wood have noted the economic uncertainties that beset debt-ridden planters and struggling merchants. For neo-Whigs, however, such commercial problems do not form the basis of an interest-oriented interpretation. Rather, instabilities in the economy are only part of the troubling ambience that led colonists to credit all the more reports of ministerial plots against their freedom.[5]

The "consensus" or neo-Whig approach of many recent writers does rectify some of the more blatant shortcomings of the Progressive reading of the revolutionary era. It helps explain, for instance, the achievement of Independence with only minor changes in the structure of society. It avoids as well the contorted explanation of the Progressives, with first the upper classes, then a noble-minded lower class, leading the Revolution. And the neo-Whig approach readily incorporates the conclusion of the

Imperial School that the Navigation Acts did not constitute a long-standing grievance.

But criticism may be directed at the neo-Whigs even more devastating than that leveled at the Progressives. Basically they do not explain what happened. They do not explain, for example, why protests against the important Revenue Acts of 1764 and 1766 were so mild, and why colonists duly complied with these measures down to the eve of Independence. These laws placed a duty on West Indian goods but explicitly declared in their preambles their purpose of raising a revenue to support English placement in the colonies rather than merely regulating trade. And if neo-Whig emphasis on principle and consensus makes plausible the leading role played by certain merchants in the revolutionary movement, it fails to explain the large Tory element among the traders and the subsequent loyalist exodus. The conflicts in the years after 1763 seem either inexplicable or irrelevant as a result. The forward part played by the Northern Neck of Virginia in pushing that colony toward Independence demands an investigation of colonial society far beyond treatises on Whig ideologies, just as the presentation of America as a nation of prosperous middle-class farmers overlooks a diversity of sharply differing regional economics. Similarly, the treatment of economic problems in psychological terms can be misleading if done in the context of the most facile economic analysis. At least the Progressives tried to grapple with these economic questions. If they failed to clarify the issue in every case, they nonetheless realized the problems involved.

Finally, the debates between the defenders of the several schools have a fixed and unproductive air about them. As in the case of the interminable disagreement over perennials such as "Was plantation slavery profitable?" attackers and defenders of the Progressive or neo-Whig positions concern themselves with equally hoary questions such as "Were the Navigation Acts a burden?" and "Were the ideas of the Revolution radical or conservative?" A new approach is in order.

This dicussion of the historiography of the Revolution points up the contributions of earlier interpretations as well as the problems with which any new explanation must deal. The following discussion addresses itself to these considerations and focuses on three broad interrelated developments in the decades preceding 1776. Together, the three, in the light of post-1763 British policies, form the necessary and sufficient conditions for the Revolutionary movement. Two of the developments have received lengthy treatment by other historians and, while an important part of this reinterpretation, will be mentioned only briefly in this paper.

The first of these is the growth of a self-conscious, powerful colonial elite composed of merchants and wealthy landowners in the North, and planters and merchants in the South. At odds with themselves on some issues, on most questions touching local control these colonial elites had successfully asserted their autonomy from the crown. Further, the Whig elite had developed an ideology, a widely-held set of political and constitutional beliefs, that had been shaped and tested in colonial resistance to British men and measures in the past. This ideology became in turn an important element in later conflicts as a means of uniting and motivating the elite, as well as other members of the colonial middle classes. By the eve of the Revolution, a class or group consciousness that had evolved was essential to the mentality of the Whig elite.

The second development was the active and self-conscious involvement of the "lower orders" in the revolutionary movement. The "mob" had been an element in the volatile mix of colonial politics dating back at least to the early eighteenth century. But the decade or two before Independence saw the "poorer sort" of the city and the less wealthy landowners articulating their own interests and seriously questioning long-held assumptions about society and politics. The "lower orders," to be sure, never gained control in a society that was always dominated by the upper classes. However, the new demands they voiced, and the important role they played in the revolutionary movement, frightened many of the wealthy. This will be touched on later.

The third development forms the heart of this paper. During the eighteenth century, broad economic changes transformed the Atlantic economy. The impact of these changes on the several colonial regions and classes of people forms a crucial background for an understanding of the Revolution. Only from this vantage does the actual response of the colonists to British measures, from the Currency Act of 1751 to the Tea Act of 1773 and beyond, become intelligible.

The fundamental change affecting the Atlantic economy was that during the period 1720 to 1775 trade grew in two long swings. The areas involved included the British Isles, the slave coast of Africa, the British West Indies, and the American mainland colonies. These swings may be roughly dated 1720 to 1745 and 1745 to 1775. The first wave of growth was gradual, the second marked by an unprecedented expansion. Not all flows of goods took part in these two waves of growth, but the areas and trades included were significant: the export of British manufactures to Africa and the American colonies; the export to the West Indies of slaves from Africa and provisions from the mainland colonies; and the flow of sugar products to Britain. Exceptions to this pattern of growth were exports of tobacco and, in general, shipments from the American colonies to Britain. This rapid expansion after 1745 seems to have been produced by the strong growth of the British economy which was able to transmit significant new purchasing power to its trading partners across the Atlantic.

The impact of this commercial expansion on the American colonies is best considered by regions. There are, of course, several ways in which the North American colonies may be grouped, but with respect to the impact of British export policies a twofold division seems most useful. First are those areas in which the distribution of British goods was handled by an urban center controlled by a strong native merchant community. Four colonial ports with their respective hinterlands may be singled out in this regard: Boston, New York, Philadelphia, and Charles Town. Baltimore joined this list at the very end of the colonial period. Second, one may delineate that region where the distribution of British goods occurred within a decentralized marketing and credit structure—namely, the broad area of tobacco cultivation that included Virginia and parts of North Carolina and Maryland.

Before examining more closely the economic and political impact of this post-1745 expansion, we must turn briefly to the sources of this study, for the question may well be asked: Is there sufficient evidence to depict short- and long-run economic changes in colonial America? The answer is an unequivocal yes. Indeed, what is surprising given the excellent work being done by scholars on the nineteenth-century United States is the almost complete lack of detailed analysis of the eighteenth-century economy.

Of first importance are the extensive collections of business letters, journals, and diaries that give an excellent day to day picture of colonial economic life. Of the commercial centers, only Baltimore and possibly Charles Town in the late colonial period lack a solid run of documents. For the tobacco colonies, letters and diaries of planters, and letterbooks and ledgers of both British factors and local merchants, offer a solid basis for an economic study. The exception is North Carolina, for which we have little business correspondence.

In addition to these sources, there is a surprising abundance of quantitative data which allows for a more precise demarcation of short-run changes. Price series for North American and West Indian goods, for instance, are available, or easily derivable, for most of the regional economies. Data for overseas trade is provided by both British customs records and by an examination of the ship movements recorded in most colonial newspapers. Indeed, the newspapers are a virtual mine of information for examining fluctuations in the economy. Changes in merchant credit policy may be observed from a careful study of advertising, while sheriffs' sales and announcements of repossession are important indicators of periods of contraction and expansion. Another valuable and generally unused source is merchants' account books. These make possible not only the calculation of the success of individual firms but also the derivation of the cost and selling price of dry goods. As an example, the chart below presents the changing markup in Philadelphia for linen and cotton checks. Reflected in the figures are the prosperity of the late 1740s, the depression of the first part of the 1750s, the flush times of the early war years, the depression of the 1760s, the recovery during nonimportation in the late 1760s, and the slump of 1772 to 1774.

AVERAGE MARKUP BY PHILADELPHIA CLOTH IMPORTERS

Year	Percent	Year	Percent	Year	Percent
1747-1749	39	1758-1759	33	1766-1768	28
1750-1753	29	1760-1762	16	1769-1770	42
1754-1757	27	1763-1765	13	1771-1773	16

Sources: Selling prices in Philadelphia are culled from the daily entries in John Reynell Day Brooks, 1747-1773; Thomas Biddle Cash Book, 1772-1773; Henry Drinker Day Book, 1773. English prices, freight, and insurance rates are drawn from invoices in the following collections: Reynell Papers, 1747-1761; Wharton Manuscripts, 1754-1760; Richard Waln Invoice Book, 1763-1771; William Pollard Letterbook, 1772-1773. All manuscripts are in Historical Society of Pennsylvania. Interpolations in the series for English prices are on the basis of fluctuations in the cost of other fabrics. Final calculations are in sterling, and Philadelphia prices are reduced by the exchange rates presented in Bezanson, et al., *Colonial Prices*, 431, as modified by the authors.

These series amount to only a suggestion of the sources available for economic analysis. Wills, inventories, court records—both of the provinces and, later, of the early states and the federal government—and the various records of local chambers of commerce, poorhouses, insurance offices, and manufacturing establishments offer data of significant value for a detailed study of the colonial economy.

The sharp expansion of British commerce during the second long swing (1745-1775) was first felt in the colonial cities with the cessation of hostilities in 1748. British imports surged to record levels, increasing in the northern colonies by a full 40 per cent per capita between 1740 to 1744 and 1750 to 1754. The result, despite some improvement in the markets to which the colonists shipped their produce, was a depression of unprecedented magnitude. Dry goods piled up on shelves; profit margins for the merchants were small or nonexistent. Bankruptcies were common. This was the beginning of a quarter century in which established merchants became increasingly concerned about their survival as a group.

Why, it may be asked, did merchants import such large quantitities of goods when the results were so manifestly disastrous, and why did these importations persist at such high levels despite uniform complaints of depressed conditions? To some extent, established merchants were encouraged to take more goods by liberal offers of credit from the English suppliers, who, backed by a burgeoning economy, found that they could deal more generously. But far more important in facilitating this swollen flow of goods were structural changes that threatened wholly to transform the trading communities in the colonial cities. Increasingly, British houses were bypassing the established colonial merchant to promote the sale of dry goods. This period was marked by the growth of vendue or auction sales. These sales had been an integral part of colonial life before 1748, but most often their role had been to aid in the disposal of damaged or outmoded goods rather than to serve as a major wholesale outlet. Now new merchants began importing directly for auctions to sell off large quantities of goods with only fractional profits on each sale. A careful study of mercantile advertising in Boston indicates that during depressions there was a sharp rise in vendue sales and a parallel decline in the offerings of the established merchants. Not surprisingly, the larger importers were angered by the new prominence of auctions and undertook campaigns to regulate public sales. Such regulation as was adopted, however, generally proved ineffective.

British firms also increasingly entered into direct dealings with shopkeepers and other marginal importers in the urban centers, importers who normally would have bought from one of the established merchants. By the 1760s and 1770s it was not uncommon to find numerous English "agents" in any colonial city drumming up business for their parent firms and seeking liaisons with the smallest shopkeeper along with the largest importer. A major London house might have as many as one hundred fifty correspondents in a single northern port. This practice of direct dealing riled the established merchants and provoked a stream of angry letters. "I would have you not bee too forward in pushing goods upon people," Philadelphia importer John Kidd wrote to the London house of Neate and Neave. "I shall also take the liberty to inform you that your supplying the shopkeepers at all is more harm than good to you, which I saw long ago but was afraid to mention it for fear you should think it was a sinister view for my own interest. For these merchants that probably might be inclined to correspond with you or at least say nothing to your disadvantage, take the liberty to ridicule you in all companies."[6]

Nonetheless such complaints counted little when weighed against the desire for profits on the part of the English exporters. Attempts of colonial legislatures to ease depressed conditions and to aid the merchants were checked by the tight hand the Privy Council and royal governors kept on colonial currency and banking practices. War proved to be, at least, temporarily, more efficacious than any legislation in easing the trading community's plight. The prosperity that accompanied the campaigns of the French and Indian War assuaged the dissatisfaction and anger which had mounted among the merchants during the early 1750s. Good times, however, abruptly came to an end with Britain's victories in 1760 and the shifting of the theater of war.

By 1763 a dark pall of depression hung over the commercial colonies. Creditors scrambled for liquidity, and commercial establishments from the largest British exporters to country storekeepers contracted their affairs. The colonial importers called in debts from shopkeepers and, at the same time, frantically sought to stave off English creditors. "Thus the consumers break the shopkeepers; they break the merchants," John Dickinson wrote, "and the shock must be felt as far as *London.*"[7] Seemingly overnight, the hard money spent by the British forces drained back to the mother country. Nor was this the only difficulty faced by the colonial merchants. The curtailment of British spending and the colonial need for bills of exchange drove up the exchange rate; debts collected within the colonies were translated into smaller sums of sterling. Furthermore, American merchants, confronted on the one hand by a debt-strapped countryside, and on the other by overstocked inventories, experienced a virtual disappearance of profits in the sale of imported wares. However, neither reports of these conditions nor the difficulty of collecting debts from their colonial correspondents deterred British houses from renewing their former practices. Exports to the commercial provinces climbed sharply in 1764 despite a wave of bankruptcy that brought down some of the largest colonial houses.

More and more the established merchants spoke of reasserting control over their commercial dealing and over the local economy in general. The strong repugnance voiced by colonial importers for British mercantile practices merged with other grievances to form an inseparable part of the protests against the new parliamentary enactments. The Currency Act of 1764 is a case in point. The emission of paper money had always been considered by the colonists as having importance far beyond the financing of government expenditures. Bills of tender were often issued by a land bank which provided the money as a rotating mortgage fund, thus facilitating agricultural expansion. In some colonies, such as Maryland, these land bank loans directly provided businessmen with a source of working capital. And, in general, local merchants saw a close link between fluctuations in the visible money supply (chiefly paper money and foreign coin) and American prosperity. While modern analysts debate the wisdom of the varying colonial monetary practices and proposals, there is no doubt that Britain's constant and jealous supervision of the colonists' currency systems seriously weakened the Americans' ability to control their own economy. The reaction to the Currency Act of 1764 reflected only a new and extreme phase of a long struggle over this aspect of economic sovereignty.

Control over currency and banking was for some in the commercial provinces the "sovereign remedy." But this was not the only stratagem pursued by the beleaguered, larger merchants to rectify structural imbalances in domestic and foreign trade. Testy letters to British houses berating them for crediting shopkeepers, or for shipping unsolicited goods, were a commonplace in the decade before Independence. The attempts of the large importers to regulate the vendues also continued, although the strenuous campaigns met with only partial success. In Massachusetts a move in 1773 to limit business to four licensed auctioneers in each town was vetoed by the Privy Council.

Another recourse for the large merchants was the encouragement of manufactures. Declining profits in the dry goods trade made investment opportunities offered by domestic industries all the more appealing. British regulations had long been ignored, and despite prohibitive legislation, colonial hats, shoes, finished ironware, and furniture competed profitably in North America and the West Indies with English products. Some industries, however, catered to, rather than competed with, Great Britain. These offered the merchant the possibility of directly reducing his indebtedness to the mother country. Consequently, in the decades before Independence there was a spurt in the production and export to England of such goods as pig and bar iron, alkalines, and whale products. Wine, soap, hemp, and flax were also encouraged, although with poor results. But the relationship of the merchants to domestic manufacturing went beyond questions of straightforward economic interest. Increasingly after the French and Indian War, the colonial importer looked upon the development of domestic industry as an integral part of a program to achieve economic sovereignty to counter the restrictions imposed by membership in the British Empire. "We are clearly of the opinion," wrote one importer in 1764, "that if our trade is obstructed or labors under any objection, it will more affect England than us, as it will put it out of our power to pay for such vast quantities of goods, as we have yearly imported from thence. And what we want more than we can pay for will be made among ourselves."[8] Reasoning in this manner, colonial merchants were willing to encourage native industries, such as the production of woolen and linen cloth, that directly competed with their importations.

Still the encouragement of manufacturing, as important as it might have been in reflecting the outlook of the merchants, absorbed only limited amounts of capital and ultimately made only a small difference in the structure of foreign trade. Control over currency and banking, regulation of vendues, development of manufactures—the stratagems used by the established importers to ameliorate conditions of glutted markets, over-competition, lack of liquidity, and falling profits—for the most part proved unsuccessful despite the strong support of merchant communities. None-theless, these efforts sooner or later boded conflict with royal authority. The consciousness of a clash of interests made the merchants more aware of the identity of economic and political goals.

One course of action that did offer the larger merchants immediate benefits and tangible relief from depressed conditions—at least in the short run—was the nonimportation of British goods. Nonimportation permitted the merchants to dispose of their inventories at higher prices and to retrench. "You will have a good price for all your dead goods which have always been unprofitable," an anonymous writer reminded his merchant readers in the November 1767 issue of the *Pennsylvania Gazette*. "You will collect your debts and bring your debts in England to a close, so that balances would hereby be brought about in your favor which with-out some such method must forever be against you."[9] Equally important, nonimportation meant the elimination, if only temporarily, of the upstart trader with his smaller stock of goods. Finally it meant that bills of ex-change, the international currency of the eighteenth century, would be cheaper so that debts could be paid to England without a sharp discount. As a consequence, merchants in the northern colonies adopted nonimpor-tation in 1765 and again in 1768. In Charles Town's rice and naval stores economy, local conditions made for somewhat different timing, and there the second boycott was decided upon in 1769.

In sum, nonimportation was only incidentally designed to compel Parliament to repeal obnoxious legislation. Without understanding the economic background, the timing and the nature of the boycotts is almost inexplicable. The agreements adopted in Boston in 1768 and Charles Town in 1769 were intended to run for no more than a year, even if Parliament took no action whatsoever. Nonimportation was not applied to the West Indian trade until 1774, and the taxes on tropical goods were always paid despite Britain's avowed intention of raising a revenue, rather than regulat-ing commerce, with those duties. American merchants would not curtail their commerce with the Caribbean because in their dealing with the islands they enjoyed persistently favorable balances to pay for British goods.

Nor were the merchants reluctant, at least in private correspondence, to express their reasons for supporting the boycott. John Chew frankly discussed the desire of Philadelphia merchants for nonimportation. In a letter of November 7, 1765, he wrote: "Indeed we are well convinced something of this sort is absolutely necessary at this time from the great much too large importation that has for sometime past been made. There will be no wanted goods for a twelve month."[10] The nonimportation agreements of 1765 and 1766 were short-lived, ending in the jubilation that accompanied the repeal of the Stamp Act. But they had beneficial results, bringing down exchange rates and clearing glutted inventories. By 1767 and 1768, conditions had worsened once more, and importers were beset by the same broad spectrum of problems. Again, merchants turned to nonimportation for motives avowedly economic. "I believe the gentlemen in trade are one and all convinced," Thomas Cushing of Boston observed in 1768, "That it will be to no good purpose for them to import English goods as usual. They despair of ever selling them and consequently of ever being able to pay for them."[11] His sentiments were echoed by a Philadelphia importer in April 1769: "A time of leisure seems now approaching and the commercial intercourse with Great Britain is inhibited for a season. It is a very general wish amongst the merchants that it may continue at least one year in order that they may dispose of the great quantity of goods on hand, and contract their affairs. This is agreeable to my private interest."[12]

When the majority of the merchants sought to abandon nonimportation in 1770, charges of self-interest filled the press, and rightly so. As far as questions of principle were concerned, the only change occurring in 1770 was the partial repeal of the Townshend duties. There had been no serious revision of restrictive British legislation, and it could well be argued that the tax on tea was as serious an insult to Americans as the tax on painters' colors, glass and tea. The point remains that merchants had instituted the boycott for reasons other than abstract principle and, having disposed of their inventories, easily separated themselves from the ideologues to resume trade at the end of 1770.

What was lost for the moment on those who railed at the merchants in 1770 was the profound and growing commitment of the colonial importers to the achievement of sovereignty, economic and political. It is in this light that many of the conflicts between the colonists and the British within the third quarter of the century must be viewed. The struggles over the Currency Act, the Stamp Act, the Revenue Act, and the Townshend Acts in the 1760s reflected a strengthened commitment to economic autonomy and an increased awareness of the close ties between the world of colonial business and imperial politics.

Although the nonimportation agreements of 1769 and 1770 significantly ameliorated depressed markets, as had the trade stoppage during 1766, by 1771 commercial centers from Charles Town to Boston were inundated by unprecedented quantities of English goods. The ensuing depression was the last, and perhaps the worst, of the colonial period. The proliferation of small importers, the wholesale dumping of goods by English houses, the sharp rise in vendue sales—all made American importers bitter once again. The fitful, angry reaction to the Tea Act of 1773 must be understood in this context. The East India Company's decision to sell directly to American agents was not viewed by the colonists as a chance to buy cheaper tea. Rather, for many colonial traders it was another instance of a British exporter seeking to swell his trade by dealing outside the established channels.

In the swirl of events that followed the "tea parties," the established importers played a crucial role, both in positions of leadership and in the day to day administration of programs adopted by provincial and continental congresses. Such vital, if secretive, actions as securing munitions and finding markets for America's cash crops performed by patriotic merchants made possible the final break from England. Hence, an understanding of the colonial merchants' long-term struggle for economic sovereignty is necessary to explain the nature of the revolutionary movement in the commercial colonies and the leadership provided by the merchant class after Independence.

Compared to those colonies with developed urban centers, the tobacco growing area—basically Virginia, along with adjacent regions in Maryland and North Carolina—was the more thoroughly penetrated by the British imperial system and the less able to adapt stratagems to counter the threatening developments in the Atlantic economy after 1745. The second long swing of trade from 1745 to 1775 brought to an end a lengthy period marked by a persistently favorable balance of trade with the mother country. After 1745, imports increased dramatically, facilitated by a heavy inflow of British capital.

This inflow of capital was accompanied by far-reaching changes in the relations between colony and metropolis. The most striking aspect of these changes was the rapid growth of planter indebtedness. There was considerable alarm among colonial Virginians and Marylanders over the growing burden of debt, and Progressive historians such as Isaac Harrell and Schlesinger echoed this concern, seeing in the accumulated indebtedness grounds for revolution.[13] Neo-Whig critics, however, have rejected that conclusion as a crude piece of "economic determinism" because there is scant evidence directly linking the debt question to Virginia's revolutionary movement. But if advocates of the "Planter Indebtedness" thesis failed to make a convincing case, it was only because they did not pursue their argument far enough. A detailing of debts reveals little by itself, for a debt may be either a boon or a disadvantage depending on the structure of the credit system and the dynamics of economic change. It is these latter questions that must be investigated to understand fully the significance of the growing burden of debt.

By the late 1740s, the intimate and relaxed relationship between the large planters and the English consignment of merchants (to whom the planters shipped their tobacco to be sold on the English market) was breaking down. Replacing it was a new credit system managed by local factors of the great Glasgow tobacco houses. The distinguishing mark of the new system, whose real development accompanies the second period of imperial economic growth (1745-1775), was the establishment of chains of stores stretching along the great river valleys. These Scottish firms soon dominated the tobacco economy in the Piedmont and made serious inroads into the trade of the older Tidewater areas. The reason for the success of the Glasgow merchants was that they financed their exports to Virginia out of pocket by advancing the Virginians credit to make up trade deficits; the factor at each store bought tobacco, sold dry goods, and extended credit.

The planters reacted with mixed emotions to the ever-expanding dealings of the Scots factors. On one hand, the credit these storekeepers proffered was the lifeblood of the plantation economy. It allowed the planter to defer payment for European goods and at the same time freed cash for the purchase of land and slaves, the basis of economic expansion and social position. The imperative to enlarge one's holdings remained constant and so did the demand for credit. On the other hand, the power of the Scottish merchants went far beyond these commercial dealings and threatened the planter elite on the most basic levels of political, social, and economic power. As James Madison once expressed it, the "essential legislation" of Virginia was passed by Scots traders at court days in Williamsburg, when they set tobacco prices, fixed exchange rates, and settled accounts.[14] In addition, the Scots challenged the planter elite's power even more directly. First in Whitehall, then in Virginia itself, the Scottish firms and their factors sought to block unfavorable legislation by the planter-dominated House of Burgesses. From 1759 on, for instance, the Scots, together with some of the larger London tobacco houses persisted in using their influence on both sides of the Atlantic to regulate Virginia's paper money practices in their own interest. Thus members of the planting elite were faced with a dilemma: how to maintain their place in a society that valued social and economic independence without becoming pawns to that "plague of Egyptian locusts," the hated Scots.

Further, the Scottish factors' practice of dealing directly with the myriad of small tobacco producers threatened the sovereignty of the larger planters, who under the consignment system had handled the output of these smaller farmers, including it with their own consignments. A basis of unity was forged between the great planters and the farmers, both of whom now dealt directly with representatives of British capital.

If these institutional shifts accompanying the transformation in the system of credit and trade elicited loud outcries against the Scots as well as imperial authorities, the sudden collapse of credit in 1762 produced even greater strains. At a time of general financial calamity in Europe, tobacco houses in Scotland and England began to cut back their short-term loans to Virginia and to press for payment of back debts. Meanwhile, the low price for tobacco and the prospect of an end to the French and Indian War, which was expected to lower prices even further, prompted a temporary abatement of tobacco imports. The overall effect was to reduce sharply the amount of credit and foreign exchange available in Virginia at the very moment the demand for sterling remittances was greatest. Many planters now refused to pay debts. General suspension of court proceedings involving debt cases soon followed, and public loans and similar expedients were urged.

Some of the cures posed were more radical. There was discussion, for instance, of exploiting new markets through the diversification of agriculture, and of encouraging secondary manufactures in items such as flour and bread. In addition, some planters raised anew the possibility of totally reorienting the local economy by accelerating the shift out of tobacco and into foodstuffs through the creation of a highly commercialized urban marketplace. The idea here was to lessen the dependence on resident Scots factors through the establishment of new urban-commercial hubs that would function as Philadelphia did in the North. Such centers were to be kept firmly in the hands of local Virginians. The outcome of these various schemes proved disheartening. Despite discouragements, the planters showed an increasing concern with economic sovereignty. Furthermore, they came to feel that the restriction imposed by Parliament and the credit system of the Scots made changes in this direction unlikely. Economic strains in Virginia fast became an inseparable part of the struggle against the new British postwar policies.

The economic situation worsened again after 1772 following the collapse of credit for the second time in a decade. The cry of the planter caught in a seemingly hopeless web of debt grew more shrill. With significant economic change an unrealized dream, the financial panic of 1772 and 1773 removed lingering hopes of a solution within the existing framework of the imperial system.

Especially in those parts of Virginia, such as the Northern Neck bordering on the Potomac, where progressive planters were already making strenuous efforts to diversify their agriculture and establish commercial relations apart from the ubiquitous Scottish store system, more and more wealthy Virginians became convinced of the need for a radical change in imperial relations and for control of their own economic destiny. Even planters who hoped for moderate reform within the empire were willing to take an active part in the frenzied politics that followed the depression of 1772 and 1773. Planters throughout the tobacco colonies stood shoulder to shoulder in a movement directed in large part against the Scottish mercantile community. It is no surprise to find the planting elite in the forefront of Maryland's and Virginia's revolutionary struggle.

If two developments—the long-term growth of the Whig elite's self-conscious strength, and second, the increasing awareness of a need for economic sovereignty in the face of the post-1745 spurt in British exports and of new British policies after 1763—called into existence the revolutionary movement, a third factor, the involvement of the urban "lower orders" and the smaller farmers, was crucial in determining the nature of this movement.

The participation of the urban lower classes in the Revolution is a familiar theme; it was, of course, one of the Progressive historians' chief concerns. Most writing has stressed, with some validity, that tradesmen, sailors, and laborers were initially brought into political activity during the 1760s at the behest of the Whig elite. The wealthier patriots in the cities, it has been argued, used the colonial "mob" to their own ends, directing its furies against stamp distributors and customs officials. What we emphasize here in addition is that to a great extent the involvement of these lower classes resulted from their own economic grievances. To begin with, city dwellers were the first to be encouraged to buy with liberal offers of credit and the first to feel the bitterness of depression and debt contraction. Nor were tradesmen and artisans merely the first to be pressed for payment; they were also frequently the last to be paid in a time of stringency. "The poor industrious tradesmen, the needy mechanic, and all men of narrow circumstance," an observer of events reported to the readers of the *New-York Gazette* in November 1767, were facing "impending ruin." The "money'd men" were holding on to whatever cash came their way, refusing to pay their bills and bankrupting the small tradesman and artisan.[15] Also, during periods of business contraction, sailors and day laborers increasingly found themselves without work. Thus beginning in the 1750s, and later paralleling the merchants' nonimportation movement in the 1760s, the urban lower classes organized and agitated for agreements promoting nonconsumption and domestic manufacturing. Such compacts served both to allow the debt-ridden citizenry to retrench as well as to boost local employment. For some among the urban "lower orders" these agreements marked their initial entry into active political life; for others they offered one additional, important reason for participation in the revolutionary movement.

As the urban lower classes became more involved in the pursuit of their own interests through such programs as nonconsumption and domestic manufacturing, they also became more vociferous in articulating other demands of their own, demands for the further democratization of colonial society. This new militancy frightened many of the merchants who now saw the threat of social upheaval. Admittedly, in historical retrospect, there was little change in the structure of society, though some in institutions. But there was ample justification for the fears of the wealthy, as numerous editorialists called for far-reaching changes in the nature of government. The mere airing of these demands was enough to convince many in the upper classes that the Revolution had gone too far and that it was better to bear the burdens of membership in the British Empire than to risk social disruption at home. This lower-class militancy helps explain the existence of important loyalist minorities in each of the port cities. On the other hand, most of the Whig elite felt with some prescience that the situation could be kept well under control.

Apart from the area of tobacco cultivation, the protests against Britain centered in the cities. Any recounting of the revolutionary movement must necessarily focus on these centers and recognize the significance of the urban classes, merchant and laborer alike, which went far beyond the weight of their numbers. Yet, the bulk of the population was composed of farmers, and only with their involvement was war with Britain possible. Most farmers of the northern colonies and of the Appalachian plateau stood outside the revolutionary movement until 1774. In part, this reflected the pacifism of certain religious sects as well as the difficulty of informing and organizing a population spread out over a large area. More significantly these farmers did not share the economic grievances of either merchants and tradesmen of the coastal cities or of the tobacco growing planters of Virginia and Maryland. The dry goods sector of the economy suffered from chronic depressions after 1745, strapping those who either handled goods or relied directly on British capital. However, those who raised wheat or other provisions experienced generally good times, selling their products to a constantly expanding world market and receiving prices which steadily appreciated in terms of West Indian and English goods. As the value of holdings constantly rose, it was only the improvident, or the heavily mortaged, husbandman who suffered from the postwar contradictions that beset the colonial credit supply and the dry goods sector.

After 1774 the small farmer took a more active role in response to the increased presence of British forces and the impassioned pleas of continental and provincial congresses. His loyalty depended on a variety of considerations: the advantages offered by the new state governments, the traditional relationship of the backcountry to the dominant groups on the coast, and often, simply the question of which army was in the neighborhood. In states like Pennsylvania, where Independence was accompanied by a new state constitution giving the backcountry more just apportionment and control over local affairs, the farmers became enthusiastic patriots. In the Carolinas, where the new government, like the old, showed less interest in mollifying backcountry discontent, there were significant Tory elements among the small farmers.

One group of agriculturists serviced by an urban center had been active in the revolutionary movement throughout the decade before Independence: the South Carolina rice and indigo planters. These slaveholders, like the wheat and provision farmers of the North, imported and exported their goods through a city and dealt with a merchant community composed predominantly of native merchants rather than foreign factors. Like northern farmers, rice planters sold to an expanding world market and enjoyed generally rising prices. But South Carolina planters differed in important ways from those who cultivated wheat and provisions, for rice and indigo planting required far greater inputs of capital, chiefly in the form of slaves, than did the production of grain. This means that rice and indigo planters were involved to a greater degree in local money markets than were northern farmers, and hence were more seriously affected by the currency and credit contractions that plagued the South Carolina economy in the 1760s and especially in the 1770s. Also, planters of coastal South Carolina, as men of wealth and stature, had long been active in the struggles with royal governors and British policies. This different background helps explain their more active role in the years before 1774.

The upper-class Whigs who stood in the forefront of the revolutionary movement retained their coherence and their momentum after 1776. Independence was no more their ultimate goal than was the repeal of any specific piece of British legislation. The control over the American economy that they sought required a restructuring of government and a comprehensive program of legislation: for those in urban centers, a national banking system and American navigation acts, and for the tobacco planters of the South, the encouragement of national cities. In addition, upper-class Whigs showed a continued concern for challenges from the "lower orders." The Constitution of 1789, from the Whig elite's viewpoint, was the culmination of the movement for Independence, not its antithesis.

Interpretations of the revolutionary decades have changed much during the twentieth century. Progressive scholars offered a broad explanation which on closer scrutiny has been found wanting. Lower-class movements and social upheaval may in part characterize the revolutionary movement; they do not explain it. Since the Second World War, a generation of neo-Whig scholars has completely rewritten the history of these years. Ideas rather than social classes, unreasoning fears rather than rational self-interest, have become keynotes of the Revolution. But if the pitfalls of the Progressive approach have been avoided, more glaring shortcomings have appeared. While neo-Whig interpretations have shown an increasing concern for the "inner world" of a select group of publicists, they have at the same time shown less concern for the specific events, issues, and interests of the period. The time has come to reassert the essential reasonableness and necessity of the American Revolution in terms of the overall economic situation of the colonies and of the specific interests of the actors. In this way historians may be better able to explain both the ideas and the events that marked the decades of the American Revolution.

Part Three

THE AMERICAN REVOLUTION?

These chapters concentrate on the preconditions for and the precipitants of the American "Revolution." Jack Greene (chapter 10) presents a perceptive overview of the broad preconditions for revolution in America through a book review that is really an essay on the conditions leading to the break in 1776. Max Savelle (chapter 11) discusses British nationalism in America and all that connoted in terms of rights and obligations felt by the colonists. He chronicles the divided views that grew in the colonies over what nationalism meant—views of Tories, Whigs, and radicals—and what reactions should be to the increasing British challenges to the Americans as British nationals. The growth of the concept of an American nation is Savelle's theme. Although considerations of space necessitated editing out some of his examples, his basic conclusions remain.

Rhys Isaac (chapter 12) and Bernard Bailyn (chapter 13) present two aspects of the precipitant events that brought the rebellion of 1776. Isaac gives a view from the bottom, the movement to mobilize the unlettered masses by "dramatizing" the dynamics of the emergent "cause." The gentry of Virginia are shown leading the freemen within an open system of communication and participation. It should be noted that much of the first part of this article, containing the theoretic base and significance of localized courthouse sociopolitical interaction, has been edited out; the remaining narrative specifics of Virginia fulfil our purpose most graphically.

Bernard Bailyn outlines the other end of the spectrum: the importance of ideas disseminated by the literate through the literature of the period— the leadership of ideas. Bailyn argues that social and institutional reforms had already taken place in America; thus the Revolution (he still calls it so) "was a matter of doctrine, ideas, and comprehension."

Winthrop Jordan (chapter 14) provides a thorough, complete analysis of the final step to rebellion—the "killing" of the king. Thomas Paine's

Common Sense *psychologically and symbolically culminates the commitment to the break with Britain.*

And, finally, Thomas Barrow's article (chapter 15), though a bit shaky on the definition of revolution (stability replaced by instability), hits at the persistent point of the editor: the "Revolution" was not revolutionary; rather it was a war of colonial independence. It was "the completion, or fulfillment of an existing society rather than its destruction." Note also the distinction made by Jordan between a settler colony (citizens of the center) and exploitive colony (subjects). Though Barrow's conclusions are not specifically those of the editor (see introduction), they reinforce those views and provide the closing argument.

Jack P. Greene

10 FROM RESISTANCE TO REVOLUTION

Over the past quarter century, there has been a massive and wholly unprecedented outpouring—almost a deluge—of detailed studies on most aspects of the origins of the American Revolution in both Britain and America. Eight major questions have been identified, and it may be useful to take stock of present scholarly opinion upon them. Despite many disagreements about emphases and points of detail, a rough consensus has emerged over the past two decades on two points. First, Americans were not, before the 1760s, sufficiently dissatisfied with either the economic or political relationship with Britain to think in terms of separation. Membership in the empire worked to the colonists' advantage down to 1763; the colonists had long since found ways to live with (when they could not evade entirely) aspects of the imperial system they found objectionable, and, in any case, were tightly bound to Britain through close ties of interest, habit, affection and patriotism. A second point on which a general agreement has emerged is that what did create widespread American discontent, resistance, and eventually a movement for separation, were the many efforts by metropolitan authorities, beginning in the early 1760s, to tighten control over colonial economic and political life through parliamentary taxation and a variety of other legislative and administrative restrictions.

This essay is an adaptation by the author of a review of Ian R. Christie and Benjamin W. Labaree, *Empire or Independence: A British-American Dialogue on the Coming of the American Revolution* (Oxford, 1976), from which most of the quotations are taken.

Much more controversial are six additional questions: 1) why the Bute and Grenville governments undertook the new restrictive measures in the first place; 2) why the colonists resisted them so vigorously from so very early on; 3) why successive British governments persisted in such measures in the face of such animated and widespread resistance; 4) why no British government could see that there might be some middle ground between total subordination and complete independence; 5) why, given the depth and extent of their opposition, the colonists waited so long to opt for independence; and 6) what bearing social and political tensions within the colonies had upon the colonial response.

The first question has received little systematic attention. Yet it is in many ways the salient question about the Revolution. If the colonists were in fact acclimated to the imperial system by the 1760s, and if it was only the new British measures thereafter that drove them to resistance and revolution, then the question why the metropolitan government chose to tamper with a system that had yielded Britain such extraordinary economic and strategic returns at so little cost—before 1756 Britain had kept no effective military force in the continental colonies—is one that demands careful scrutiny.

The conventional answer has been that the Seven Years' War and its successful outcome either revealed or created a whole series of problems that required more active and qualitatively different metropolitan involvement in colonial affairs: the vast new territories acquired from the French and Spanish by the peace of 1763 had to be organized and administered, trade regulations in the colonies had to be enforced, the army in America had to be provided for, British merchants had to be protected against the inflation of colonial paper currencies, and, most important of all, the vast debt incurred as a result of the war had to be paid.

While not underestimating the importance of such considerations, several scholars, in a commendable effort to go beyond the traditional explanation, have recently traced the new policies to a deep-seated and broadly shared suspicion "that the colonies were thrusting towards independence," and a corresponding fear that colonial independence would inevitably affect national security adversely; that, as one official put it, in 1774, national "destruction must follow disunion." America was thought to have provided Britain "with the balance of strength which gave her the edge over her formidable French rival," and it followed that without America "the country would no longer have the power to keep itself safe in the jungle of international politics."

But it is possible to go ever farther in the search for an answer to this question. Quite as much as strategic, economic considerations, a growing awareness within Britain of the enormous and ever increasing economic worth of the colonies, especially as markets for British exports, would seem to have animated the fears of independence. Increasingly, reiterated through the middle decades of the eighteenth century, such fears, long in evidence but previously largely latent, seem to have been activated as early as the late 1740s by the simultaneous eruption of severe political disturbances in several colonies and mounting evidence of metropolitan weakness in many others. Despite the expenditure of much time and effort, metropolitan authorities were unable to deal with these problems through existing mechanisms of colonial administration and this ineffectiveness further intensified fears of loss of the colonies and led, well before the Seven Years' War had further underscored the weakness of metropolitan control, to a widespread conviction among people in power in Britain that Parliament itself would have to intervene before metropolitan authority could be securely established. By making it less necessary to court colonial co-operation for purposes of imperial defense, the removal of the French and Spanish from eastern North America as a result of the war gave later British governments a much freer hand to undertake a broad program of colonial reform while the presence of seventy-five hundred royal troops in the colonies seemed for the first time to give them the might necessary to suppress any colonial opposition.

Why American resistance was so vigorous and so immediate is an equally complex question. Current scholarly orthodoxy attributes it largely to the traditional British suspicion of unlimited power. But it is important to add that that suspicion derived not merely from the colonists' experience with politics inside the colonies, but also, as an older generation would have appreciated, from the ambiguous constitutional arrangements that obtained within the empire. Having repeatedly tried and failed before 1730 to obtain explicit constitutional guarantees that would put them on a comparable footing with people in the home islands and secure their liberties and property from any possible misuse of the new unlimited might of the metropolis, the colonists had been left with no stronger defenses than local custom (in no case of more than 150 years' standing) or their uncertain claim to the traditional rights of Englishmen, however those rights might or might not be applicable to distant colonies. Anxieties arising from this constitutional insecurity were largely dormant after 1725 as a consequence of the relaxed colonial administration under Walpole and his immediate successors. But they remained close to the surface, and were easily activated when imperial reorganization after 1763 "inevitably involved the use of power in ways which had not hitherto been customary."

The apparent significance of this reorganization was also important to most politically informed Americans. It seemed to be an arbitrary and dangerous breach of the traditional relationship between them and the metropolis; it threatened both to deprive them of effective control over the internal affairs of their own political societies, and to reduce them to a status within the empire that was equivalent to that of the politically excluded classes in the home islands. Such a status might be fitting for servants and slaves, women and children, the propertyless and the incompetent. But it was scarcely suitable for independent adult male Britons. In colonial America, quite as much as in early modern Britain, civil emasculation was a familiar condition. With the vivid and omnipresent example of the unrepresented African slaves (who were not yet confined to the southern portion of the continent) and other dependent groups in their own societies constantly before them, the colonists' complaint that taxation by, without representation in, Parliament would reduce them to slavery came directly from the heart. Far from being empty rhetoric or mere cultural mimicry, it was expressive of the most profound fears and anxieties. Not just their liberties and property but their identity as freeborn Britons, their manhood itself, seemed to be threatened by the metropolitan posture toward the colonies.

The timing of the new measures, moreover, further stimulated colonial opposition—and not just for the familiar reason that the recent removal of the French and Spanish from the eastern half of North America made the colonists less dependent upon Britain for protection. For the colonists, the Seven Years' War had been a psychologically liberating and reinforcing experience. That so much of the war had been fought on American soil, and that the British Government had made such an enormous effort to defend the colonies, gave rise to an expanded sense of colonial self-importance. In addition, no matter how it appeared in London many of the colonies had contributed a substantial amount of money and a significant number of men to the war effort. Virginia and Massachusetts, the two colonies that, in all probability not accidentally, subsequently took the lead in the resistance, had, in terms of liquid economic resources, virtually bankrupted themselves in voting men and money for the war. For the colonists, the knowledge that they had made such an important contribution to so great a national cause increased the immediacy and the strength of their ties with Britain and created heightened expectations for a larger role and a higher status within the empire. The new measures after 1763 thus tended to create a classic situation of frustrated expectations and to heighten the intensity of the colonial response.

Why various governments persisted in such measures in the face of such intense opposition, and why none of them were able to find a peaceful solution to the controversy that would satisfy the protesting colonists are closely related questions. What historians have described is a situation in which an underlying resentment against what seemed in Britain to be the more favored fiscal position of the colonies interacted with increasing outrage at American resistance to metropolitan authority, misconceptions about the character and thrust of that resistance and an almost xenophobic contempt for the colonists' capacity to offer effective opposition to British arms. Successive British governments moved progressively further away from the conciliatory posture that had traditionally characterized metropolitan behavior towards the colonies (and was still manifest in the repeal of the Stamp Act in 1766 and of most of the Townshend duties in 1770) towards a growing feeling in 1774-76 that firmness and coercion were the only effective instruments to secure colonial obedience to metropolitan authority.

The most universal commitment within the British political nation— a commitment that extended even to advocates of conciliation such as Chatham and Burke—to the beliefs that sovereignty was indivisible, that, as the embodiment of that sovereignty, the King-in-Parliament was supreme throughout the whole of the British Empire, and that economic control over distant colonies could not be maintained without political hegemony, meant that colonial resistance would be widely interpreted in Britain as a fundamental and dangerous challenge to both the existing constitutional system, the universally praised Revolutionary Settlement of 1688-1715, and to the prosperity and security of the nation. So deep and widespread was this commitment that no political group following the Stamp Act crisis could risk giving "the impression that it might be lax towards the Americans"; and no significant element within the political nation could perceive that colonial demands for exemption from parliamentary taxation and, after 1774, for autonomy over their internal affairs, could lead anywhere except to the nullification of the navigation system, colonial independence, and, for the metropolis, a rapid slide to the bottom of the international status hierarchy.

Most recent analysts have taken pains to insist that the "events of 1775 and 1776 were not inevitable." Yet the failure of anyone in or close to power in Britain to come up with a solution that might have been acceptable to the colonists strongly suggests that the odds against finding such a solution were so high as to be practically nonexistent. A few people in opposition—Barré, Burke, Cavendish, Chatham—understood the fundamental political truth that "that country which is kept by power is in danger of being lost every day" and, recognizing that "a great Empire" could only be governed "by consent," advocated bringing over "the affections of all of our colonies by lenient measures." But not a single one of the conciliatory schemes they produced came close to meeting the American demands, made in response to the Coercive Acts of 1774, for a constitutional settlement that would provide Americans with strict guarantees of their liberties and property and complete autonomy over their internal affairs. And even these limited schemes went vastly too far for the overwhelming majority of the metropolitan political nation, who agreed with George III that there could be no halfway between submission and independence. In rejecting conciliation in favor of force, the Government "was carrying out Parliament's—indeed, the Country's—will."

The inability of anyone—either in office or in opposition—to perceive the viability of the American proposal for an empire of coordinate polities united through a common monarch, a proposal that was essentially similar to the Commonwealth system worked out less than a century later, strongly suggests that the political failures of the mid-1770s were attributable less to the political myopia of most of the men involved, as has so often been asserted, than to the political culture that permitted, even demanded, that myopia; a political culture that was so widely celebrated and so successfully repressive as to preclude any possibility of the sort of flexibility required by conditions in 1774-76. The kinds of innovations demanded by the Americans could not be seriously entertained until mercantilism had given way to free trade, and the power of the monarchy had so far declined as to allay the residual fears of prerogative that underlay the widely expressed anxiety that the crown might deploy its colonial resources in such a way as to render monarchy independent of Parliament and Parliament unnecessary to the monarchy.

But such changes lay far into the future. During the late eighteenth century, the extreme structural or systemic rigidity of British political culture meant that, once the Americans had determined to accept nothing less than explicit metropolitan renunciation of the doctrine of parliamentary sovereignty over the colonies, the British decision to use force, the political revolution that followed that decision, and the eventual demise of the First British Empire were, as Sir Lewis Namier suggested almost fifty years ago, virtually as certain as "the revolutions of planets . . . the migration of birds, and . . . the plunging of hordes of lemmings into the sea."

On the American side, the Stamp Act crisis made the colonists profoundly suspicious of metropolitan intentions, but it did not inaugurate a movement for colonial independence. "Should [the British] government be so temperate and just as to place us on the old ground on which we stood before the Stamp Act," Samuel Cooper wrote to Benjamin Franklin from Boston as late as 1771, "there is no danger of our rising in our demands." Resistance did not become revolution until the outbreak of hostilities at Lexington Green on April 19, 1775. Why it took so long for a revolutionary movement to develop is to be explained primarily by the presence of several powerful deterrents.

Some of the best known of these include fear of British power, the persistent parochialism of the individual colonies, the lack of political institutions capable of coordinating a central resistance movement, the continuing willingness of the metropolitan government to eschew the search for the final solution to the knotty problem of Parliament's authority over the colonies, the illusion among the colonists that they had a large reservoir of political support in Britain and, most important of all, the great residue of affection felt by so many colonists for Britain. Another deterrent was the fear among traditional leaders in the colonies that the removal or attenuation of British authority might mean loss of political control by local elites, domination by the French or the Spanish, or a republican form of government—all or any of which might lead to political chaos and a tyranny far worse than any they might, on the basis of their experience before the mid-1770s, expect to suffer at the hands of the metropolis.

The rapid spread within the colonies of a generalized belief in the evil intentions of men in power in Britain and in the corruption of the central governing institutions of the empire contributed to the gradual alienation of colonial affections for Britain between 1766 and 1774, while other important developments helped to weaken the force of still other deterrents over the same period. The inability of the metropolitan government to enforce its will in the colonies at any point in the long controversy led to gradual weakening of respect for British power among the colonists. The increasing politicization of the colonies around a central focus of opposition to British policy effectively mobilized large groups of previously politically inert people without resulting in political or social chaos. The alienation of the overseas trading merchants in Britain, the colonists' main allies in the metropolis, by the adoption of economic boycotts during the late 1760s and again in 1774, removed the one most effective voice for moderation in metropolitan circles. The Continental Congress, the revolutionary conventions at the state level, and the committees of safety in the localities provided the colonists with the necessary organization for a unified resistance movement and, through their successful functioning, helped to allay fears that separation from Britain and republican political institutions would result in political collapse. Finally, the course of the war during the first year and the increasing prospect of French aid encouraged the colonists in the belief that they might successfully oppose British military might.

A final question, the relationship between social and political tensions within the colonies and colonial resistance to Britain, is in many ways the most complex. Considerable research and even more theorizing has been done on this question over the past decade. Although no one has yet been able to show that the social situation in any colony was sufficiently brittle as to make internal revolution very probable without the altercation with Britain, they have demonstrated clearly that the peculiar socioeconomic character of each colony affected both its response to the controversy with Britain and its behavior following independence; the many variations in the "face" of the Revolution from one colony to the next can only be explained in terms of the widely differing character of political society in each.

The view that better communications might have produced a clearer understanding on both sides of the Atlantic of the intentions of the protagonists, an understanding which presumably might have averted the dismemberment of the empire, has gained much currency over the past few years. But is it really very plausible? To be sure, each side misunderstood the motives of the other. But the role the British actually envisioned for the colonies, which was not so widely misunderstood in the colonies as has recently been contended, was no more acceptable to the colonists than American demands for a more equivalent and autonomous role within the empire were to the British political nation. It can be argued at least as plausibly that better communications would have hastened rather than prevented revolution.

Max Savelle

11 NATIONALISM AND OTHER LOYALTIES IN THE AMERICAN REVOLUTION

Loyalties of one sort or another have always been powerful causal forces in human history. It was the personal loyalty of the vassal to his lord that gave to medieval feudalism its cohesive force; it is individual and collective loyalty to the nation which, today, holds the national societies of the modern world together. This peculiar form of loyalty did not become a major factor in the history of the Western world until about the middle of the eighteenth century. Nor could it have been until the concept of the nation had become a reality in the ideologies of Western societies since nationalism is a form of loyalty whose object is the nation.

But what is a nation? No one has ever seen a nation; no one has ever touched one. The nation has no existence in the physical world. Its existence, therefore, while nonetheless real, is entirely metaphysical, or mental; the nation exists only as a concept held in common by many men. It is the emotional loyalty of men to this always changing concept, the nation, that constitutes nationalism. Without the concept, the loyalty could not exist.

The concept of the nation appeared in the Western world apparently as a by-product of the emergence of the modern integral state. One of those who, as it were, first seized upon the mental image of the nation was Jean Jacques Rousseau, who stated it clearly in his "Considérations sur le gouvernement de Pologne . . . ," when he said, "A child on opening its eyes for the first time should see the nation, and until death he should see nothing but her. Every true national imbibes with his mother's milk the love of *la patrie*. . . . This love encompasses his entire existence; he sees only the nation, he lives only for her; alone, he is nothing; the moment he is without the nation he ceases to exist. . . ."[1]

Lord Bolingbroke skirted the same concept in his essay on "The Idea of a Patriot King" and elsewhere, and Edmund Burke apparently had in mind a clear concept of the British nation—a nation he was trying desperately to hold together—when he made his famous plea for reconciliation with the colonies on March 22, 1775:

My hold of the Colonies is in the close affection which grows from common names, from kindred blood, from similar privileges, and equal protection. These are ties, which, though light as air, are as strong as links of iron. Let the Colonists always keep the idea of their civil rights associated with your government;—they will cling and grapple to you; and no force under heaven will be of power to tear them from their allegiance. . . . Deny them this participation of freedom, and you break that sole bond, which originally made, and must still preserve, the unity of the Empire. . . . It is the spirit of the English Constitution, which, infused through the mighty mass, pervades, feeds, unites, invigorates, unifies every part of the empire, even down to the minutest member. . . .[2]

It is to be noted that the concept of the British nation and of loyalty to it, here appealed to by Burke, was expressed in the term "the Empire." This term was also used by the Americans down to 1776, and it was borrowed, as "the American Empire," to indicate the American nation as that new concept grew in the minds of Americans after independence. The psychological, the emotional cement that bound together the members of the British nation wherever they were was for Burke and other British nationalists the English mythos, the central, essential element in which was the belief in the reality of an Anglo-Saxon love of liberty.

The Britons of Anglo-America shared in this Burkean type of nationalism. They gloried in the name of Briton, and they felt a genuine emotional identity with this concept of the British nation. William Douglass, for example, expressed this American-British loyalty in his *Summary, Historical and Political . . . of the British Settlements in North America*: "The high encomiums of our militia ought not to give any umbrage or jealousy to the British government or mother-country; that in case of any general (maritime powers) war, they cast themselves into the arms of the French or Dutch; . . . the people here [Massachusetts] are so loyal to the crown, and so affectionate to their mother country, that this cannot be supposed. . . ."[3] Benjamin Franklin echoed this sense of common nationalism during the Seven Years' War as he wrote to Lord Kames in January 1760: "No one can more sincerely rejoice than I do, on the reduction of Canada; and this is not merely as I am a colonist, but as I am a Briton. . . ."[4] A little later in the same year, in his famous pamphlet on

"Guadaloupe" [*sic*] , he made his British nationalism sharply clear when he remarked that "if ever there was a *national* war, this is truly such a one: a war in which the interests of the *whole* nation is directly and fundamentally concerned."[5]

This feeling of "affection" for the mother country persisted into the years of crisis, right down to the eve of independence, in the minds and feelings of both American Whigs and American Tories. It ended for the Whigs with Independence; it continued to dominate the thought and feeling of the Tories through and beyond the Revolution.

Yet the Americans distinctly felt themselves to be different from other Britons, and in many ways. Jonathan Mayhew, celebrating the triumph of British armies in the Seven Years' War, enumerated the peculiar satisfactions of being a member of the British nation: "We Britishers are still farther distinguished and favored of God, by having been born and bred in a *protestant* country, and a *reformed* part of the christian church. . . ."[6] But if it was a peculiar privilege to be born a member of the British nation, this special favor of God reached superlative heights in one's being born a Britisher of New England. "If we come to our own country in particular; we have here enjoyed of late, almost all the blessings of peace, in a time of war and tumult among the nations of Europe. . . ."[7] Mayhew, in speaking of "our own country," as his contemporaries were accustomed to do, had in mind his native New England. He was proud to be a Briton, and he loved the ideals that, to him, made the British nation the happiest and best in the world. But it was the "New-English" Britons who enjoyed, more than any other, the national values, the most precious of which were the civil rights and privileges that were theirs as members of the British nation.

It was this coupling of a sense of identity with the British nation with a distinct consciousness of differentness and a certain smug self-satisfaction in it that characterized the "British" nationalism of the colonial Americans. The citizen of any one of the colonies looked upon that colony as his "country," and he felt a distinct patriotism, or love of his land, toward it. Some of the colonists even spoke of "America" as the aggregate of the colonies, and betrayed, on numerous occasions, an active and enthusiastic sense of the "manifest destiny" (to use a later phrase) of the American segment of the British nation.

This consciousness of being a different "country" was apparently a strong germinal factor in the origin and, later, the emergence of a self-conscious American nationalism. In the years following the Seven Years' War it enjoyed a new burst of enthusiastic, emotional expression. But this feeling for one's "country" (colony) and for America in a collective or pluralistic sense was always focused upon the new land only within the larger context of the Empire. The colonial Americans were never less than loyal to their nation—the nation of Britons everywhere; their loyalties to America were always subservient to and integrated in their greater loyalty to the "Empire" and its ideals.

The history of loyalties in Anglo-America in the years between 1763 and 1775 is not one of divided loyalties, but, rather, a history of two separate, distinct, and rival series of efforts to preserve the old American loyalty to the British nation. The American Whigs stood for the maintenance of the old loyalty to the British national ideals, as they understood them, *against* the policies and actions of what they took to be a series of misguided ministries; the Tories clung to the old loyalty *despite* the policies of those same ministries, however misguided. For the Tories, as contrasted with the Whigs or radicals, British national symbols, ideals, and loyalties, in the Burkean sense were everything. If worse came to worst, they would submit to the ministry rather than split the British nation and precipitate it into civil war. The Whigs always maintained that their loyalty to the British nation, and to the crown as its symbol, was just as strong and devoted as that of any other Britons, and they demonstrated their sincerity in their writings. John Dickinson, for example, in the midst of American fury over the Townshend program, betrayed a deep emotional fear of rending of the "body" of the British nation:

Resistance, in the case of colonies against their mother country, is extremely different from the resistance of a people against their prince. A nation may change their king, or race of kings, and . . . be gainers by changing. . . . But if once we [the colonies] are separated from our mother country, what new form of government shall we adopt, or where shall we find another Britain, to supply our loss? Torn from the body to which we are united by religion, liberty, laws, affections, relation, language and commerce, we must bleed at every vein.[8]

A few years later, Samuel Adams, in his debate with Thomas Hutchinson, pointed out that all the American Whigs insisted upon was some sort of constitutional reform that would ensure to the Americans the same constitutional guarantees that the Britons living in England enjoyed. Given this guarantee, he said, the loyalty of the Americans to the British-imperial national ideal would remain true and undiminished. Persistent wrongheadedness by English ministers might destroy American loyalty to the "empire," but enlightened constitutional reform—even just the honest recognition and institutionalization of the real status quo—might be expected to preserve and encourage American loyalty to the national ideal indefinitely.

A similar effort to fit the expediency of constitutional reform into a generally received concept of and loyalty to the British imperial nation is to be observed in the the writings of John Adams in 1774 and 1775. In the first of his *Novanglus* essays, for example, Adams introduced his series of replies to Massachusettensis (David Leonard) with: "A writer, under the signature of Massachusettensis, has addressed you, in a series of papers, on the great national subject of the present quarrel between the British administration and the Colonies."[9] Adams here used the term "national" to indicate the totality of British imperial society. He recognized clearly the fact that there were two segments of that society, the English and the American, but the whole British national society on both sides of the Atlantic was one, and he was loyal to it. It is a notable fact that Leonard's concept of the British nation was basically the same as that of Adams. Their difference arose chiefly over Adams's insistence that the Americans were entitled to different, special treatment as Britons, a treatment that could be administered only by their own colonial governments and some sort of continental congress.

Thomas Jefferson, evidently, was thinking along similar lines. In his "Draft of Instructions to the Virginia Delegates in the Continental Congress" of July, 1774, he proposed a "humble and dutiful address" to the King, presenting the strong American discontents on the encroachments of "the legislature of one part of the empire upon those rights which God and the laws have given equally and independently to all."[10] And in the Resolution of the Virginia Convention of August, 1774, the Virginians avowed their

. . . inviolable and unshaken fidelity and attachment to our most gracious Sovereign, our Regard and affection for all our Friends and Fellow Subjects in Great Britain and elsewhere, [and protest] against every Act or Thing which may have the most distant tendency to interrupt, or in any wise disturb, his Majesty's Peace, and the good order of Government within this his ancient Colony, which we are resolved to maintain and defend at the Risk of our Lives and Fortunes. . . ,[11]

This was not the language of American nationalism. It was British nationalism. And the Virginians surely meant what they said.

James Wilson expressed similar sentiments.[12] He asked, after a review of American resistance, "Are these measures, Sir, the brats of disloyalty, of disaffection? . . . [No!] Is this scheme of conduct allied to rebellion? Can any symptoms of disloyalty to his Majesty, of disinclination to his illustrious family or of disregard to his authority be traced in it?" No. American opposition to the mistaken measures of the ministry was entirely constitutional; the Americans had never shown disloyalty "to his Majesty"; they were not "enemies to the power of the crown." Alexander Hamilton said much the same thing in his dispute with the Westchester Farmer (Samuel Seabury): "I deny that we are dependent on the legislature of Great Britain; and yet I maintain that we are a part of the British

Empire—but in this sense only, as being the freeborn subjects of his Britannic Majesty."[13] John Hancock, on March 5, 1774, cried out for "patriotism" against the tyranny of British ministers. Like Wilson, he applauded the steps that had been taken to organize the colonies in a federated common front against the actions of an unwise ministry, steps that he hoped might culminate in a congress of all the continental colonies:

At such a congress a firm foundation may be laid for the security of our rights and liberties [,] a system may be formed for our common safety, by a strict adherence to which, we shall be able to frustrate any attempts to overthrow our constitution; restore peace and harmony to America, and secure honor and wealth to Great Britain, even against the inclination of her ministers, whose duty it is to study her welfare. . . .[14]

Even as late as November 4, 1775, the council of the town of Watertown, Massachusetts, issued a "Proclamation of Thanksgiving" urging the people of the town to render up thanks for their liberties and for the union of the colonies to defend them, "and to offer up humble and fervent prayers to Almighty God, for the whole British empire; especially for the *United American Colonies* . . . that He would give wisdom to the American Congress equal to their important station. . . ."[15]

Finally, the Continental Congress, itself, was still protesting its loyalty in July, 1775:

Attached to your Majesty's person, family, and government, with all devotion that principle and affection can inspire, connected with Great Britain by the strongest ties that can unite societies, and deploring every event that tends in any degree to weaken them, we solemnly assure your Majesty that we not only most ardently desire the former harmony between her and these colonies may be restored, but that a concord may be established between them upon so firm a basis as to perpetuate its blessings, uninterrupted by any future dissentions, to succeeding generations in both countries. . . .[16]

Surely there is no reason to think that these men in the colonies did not believe what they said. They did mean it, apparently; there is even a sort of pathos in their repeated and fervent protestations, as though they deeply feared to lose a connection with the British nation which, to them, was a highly precious thing. . . .

The evidence thus appears to be overwhelming that, at least until late in 1775, there was no significant split in the loyalties of the Americans. All Americans, Whigs and Tories alike, were genuinely and deeply loyal to the "British empire" or nation, to its ideals, and to its king. The divisions among them were divisions as to practical constitutional reforms, their validity and their importance, not as to national British ideals or loyalty to those ideals. . . .

But if radical and Tory were both British nationalists, differing chiefly as to the need and the nature of constitutional reform and not in their basic loyalties to the nation and its symbols, the logic of the course of events was driving them further and further apart in their reactions to expediency, and even nearer to the break from beyond which there could be no return: the final abandonment, by the Whigs, of their long-persevering loyalty to the British nation and their consequent search for new concepts and new symbols toward which to direct new loyalties.

Despite the fundamental assumption of both the earliest colonial entrepreneurs and the crown that the American colonial societies were but extensions of the society of England, de facto British colonial policy, almost from the beginning, had treated them as somehow different and separate. Wisdom, in the handling of the colonial problem, had seemed to dictate a special set of laws to channel colonial commerce and limit colonial manufactures, special regulations affecting internal colonial affairs such as postal service, fiscal affairs, and military defense, special instructions to colonial governors to administer their duties in ways that differed widely, in some aspects, from the functioning of analogous political mechanisms in England, and so on. This old set of legal and de facto assumptions as to the differentness of the colonies and the consequent necessity for special laws and institutions for their administration underlay the whole series of ministerial colonial programs in the sixteen years preceding independence, and it reached its culmination in the American Prohibitory Act of December 22, 1775, by which the Americans of thirteen continental colonies were declared to be enemies of England and were ordered to be treated as such. As the climax of a centuries-long series of *voies de fait*, this act was something like childbirth, actually forcing the offspring out of the body of the parent.

Nor had the Americans failed to be conscious of the fact that the colonial societies were, in very truth, highly different from that of the mother country. They had steadily grown toward the conviction that they alone could understand their internal problems and that, therefore, the mother country must recognize the sort of autonomy they were separately demanding and the sort of federative principle of empire being expounded, between 1765 and 1774, by Richard Bland, Franklin, Wilson, and others. Significantly, as has already been noted, many Tories, such as Galloway, Seabury, and Randolph, recognized the inevitability of some degree of colonial autonomy and even of colonial federation. Thus, on the American side, the whole history of the colonial period reached its climax in the actions of the state conventions and the Continental Congress in the years 1774 and 1775, in the course of which the American Whigs still protested, again and again, their loyalty to the ideals of the British nation and to its symbol, the British King.

It appears, thus, that both English policy and American evolution, during 169 years, had been moving steadily and inevitably toward a political and institutional revision of the imperial constitution that would effectuate an adaptation to these facts. Such a revision, however, did not necessarily mean a dissolution of old, established loyalties.

From the viewpoint of the American Whigs, the accommodation could be made without disturbing old loyalties; on the contrary, the successful transformation could only redound to the greater intensity of the loyalty of the Americans to the British nation and a glorification of its wisdom. For some of the Tories, such a revision was possible; for others, it was not. But for all the Tories, if it ever came to a choice between constitutional revision and their imperial (national) loyalty, the revision must be sacrificed to the higher national values. The break, when it came, derived from the determination of the Whigs that they must have the revision; if within the framework of imperial loyalty, well and good; if not, then outside it. For them, their own deepest convictions centered about their sense of need for self-government and the values they identified with that.

This was not yet, in 1776, American nationalism. It was expediency versus loyalty, or British nationalistic idealism. The Tories were idealists; the Whigs were realists. . . .

The one thing to which all Americans on the side of independence could, indeed, direct a fervent loyalty was "the Cause." Even Thomas Burke complained against the "jealousies" of the states as injurious to "our common cause."[17]

It was "the Cause" apparently, rather than any clearly ascertainable national ideal, for which Thomas Paine was propagandizing in the early numbers of *The Crisis*. He certainly saw clearly, and used, the concept of a nation in his criticism of Great Britain:

There is such an idea existing in the world, as that of *national honor,* and this, falsely understood, is oftentimes the cause of war. . . . It is, I think, exceedingly easy to define what ought to be understood by national honor; for that which is the best character for an individual is the best character for a nation; and whenever the latter exceeds or falls beneath the former, there is a departure from the lines of true greatness.

I have thrown out this observation with a design of applying it to Great Britain. . . . Her idea of national honor seems to consist in national insult, and that to be a great people, is to be neither a Christian, a philosopher, or a gentleman, but to threaten with the rudeness of a bear, and to devour with the ferocity of a lion.[18]

Obviously Paine's concept of a nation—in this case, the British nation—is crystal clear. Yet he did not quite arrive at the same clarity of national integrity with regard to the United States. His chief concern was for "the Cause": "All we want to know in America is simply this, who is for independence, and who is not?"[19] As yet he was apparently a fervent devotee of "the Cause"; he had not yet achieved the mental image of the nation that characterized the last few numbers of *The Crisis*. . . .

Many forces were at work, then, to create an American national image, to disseminate it among the people of the states, and gradually to arouse a universal loyalty to it. Some American leaders caught the vision, as it were, gradually, and, by the end of the war, were recognizable American nationalists.

The most famous outburst of this sentiment, of course, was Patrick Henry's impulsive exclamation to the Continental Congress in 1774 that "The distinctions between Virginians, Pennsylvanians, New Yorkers, and New Englanders, are no more. I am not a Virginian, but an American."[20] But there were others.

One such was that of Peter Thatcher of Watertown, Massachusetts, who delivered an impassioned oration on March 5, 1776, four months before the Declaration of Independence: "The tender feelings of the human heart are deeply affected with the fate of [General Richard Montgomery] and the other heroes who have bled and died, that their country may be free; but at the same time, sensations of indignant wrath are excited in the breasts of every friend to freedom. . . ."[21] Here was loyalty to a cause, but it was also an appeal to the loyalty of his hearers to "the rising empire of America". . . .

The development of Paine's thought and feeling, traced through his writings from the period of 1775 when he was writing for the *Pennsylvania Magazine*, through *The Crisis* essays, shows a clear progression from the position of an English nationalist to that of an American nationalist. The metamorphosis was not sudden or abrupt, but it did take place. In this fact, Paine was probably typical of many, if not most, Americans. . . .

It seems evident, then, that the concept of an "American empire," or nation, which replaced the image of the British imperial society to which men had given their loyalty before 1775 in their minds and hearts, was the product of a slow intellectual and emotional growth. It began, perhaps, in the sort of patriotism toward the provinces expressed by colonial writers or, it may be, in the devotion to "America" felt by Galloway. But it was many years before the image of the British empire-nation of the colonial era was fully and perfectly replaced in the minds of all Americans by the image of a genuine integral American nation. The war years, 1776–1783, constituted what might be called the period of its gestation and, toward the end of the war, its birth.

Rhys Isaac

12 DRAMATIZING THE IDEOLOGY OF REVOLUTION
Popular Mobilization in Virginia, 1774 to 1776

The Revolution began in Virginia with two solemn rituals enacted by the county representatives gathered at Williamsburg—the "courthouse" of the province. On May 24, 1774, the House of Burgesses resolved to keep the first day of June (the date for the enforcement of the act of Parliament closing the port of Boston) as a day of fasting and prayer for "divine Interposition that the Minds of his Majesty and his Parliament . . . may be inspired from above with Wisdom, Moderation, and Justice." Faced with such calculated dramatization of identification with Boston and opposition to Parliament, Governor Dunmore felt obliged to dissolve the assembly. Eighty-nine of the burgesses met the next day in an assembly room near the capital, to subscribe solemnly to an "Association" for common action in the crisis.[1] This public signing revived a form of behavior that was to become an important ceremonial means of mobilizing the populace behind the patriot cause. On June 1 the burgesses, led by their Speaker and preceded by the mace, walked in a procession to the parish church on the governor's palace green, there to hold their fast-day service. By that time some of their number had already gone home; these added the weight of their dignity to the little replications of the Williamsburg enactment that took place in many of the parishes throughout the province. George Mason could not return to Fairfax County, but to his family he sent instructions that reveal the striving of the gentry for dramaturgical effects. They were "to pay strict attention" to the fast, and his three eldest sons, with his two eldest daughters, were to "attend church in mourning."[2]

There followed a brief but tense period of suspense. Nearly ten years had passed since the Stamp Act crisis had occasioned an astounding demonstration of Virginia's potential for patriot mobilization. During the intervening period the commitment of the leading gentry, as demonstrated in formally drafted resolves and remonstrances, had not been matched by the overall performance of either the gentry at large or the common folk. The nonimportation movement of 1769 had quietly weakened, and after attempts to revive it had failed, it was simply allowed to die.[3] The crisis of 1774 arose over events in the remote city of Boston and over acts of Parliament directed at Massachusetts; it was far from certain that Virginians generally would respond with vigor. Philip Fithian, a New Jersey tutor residing in Westmoreland County, noted in his journal for May 31: "The lower Class of People here are in tumult on account of Reports from Boston, many of them expect to be press'd and compelled to go and fight the Britains!"[4]

It was imperative for the patriot gentry to communicate to the populace not only their dark and fearful view of what awaited Virginians should they remain supine but also their vision of the good life in the pursuit of which they would lead the struggle. At stake were "fortunes . . . liberties . . . and every thing that is held most dear among men," the heritage of "a brave, virtuous and free people." "Virtue," at the heart of patriot aspirations, was not just a moral quality or disposition; it was a program for the preservation and regeneration of society. The threatened British constitution was "the Gift of God . . . to relieve Virtue from every Restraint to its beneficent Operation, and to restrain Vice. It elevates the Soul, by giving Consequence to every Individual, and enabling him to support that Consequence."[5] By the operation of virtue the necessary ranking of society could be rendered compatible with the dignity and worth of free men. It was to this vision that the patriot leadership thrilled. The means by which they were able to communicate that thrill, so as to make it the basis for popular action are the principal subject matter in this case study of Virginian mobilization.

The newspaper in which the burgesses' responses to the closing of the port of Boston were announced is revealing of the communication dynamics of the period. A small-print notice in Dixon and Hunter's *Virginia Gazette*, following news from London, Boston, New York, and Philadelphia, presented only a simple outline of the steps taken by the burgesses and the governor. We might be inclined to suppose from the absence of typographic dramatization that contemporaries did not attach great importance to these actions. There is abundant evidence, however, of an immediate and widespread sense of their momentousness.[6] It is, indeed, in the very rapid spread of shock throughout Virginia that the explanation for the seeming nonchalance of the newspaper lies, for the press served, especially in connection with local news, rather to authenticate reports passing by word of mouth than to carry news in its fullness. The newspapers of that time, with their fine print, their long reports from the courts of Europe, and their polemical exchanges in learned literary style, replete with Latin quotations, were not directed to the general populace. Persons of this rank were expected to receive the more important messages contained in the fine print through reading aloud and through conversation at courthouses, ordinaries, and other places of assembly as news became part of the common stock of knowledge, opinion, and feeling.

There are a few records of explanations and exhortatory verbal forms addressed directly by the patriot gentry to ordinary men. On June 6, 1776, Landon Carter felt impelled to go to the Richmond County courthouse:

[T]here I endeavoured by my Conversation to Convince the People that the case of the Bostonians was the case of all America. . . . I farther hinted to our own Peo[ple] that as the People of Great Britain had seemed to be quite Patient under this Arbitrary Proceeding of their Parliament, it behoved us to have a little Commerce with them as Possible, and farther to refuse to do them the service to determine their suits for their debts since they had consented to a Manifest Violation of our whole Constitution. There seemed to be an assent to all I said and I do hope that at some meeting that our two representatives will be active soon in getting together [.] We shall all be Pretty unanimous in Associating against any Commerce or use of . . . Manufactures of Great Britain or of any Place that shall be passive in this grand affair of Liberty.[7]

Eleven days later it was reported to Carter that the common people felt that since they did not drink tea they were not involved in the current disputes.

A single text of a courthouse oration survives from the initial period of uncertainty. It was probably delivered in the summer of 1774 and was later sent to the printer with the explanation that it was "an address delivered to the inhabitants of a certain county in this colony . . . adapted to the understandings, and intended for the information of, the middling and lower classes of people." It was directed explicitly to those who lived primarily within the oral medium as may be seen from the observation that "your circumstances in life are such that you have little to do with *letters.*" The basic strategy was to open with an expatiation on the happy state of affairs before 1763 and on the willing and loyal compliance of Americans with the restraints placed upon them, and then to recite the list of British attempts at exploitation and encroachment, concluding with a series of rhetorical questions to which the orator supplied the response:

"But methinks I see the blood of *true Britons* swelling your veins, and hear you cry, with one voice, *We will be free.*" The heroic strain was muted, however, by the difficulties with which the speaker felt he had to deal. Social distance and social tensions were a significant part of the initial lag in the translation of the patriot gentry's sense of crisis into forms of communal action. "You are told, that the present dispute . . . is concerning the duty on *tea.* . . . Perhaps some of you may now tell me that it is a dispute with which you have nothing to do, as you do not make use of that commodity, and . . . that the *high-minded gentlemen* are . . . bringing you into difficulties to support their extravagance and ambition." But the courthouse orator firmly directed attention away from insignificant causes: "Is it possible that you can be so blind to . . . the oppression daily coming upon you from Britain? Can you suppose the *gentlemen* of all *America* would be so mad as to risk their lives and fortunes merely to save a trifling duty? . . . Are not the *gentlemen* made of the same materials as the lowest and poorest amongst you? . . . Have you found, in the course of your observations, that the *gentlemen* (as they are styled) are so very frugal and saving of their money as to bring themselves into the smallest difficulties for so small an advantage?" The speaker exhorted all ranks to unite "to preserve freedom to our posterity. Fortunes we shall not leave them, but we shall be despicable indeed if we tamely suffer them to become *slaves.*" The oration concluded with a tirade against the coercive acts, and an admonition: "On the virtue and courage of the people of these colonies does it depend whether we shall be happy or miserable."[8]

It is hard to judge speech from a written text, and the few reports we have cannot constitute a sample, but it does not appear that oratory was an important medium for the mobilization of ordinary Virginians. The language of secular political culture, in terms of which the literate gentry concerned the struggle, could not readily serve as a source of verbal expressions resonating with the worldview of a populace whose higher cultural orientations were to the Bible rather than the classics. The adulation bestowed on the one leader—Patrick Henry—who could obliterate this distinction indicates an exception so spectacular as to prove the rule. In general, it was through participation in patterned forms of communal action that the rallying process can be seen to have proceeded most effectively.

Since the coercive acts were the occasion for the crisis, dramatization of the plight of the Bostonians and of Virginia's identification with them played an important part in the activation of the patriot movement. Gentlemen like Landon Carter labored to fire such sentiments in the hearts of the freeholders, and ceremonies of concern soon began to be developed, fixing attention on the victims of oppression. Subscription lists were opened, involving the dramaturgical displays of a solemn public promise by gentlemen who, in the courthouse setting, offered an example to the community by "subscribing," in writing, to make a generous donation to the cause. The celebration of this patriotic zeal was a powerful means of intensifying commitment.

The social process involved is clearly revealed in a notice from Fredericksburg that "very liberal contributions have been made, in this place, for the relief of the poor in *Boston. Mr. Mann Page*, Junior, one of our Representatives, has taken uncommon pains to promote the subscriptions. . . ." An example of the community mobilization thus striven for is seen in the announcement late in July that "the county of Surry, from the highest to the lowest, are actuated with the warmest affection towards the suffering town of Boston . . . [and] that immediately after the meeting of freeholders and others . . . upwards of 150 barrels of Indian corn and wheat were subscribed . . . for the benefit of those firm and intrepid sons of liberty, the Bostonians." The printer went on to state that "it would be needless to recognize the particular generosity of each county . . . as . . . all Virginians are unanimous in their endeavours."[9]

Above all, when the county community was gathered at the courthouse, the quest was for unanimity. This was especially evident in what a hostile observer called "the grand meeting for signing the association." In Princess Anne County, to take a well documented example, the process evidently began in July, 1774, with "a meeting of a respectable body of Freeholders . . . at the Courthouse, for the purpose of choosing Deputies . . . and, of entering into resolutions expressive of the sentiments of the County in support of their just rights and privileges." One Mr. John Saunders alone "obstinately refused to sign the resolves though particularly solicited by some of the principal gentlemen then present." Subsequent events were to reveal the agony occasioned the county leaders by this open breach of solidarity. For this reason, perhaps, the official minutes passed over it in silence, noting that "the above resolution being unanimously agreed to, and signed . . . they then repaired to a place prepared for the occasion," where they drank a series of toasts expressive of unifying, patriotic sentiment. Three weeks later, at the courthouse again, "the Provincial Association . . . was read and offered the people that they might express their approbation by signing it." Once more Mr. Saunders dissented publicly. Eventually the county committee published an account of his recalcitrance and declared him an enemy to the American cause. (Such committees clearly embodied the traditional county community, for they contained a high proportion of the men who had formerly presided at the courthouse as justices. It was not unusual for the committees to meet on court day.)[10]

The reports of these county meetings at the courthouse reveal once again the dramaturgical possiblities available through the display of formal documents in a society where the written word was not yet commonplace. At the first meeting a set of resolutions was ceremoniously adopted. These were then embodied in a draft, prepared in a gentleman's library and cast in the Latinate language of the literary-legal culture of that age largely opaque to common folk, who, if they had any instruction in reading, had it in the very different language of the Bible. At the second meeting, three weeks later, the printed text of the Provincial Association, composed by some of the colony's most cosmopolitan gentlemen, was formally read aloud. This procedure was strongly calculated to dramatize the dominance of the culture of the gentry. Later, when the copies of such papers were handed about, literary and body-language media were spliced together, as public signing in a communal context gave to writing the character of dramatic gesture.

The account given by the Association committee of Princess Anne County of their tireless but unsuccessful efforts to persuade Mr. Saunders to adhere to the nonimportation agreement reveals the depth of the patriot yearning for communal unanimity and the special importance attached to the public dissent of a gentleman. His ultimate publication as an enemy to American liberty was a boundary-marking ceremony. Ostracism formally restored consensus by putting the dissenter outside the community. For a movement that conceived of itself initially as a defensive mobilization to preserve the threatened status quo, such rituals of detestation were of primary importance in defining the danger and amplifying the community's alarm at it.

The execution of symbolic figures in effigy had constituted, from the time of the Stamp Act, an important part of patriotic rituals in urban centers of other colonies. In Virginia such ceremonies were seldom staged, and on the occasions when they were attempted, they seem to have had little impact. There was at least one episode, made famous by the participation of the young James Madison, when a bundle of confiscated Tory pamphlets was ordered by the Orange County committee to be publicly burned, "which sentence was speedily executed in the presence of the Independent Company and other respectable inhabitants . . . all of whom joined in expressing a noble indignation against such execrable publications, and their ardent wishes for an opportunity of inflicting on the authors . . . and their abettors, the punishment due to their insufferable arrogance, and atrocious crimes." This was, however, an isolated instance; in Virginia such communal displays of execration almost always took the form of the socially and economically ruinous ostracism of enemies discovered within the community.[11]

It was more reassuring, and therefore more confirmatory of the values of communal harmony, when the denunciation of deviants was the preliminary, not to exclusion from the benefits of society, but to a public act of contrition on the part of the offender. The offenders might be moved by the general fervor for the cause to purge their guilt by confession. Thus "Silas Kirby, James Ingram [and others] Voluntarily appeared before [the Southampton County] committee, and acknowledged they had been guilty of violating the . . . association, by gaming . . . that it was an error they were unthinkingly led into, and are convinced of its evil tendency." The committee magnanimously declared that, although these men had been guilty, "yet, in consideration of their candid behaviour," they hoped that "the public will join in considering the aforesaid persons as not inimical to American liberty."[12]

Elaborate acts of contrition might be demanded, as in the case of Andrew Leckie, who had "attended at the courthouse for colonel EDMUND PENDLETON'S address to the people of Caroline County." After "the resolutions of the association were read in a company of people convened for the purpose of acceding to the association, and of raising contributions for the town of Boston," Leckie "was so unguarded and imprudent as to address [himself] . . . to a negro boy who was present in this indecent manner: 'Piss, Jack, turn about, my boy, and sign.'" For this indelicacy he was made to read before the committee and "a great concourse of people" on Caroline court day a full detailed confession and a hearty avowal of friendship to the principles and measures of the patriots, concluding with an open supplication "to regain the favour and good opinion of the public, an assurance of which would be the greatest consolation . . . under the insupportable weight of public censure and public hatred."[13]

The rituals of detestation and the striving to bring deviants into conformity were, in some sense, negative celebrations of harmonious community. Yet as popular enthusiasm became engaged, the movement also elaborated a set of rituals whose tendency was to affirm, in the face of doubt, the "virtue" of challenged Virginia society. The most direct of these rituals of affirmation were the enactments of frugality and industry. These were of particular importance because they served as palliatives to nagging doubts concerning the moral soundness of Virginia—anxieties over indebtedness (supposed to arise from luxurious extravagance) and over slavery (supposed to be the source of a debilitating indolence that exacerbated the same extravagance). Public declarations of frugality through the wearing of homespun also provided the patriot gentry with a means of setting an example to their inferiors while at the same time narrowing visible social distance as signalled by richness of apparel. George

Washington had reflected in a letter to George Mason on the occasion of the proposed anti-Townshend duty association of 1769 that it would be possible to check purchases "if Gentlemen in their several Counties would be at some pains to explain matters to the people, and stimulate them to a cordial agreement." The more he considered the scheme, the more ardently he wished success to it "because . . . there are private as well as public advantages to result from it." By being "curtail'd in . . . living and enjoyments . . . the penurious Man . . . saves the money, and . . . saves his credit . . . The extravagant and expensive man has the same good plea to retrench his Expenses. He is thereby furnished with a pretext to live within bounds . . . And in respect of the poor and needy man, he is only left in the same situation he was found, better I might say, because as he judges from comparison, his condition is amended in Proportion as it approaches nearer to those above him." Encapsulated in this statement, and in its enactment in the wearing of homespun, lay an epitome of the Whig-republican ideal for society. Distinctions of rank based on material fortunes were to be ennobled and legitimated by distinctions based on moral excellence.[14]

But true virtue in that face-to-face social order could not be "private" or individualistic. Ultimately it must contribute to, and draw from, a communal harmony (itself an oral-aural metaphor), which could most readily be restored and sustained by readiness to sacrifice oneself to the general good. The ideal of harmony in community was conceived in terms of a profoundly felt analogy between it and the healthy functioning of the human body, and so in terms of a complementarity, rather than an equality, of the parts. As the sound body was ruled by the head, its rational part, so society was expected to be ruled by the learned and liberal part, the gentry. As with the healthy body, however, all the members must be responsive to each other's true needs. It was to the affirmation of virtuous harmony or bodily health of this kind that the most subtle and the most important rituals were necessarily directed in a crisis the favorable resolution of which was believed to depend upon the moral soundness of Virginia society. The rallying to the support of Boston, the Association, the purging of unsound members, and the displays of frugality all contributed to this necessary demonstration, but the vital display could best come through the dramatization of the aspect of government most dear to the patriots, namely elections.

In order to understand the dramaturgical possibilities of elections we have to divest ourselves of nearly all our current assumptions. Trials of strength between contending interests and even popular choice between rival programs were precisely the lines upon which it was believed elections should *not* be conducted. Polling was a testing, face-to-face procedure in old Virginia, with the candidates confronting the voters over the table as the latter publicly declared their preferences. The true purpose, in accordance with the organic conception of society, was to enhance the authority of virtue, or right reason combined with manly courage. The idealization according to which the election process was to be judged had been set forth with superb clarity in a paper signed NO PARTY MAN, addressed to the freeholders of Accomac County in 1771. This broadside outlined the model which the patriots would seek to represent dramatically at the county courthouses. The voters should give their suffrages to gentlemen of "penetrating Judgement," able "to scan every Proposal, to view it in every Light . . . and, piercing into Futurity, behold even how remote Posterity may be thereby effected." The ideal representative should be "able to strip every Measure of that Disguise under cover of which it may be artfully obtruded on his Mind, and penetrate through all the sinister Disigns and Machinations of the Enemies of Freedom, the Slaves of Interest. . . . It is absolutely necessary that he be a Man of Probity . . . One who regards *Measures* not *Men*" and who will follow his country's interest regardless of the effect of his course upon either his friends or his foes. To this end he must have "that Fortitude or strength of Mind, which enable a Man, in a good Cause to bear up against all Opposition, and meet the Frowns of Power unmoved."[15]

The qualities demanded of the voters who were to select such a representative were scarcely less precious. To begin with, they were to be imbued with a strong sense of their exalted roles: "It is your greatest Glory . . . that you give Being to your Legislature, that from you they receive their political Existence. This renders an American Planter [i.e. farmer] superiour to the first Minister of an Arbitrary Monarch, whose glittering Robes serve but to veil from vulgar Eyes the Chains of Slavery. Guard it then, as the most precious Pledge committed to you by the Deity. Let every Gentleman's true Merit determine his Place in the Scale of your Interest." Altogether it is an inspiring vision conjuring up a sturdy yeomanry who with dauntless honesty would elevate, by their virtuous trust, the wisest and sternest of the "Gentlemen" to give laws and "to meet the Frowns of Power unmoved."[16]

Actual representations of this scenario, dramatically affirming the virtue that inspired the patriot cause, were enacted in a series of unanimous elections at the commencement of the final crisis in 1774. A single example will convey how the vision was translated into action. Rind's *Virginia Gazette* of July 14, 1774, reported: "On Wednesday . . . came on the election of burgesses to represent the county of Prince George in the ensuing general assembly, when the people, sensible that their late representatives had discharged their duty to their country, in opposing those baneful, ministerial measures, which have been lately taken to enslave this continent, and highly applauding those sentiments of union among the colonies which occasioned the dissolution of the last assembly, unanimously agreed to re-elect RICHARD BLAND and PETER POYTHRESS, esquires, who were returned without a poll being taken." This simple courthouse enactment—the acclamation of the representatives and the explanation of the reasons for according this honor—was highly effective in dramatizing to freeholders the awful menace of British power and the noble solidarity of Americans, as well as in engendering in them a glow of virtue at their participation in this brave defiance on a world stage.

There was another possibility. The affirmation of the highest political virtues might be combined with the affirmation of frugality, by the simple inversion of the time-honored custom of the candidates' treating the voters. On July 8, 1774, a "considerable number of the inhabitants of [Williamsburg] . . . met at the courthouse" to present an address to their representative, proposing that as they were "greatly scandalized at the practice which has too much prevailed . . . of entertaining the electors (a practice which even its antiquity cannot sanctify) and being desirous of setting a worthy example . . . for abolishing every appearance of venality (that only poison which can infect our happy constitution) and to give the fullest proof that it is to your singular merit alone you are indebted for the unbought suffrages of a free people . . . we earnestly request that you will not think of incurring any expence . . . but that you will do us the honour to partake of an entertainment, which we shall direct to be provided for the occasion."[17] Five days later the freeholders met their representative, "attended by many respectable inhabitants, at the courthouse . . . to elect him again . . . when he was immediately unanimously chosen." After the election the voters "conducted him to the Raleigh, where almost every inhabitant had met, a general invitation having been given by the generous electors, whose conduct . . . will be long remembered as a laudable . . . precedent, and highly worthy of every county . . . to adopt. Notwithstanding the festivity, and the pleasing, social intercourse, which here prevailed, harmony, decency, and decorum, were strictly maintained."[18] The gentry still showed their liberality by treating and patronizing the freeholders, but their role could now be freed of "every appearance of venality," while the prevailing "harmony, decency, and decorum" were signs of virtue diffused through all the ranks of the free community.

The dramaturgical possibilities available in the celebration of local notables were even more fully realized in the feting of the heroes of Virginia and America at large. In these ceremonies they and their cause could be celebrated in such a way that their own virtue and that of the people who identified with them were simultaneously affirmed. The sense of immediate engagement in drama on a world scale (already noted in the acclamation of the Prince George representatives) could thereby be most readily intensified. The patriot leaders, of course, owed a great deal of their charisma to their own sense that they were engaged in a momentous struggle in which the destiny of mankind would be determined. Peyton Randolph, Williamsburg's representative, Speaker of the House of Burgesses, and president of the Continental Congress, had this quality of transcending local and provincial forms of authority. He combined this with the manners and outlook of a "liberal" Virginia gentleman in the traditional style—a clubman at ease with persons of all ranks. We may see these elements united in the report of a ceremony that took place on May 28 and 29, 1775:

> Last Monday, about 10 o'clock, the WILLIAMSBURG TROOP OF HORSE left this city, well accoutred, in order to meet our good and worthy speaker on his return from the continental congress. Notwithstanding the inclemency of the weather, these hardy friends and supporters of American liberty pursued their journey with the utmost eagerness, while the most unfeigned joy diffused itself in every countenance.
>
> For order, good discipline and regularity, this company was greatly applauded. Ruffen's ferry was the place where they met the object of their wishes, whom, after giving three hearty cheers, they conducted until they arrived within two miles of the city, when they were joined by the COMPANY OF FOOT, who also gave three cheers, and shewed every other mark of decency and respect. The pleasing deportment of the speaker, on account of this peculiar honour done him, animated, in the highest degree, every person that attended; and on Tuesday, about 5 o'clock in the afternoon, the whole body arrived . . . surrounding the FATHER of his COUNTRY, whom they attended to his house, amidst repeated acclamation, and then respectfully retired.[19]

In the feeling expressed through the postures adopted (or believed by contemporaries to have been adopted) toward Peyton Randolph, we catch a vivid glimpse of the war in which the patriot movement momentarily evoked (or was intended by its leaders to evoke) the spirit of the traditional, deferential social order. But, as we see also in this account, men in arms were on the march. The struggle was unleashing forces that would not find their fullest expression in marks of "decency and respect."

The preceding accounts reveal how, in a set of tableaux vivants, communicating more than words could do, there was engendered a collective consciousness of belonging to a virtuous community, unanimously roused in support of its dearest rights. The Anglo-American ideal of civic virtue was not, however, confined to frugality and political incorruptibility, for it enshrined martial valor at its heart. Military rituals and occasions for the self-presentation of the warrior that was expected to exist in every free man had ultimately the greatest potential for stirring this aggressive, contentious people. During the initial phase of uncertainty in the summer of 1774, when the Association was being promoted as a peaceful measure, involving only "some inconveniences," warlike notes were not much sounded. By December, 1774, however, the governor reported to the home authorities that every county was now "arming a Company of Men, whom they call an independent Company." We may get a sense of this new development from the record of a gathering at the Fairfax County courthouse on September 21, 1774. The proceedings reflect the valiant endeavor to produce a moral regeneration of the old order by an ostentatious assumption of public burden on the part of the gentry. The minutes show that the gentlemen and freeholders who had attended were "hoping to excite others by . . . Example." They formed themselves into "the Fairfax independent Company of Volunteers," who would meet at times appointed for "learning and practising the military Exercise and Discipline, dress'd in a regular Uniform of Blue, turn'd up with Buff, with plain yellow metal Buttons, Buff Waist Coat and Breeches and white Stockings," and furnished with a complete set of arms and equipment. Further, they would keep by them considerable stock of powder, lead, and flints. On the principle of noblesse oblige, the gentlemen, who alone could afford this dress and equipment, were setting an example of valiant patriotism and at the same time incorporating the principles of popular government into their organization by electing their officers.[20]

By February, 1775, a plan "for Embodying the People" was being circulated in Fairfax County, and a new conception of uniform heralded the intrusion of more popular styles. The drive was now for a volunteer militia, "intended to consist of all the ablebodied Freemen from eighteen to fifty Years of Age." The enlistment of poorer men rendered the prescription of uniform impossible, but the proposal did call for those who could "procure Raphel Guns . . . to form a Company of Marksmen . . . distinguishing [their] Dress . . . by painted Hunting Shirts and Indian Boots."[21]

The shifting of the balance in favor of more popular assertion, as well as the excitement engendered by the rise of martial formations, became manifest during the next phase of Virginian patriot mobilization, after the governor seized the colony's store of gunpowder from the magazine in Williamsburg on April 21, 1774. It was the morning of Monday, April 24, when news of his lordship's coup reached Fredericksburg. "This being a day of meeting of the Independent Company," the assembled volunteers angrily considered the state of affairs and "came to a unanimous resolution, that a submission to so arbitrary an exertion of Government, may not only prejudice the common cause, by introducing a suspicion of a defection of this Colony from the noble pursuit, but will encourage the tools of despotism to commit further acts of violence." They informed the commanders of the companies in nearby counties that "this Company could but determine that a number of publick spirited gentlemen should embrace this opportunity of showing their zeal in the grand cause, by marching to *Williamsburgh.*" They declared that "to this end, they have determined to hold themselves in readiness to march as Light-Horse, on *Saturday* morning; and in the mean time to submit the matter to ... the neighbouring counties."[22]

The letters conveying so clearly a body-language sense of valiant war-like posture evoked immediate responses. The Prince William company was "called together .... and had the vote put whether they would march to Williamsburgh ... which was carried unanimously." Companies began to gather at Fredericksburg for a massive display of patriotism in martial array. The excitement, and the new tone that was becoming dominant, can be sensed in the words of a young gentlemen volunteer, Michael Brown Wallace, of Falmouth, who described for the benefit of his brother how the governor's action "occasioned upwards of 1,000 men to assemble together at Fredericksburge among which was 600 good Rifle men." He was sure that "if we had continued there one or two days longer we should have had upwards of 10,000 men [as] all the frontier Countys of Virginia were in motion ... [and that] Fredericksburge never was honour'd with so many brave and hearty men since it was a Town[.] evry Man Rich and poor with their hunting shirts Belts and Tomahawke fixed of [f] in the best manner." However, Wallace also reported that "thir was a Council of war held three days saturday sunday and monday [.] [T]he third day in the evening we were all draw'd up in ranks and discharg'd—some promise of the governor's delivery of the Powder."[23]

Patrick Henry, at the head of a body of men assembled at Hanover courthouse, was not so easily dismissed. He marched toward Williamsburg until some £330 was exacted from His Majesty's receiver general by way of reprisal for the confiscated powder. Henry was uneasy for an instant at the possible consequences of his action, but addresses from courthouses throughout the province revealed that the patriot movement was ready to go decisively into military action. He and his volunteers were con-gratulated upon showing "resentment" like true Virginians. When Henry rode off soon after to the second Continental Congress, he was feted on his journey by a succession of armed escorts. Ostensibly these were to protect him from arrest or insult; they were in fact a defiant celebration of patriotism in martial array.[24]

The new tone of the patriot movement—more popular and more

martial—was sharply and dramatically signalled by the appearance of the men in hunting shirts. These "brave hearty men" had honored Fredericks-burg with their presence in early May, 1775. By June a Norfolk Tory was writing home that Dunmore would only return to Williamsburg "provided the shirtmen are sent away" and explaining that "these Shirt men, or Virginia uniform are dressed with an Oznab[urg] Shirt over their Cloaths, a belt round them with a Tommyhawk or Scalping knife." The term initially had been applied by their enemies—"the damn'd shirtmen"—and then adopted as a badge of pride.[25] The revolution in cultural orientation that was taking place is most readily seen in the contrast of the shirtmen's attire with the "Uniform of Blue, turn'd up with Buff . . . yellow . . . Buttons. Buff Waist Coat and Breeches and white Stockings," appointed for the gentlemen of the Fairfax Independent Company. For all their in-tense provincial patriotism, the Virginia gentry had always boasted a strong Church and King loyalty and, looking to the English metropolis for cultural values, had tended to despise the "buckskin" of the back-woods. Now suddenly, the rifle-men from the west were the "heroes in huntingshirts," to whom even the most cosmopolitan gentlemen looked for protection. James Madison wrote on July 19, 1775, to a friend in Pennsylvania that "the strength of this Colony will be chiefly in the rifle men of the Upland Counties, of whom we shall have a great number." This sentiment occurs in a great many places and had evidently become almost universal. The intensity of the reorientation westward and the adoption of the new woodsman identity by the gentry can be seen in a published recommendation to the burgesses, before the assembly, called for June 1, 1775, that they attend in shirtmen's attire, "which best suits the times, as the cheapest and the most martial." The advice was taken, "numbers of the Burgesses" did attend in the uniform of "Coarse linnen or Canvass over their Cloaths and a Tomahawk by their Sides."[26]

The committee for Cumberland County, meeting in May, 1775, con-sidered the news of the battles of Lexington and Concord and resolved "that the Military Powers of this County be immediately collected and . . . that Wednesday the 10th . . . be appointed for a general Muster . . . and that all free Men be summoned . . . to appear at the Court House on that day" equipped with their arms.[27] Preparation for war was now the principal source of excitement for the patriot movement. The classical Graeco-Roman attitudes so characteristic of the early phases were being overlaid by more robust and popular styles. A blend of the two may be seen in the correspondence of Col. Adam Stephens who had written August, 1774, that in the Virginia Convention he "should expect to see the spirit of the Amphyctions shine, as . . . in their purest Times before Debauch'd with the Persian Gold." Later Stephens wrote that, having heard "that Lord North has declar'd that he has a Rod in piss for the Colony of Virginia," he wished he could see his lordship in America, for "in Spite of all the armies of Commissioners, Custom house officers and soldiers, I would make the meanest American I know piss upon him."[28]

With this last we are in touch with the scatological ribaldry of the military camp. Although this form of communication appears little in the written records, it represented an important aspect of that male warrior fraternity which was more decorously manifested in the stirring resolves of the spring and summer of 1775. In this ethos the country squirearchy, many of whose members were schooled in boxing and quarter racing, could hold their own, but social distance was inevitably reduced, special advantages derived from cosmopolitan education were diminished, and distinctions of rank were rendered less sharp. By the same confusions in society at large the momentary sense of a precious harmony was drowned and defense was abased, so that by the spring elections of 1776 the celebrated unanimity with which the freeholders of many counties had affirmed community virtue was replaced by "many . . . warm contests" in which even "Colonel Mason [was only] with great difficulty returned for Fairfax."[29]

The shift in dramaturgical forms from tableaux of civic virtue and constitutional loyalties to courthouse musters of men in hunting shirts inevitably contributed to the increasing alienation of Virginians from the mother country. No accounts exist of popular ceremonies at the courthouses directed to the dramatic "killing" or dethroning of the king. There was the vehement inversion with which this essay began; and something more of the persistence of old forms—and of the readiness to see them changed—is caught in a report of April, 1776, from Gloucester County: "We hear . . . that as the sheriff was opening the court . . . he was going to conclude with *God save the King*, when, just as he was about pronouncing the words a *five's ball*, struck by a soldier of the 7th regiment, entered the window, and knocked him in the mouth, which prevented him from being guilty of so much impiety."[30] Perhaps the impropriety of regicide enactments, before an alternative locus of sovereignty was declared, inhibited more deliberate performances—or the reporting of them.

In Williamsburg there was an official celebration of the formal decision of the Virginia Convention for independence on May 15, 1776. In accordance with ancient Virginia custom, "some gentlemen made a handsome collection for treating the soldiery." After a parade and salutes to the "American independent states," to congress, and to General Washington, refreshments were taken "and the evening concluded with illumination . . . and other demonstrations of joy." The report stated that everyone seemed "pleased that the domination of Great Britain was now at an end, so wickedly . . . exercised for these twelve or thirteen years past." It had already noted that independence was "universally regarded as the only door which will lead to safety and prosperity."[31] The matter of fact, even complacent, tone suggests that anguish at denying, once so strongly affirmed, was already over.

At a Court held for Lancaster County on the 18th Day of July, 1776. In Pursuance of the Ordinances of the general Convention of this Colony of Virginia, being the first Court . . . after the Establishment of the new Form of Government . . . and the Declaration for the Independency of the American States.
   James Ball, Gent., first Justice having taken the Oath prescribed by the Convention, administered the same to John Chinn . . .[32]

We seem to be witnessing a cyclical repetition as old forms reassert themselves. The patriots' Revolution came and went, the continuities in the life that ebbed and flowed about the courthouse were very great. The question about how much was changed by the Revolution, at the level of community life, still presents itself as one of the most often asked and least satisfactorily answered in the field of early American history. Approaching the question, we need to be less exclusively preoccupied with "social structures" conceived in terms of wealth and status. It will also be necessary to extend the new and fruitful interest in ideology and the symbolic order to include the media and dynamics of communication.
   We have been taught to think of the Revolution primarily in terms of its apparently timeless statements of principle, but those statements can only be understood historically in relation to the passions of the movement of which they were the fruit. The courthouse (or its equivalent elsewhere) was the central exchange point of that movement. It was the forum for the translation of the patriot gentry's essentially literary vision into a powerful communal enthusiasm, and for the counter-assertion of popular aspirations and identifications, as in the emergence of the "shirt-men" and the new cultural orientation they represented.
   The courthouse had been the place where, through formulaic oaths and ceremonies the source and nature of authority under a customary constitution had been continually intoned, to be learned and internalized. For the system of authority conceived and sustained in this way the Revolution substituted frameworks of government, delineated in written documents, immediately cast in type, multiplied in many copies, and soon to become milestones in the literate world of cosmopolitan culture. There were three newspapers in prerevolutionary Virginia, emanating from a single center. In the 1780s twelve new ones, from eight centers, appeared. For the 1790s

thirty-one newspapers have been listed from twelve centers.[33] At the oath-taking ceremony in Lancaster County on July 18, 1776, the courthouse community was on the threshold of a world, dominated by print—modernized—as it had not been before.

Bernard Bailyn

13 POLITICAL EXPERIENCE AND ENLIGHTENMENT IDEAS IN EIGHTEENTH-CENTURY AMERICA

The political and social ideas of the European Enlightenment have had a peculiar importance in American history. More universally accepted in eighteenth-century America than in Europe, they were more completely and more permanently embodied in the formal arrangements of state and society; and, less controverted, less subject to criticism and dispute, they have lived on more vigorously into later periods, more continuous and intact. The peculiar force of these ideas in America resulted from many causes. But originally, and basically, it resulted from the circumstances of the prerevolutionary period and from the bearing of these ideas on the political experience of the American colonists.

What this bearing was—the nature of the relationship between Enlightenment ideas and early American political experience—is a matter of particular interest at the present time because it is centrally involved in what amounts to a fundamental revision of early American history now under way. By implication if not direct evidence and argument, a number of recent writings have undermined much of the structure of historical thought by which, for a generation or more, we have understood our eighteenth-century origins, and in particular have placed new and insupportable pressures on its central assumption concerning the political significance of Enlightenment thought. Yet the need for rather extensive rebuilding has not been felt, in part because the architecture has not commonly been seen as a whole—as a unit, that is, of mutually dependent parts related to a central premise—in part because the damage has been piecemeal and uncoordinated: here a beam destroyed, there a stone dislodged, the inner supports only slowly weakened and the balance only gradually thrown off. The edifice still stands, mainly, it seems, by habit and by the force of inertia. A brief consideration of the whole, consequently, a survey from a position far enough above the details to see the outlines of the over-all architecture, and an attempt, however tentative, to sketch a line—a principle—of reconstruction would seem to be in order.

A basic, organizing assumption of the group of ideas that dominated the earlier interpretation of eighteenth-century American history is the belief that previous to the Revolution the political experience of the colonial Americans had been roughly analogous to that of the English. Control of public authority had been firmly held by a native aristocracy— merchants and landlords in the North, planters in the South—allied, commonly, with British officialdom. By restricting representation in the provincial assemblies, limiting the franchise and invoking the restrictive power of the English state, this aristocracy had dominated the governmental machinery of the mainland colonies. Their political control, together with legal devices such as primogeniture and entail, had allowed them to dominate the economy as well. Not only were they successful in engrossing landed estates and mercantile fortunes, but they were for the most part able to fight off the clamor of yeoman debtors for cheap paper currency, and of depressed tenants for freehold property. But the control of this colonial counterpart of a traditional aristocracy, with its Old World ideas of privilege and hierarchy, orthodoxy in religious establishment, and economic inequality, was progressively threatened by the growing strength of a native, frontier-bred democracy that expressed itself most forcefully in the lower houses of the "rising" provincial assemblies. A conflict between the two groups and ways of life was building up, and it broke out in fury after 1765.

The outbreak of the Revolution, the argument runs, fundamentally altered the old regime. The Revolution destroyed the power of this traditional aristocracy, for the movement of opposition to parliamentary taxation, 1760-1776, originally controlled by conservative elements, had been taken over by extremists nourished on Enlightenment radicalism, and the once dominant conservative groups had gradually been alienated. The break with England over the question of home rule was part of a general struggle, as Carl Becker put it, over who shall rule at home. Independence gave control to the radicals, who, imposing their advanced doctrines on a traditional society, transformed a rebellious secession into a social revolution. They created a new regime, a reformed society, based on enlightened political and social theory.

But that is not the end of the story; the sequel is important. The success of the enlightened radicals during the early years of the Revolution was notable; but, the argument continues, it was not wholly unqualified.

The remnants of the earlier aristocracy, though defeated, had not been eliminated: they were able to reassert themselves in the postwar years. In the 1780s they gradually regained power until, in what amounted to a counterrevolution they impressed their views indelibly on history in the new federal Constitution, in the revocation of some of the more enthusiastic actions of the earlier revolutionary period, and in the Hamiltonian program for the new government. This was not, of course, merely the old regime resurrected. In a new age whose institutions and ideals had been born of revolutionary radicalism, the old conservative elements made adjustments and concessions by which to survive and periodically to flourish as a force in American life.

The importance of this formulation derived not merely from its usefulness in interpreting eighteenth-century history. It provided a key also for understanding the entire course of American politics. By its light, politics in America, from the very beginning, could be seen to have been a dialectical process in which an aristocracy of wealth and power struggled with the People, who, ordinarily ill-organized and inarticulate, rose upon provocation armed with powerful institutional and ideological weapons, to reform a periodically corrupt and oppressive polity.

In all of this the underlying assumption is the belief that Enlightenment thought—the reforming ideas of advanced thinkers in eighteenth-century England and on the Continent—had been the effective lever by which native American radicals had turned a dispute on imperial relations into a sweeping reformation of public institutions and thereby laid the basis for American democracy.

For some time now, and particularly during the last decade, this interpretation has been fundamentally weakened by the work of many scholars working from different approaches and on different problems. Almost every important point has been challenged in one way or another. All arguments concerning politics during the prerevolutionary years have been affected by an exhaustive demonstration for one colony, which might well be duplicated for others, that the franchise, far from having been restricted in behalf of a borough-mongering aristocracy, was widely available for popular use. Indeed, it was more widespread than the desire to use it—a fact which in itself calls into question a whole range of traditional arguments and assumptions. Similarly, the Populist terms in which economic elements of prerevolutionary history have most often been discussed may no longer be used with the same confidence. For it has been shown that paper money, long believed to have been the inflationary instrument of a depressed and desperate debtor yeomanry, was in general a fiscally sound and successful means—whether issued directly by the governments or through land banks—not only of providing a medium of exchange but also of creating sources of credit necessary for the growth of an underdeveloped economy and a stable system of public finance for otherwise resourceless governments. Merchants and creditors commonly supported the issuance of paper, and many of the debtors who did so turn out to have been substantial property owners.

Equally, the key writings extending the interpretation into the revolutionary years have come under question. The first and still classic monograph detailing the inner social struggle of the decade before 1776—Carl Becker's *History of Political Parties in the Province of New York, 1760-1776* (1909)—has been subjected to sharp criticism on points of validation and consistency. And, because Becker's book, like other studies of the movement toward revolution, rests upon a belief in the continuity of "radical" and "conservative" groupings, it has been weakened by analysis proving such terminology to be deceptive in that it fails to define consistently identifiable groups of people. Similarly, the "class" characteristic of the merchants group in the northern colonies, a presupposition of important studies of the merchant in the revolutionary movement, has been questioned, and along with it the belief that there was an economic or occupational basis for positions taken on the revolutionary controversy. More important, a recent survey of the writings following up J.F. Jameson's classic essay, *The American Revolution Considered as a Social Movement* (1926), has shown how little has been written in the last twenty-five years to substantiate that famous statement of the Revolution as a movement of social reform. Most dramatic of all has been the demotion of Charles Beard's *Economic Interpretation of the Constitution* (1913), which stood solidly for over forty years as the central pillar of the counterrevolution argument: the idea, that is, that the Constitution was a "conservative" document, the polar opposite of the "radical" Articles of Confederation, embodying the interests and desires of public creditors and other moneyed conservatives, and marking the Thermidorian conclusion to the enlightened radicalism of the early, revolutionary years.

Finally, there are arguments of another sort, assertions to the effect that not only did Enlightenment ideas not provoke native American radicals to undertake serious reform during the Revolution, but that ideas have never played an important role in American public life, in the eighteenth century or after, and that the political "genius" of the American people, during the Revolution as later, has lain in their brute pragmatism, their successful resistance to the "distant example and teachings of the European Enlightenments," the maunderings of "garret-spawned European illuminati."

Thus from several directions at once have come evidence and arguments that cloud if they do not totally obscure the picture of eighteenth-century

American history composed by a generation of scholars. These recent critical writings are of course of unequal weight and validity; but few of them are totally unsubstantiated, almost all of them have some point and substance, and taken together they are sufficient to raise serious doubts about the organization of thought within which we have become accustomed to view the eighteenth century. A full reconsideration of the problems raised by these findings and ideas would of course be out of the question here even if sufficient facts were now available. But one might make at least an approach to the task and a first approximation to some answers to the problems by isolating the central premise concerning the relationship between Enlightenment ideas and political experience and reconsidering it in view of the evidence that is now available.

Considering the material at hand, old and new, that bears on this question, one discovers an apparent paradox. There appear to be two primary and contradictory sets of facts. The first and more obvious is the undeniable evidence of the seriousness with which colonial and revolutionary leaders took ideas, and the deliberateness of their efforts during the Revolution to reshape institutions in their pattern. The more we know about these American provincials the clearer it is that among them were remarkably well-informed students of contemporary social and political theory. There never was a dark age that destroyed the cultural contacts between Europe and America. The sources of transmission had been numerous in the seventeenth century; they increased in the eighteenth. There were not only the impersonal agencies of newspapers, books, and pamphlets, but also continuous personal contact through travel and correspondence. Above all, there were Pan-Atlantic, mainly Anglo-American, interest groups that occasioned a continuous flow of fresh information and ideas between Europe and the mainland colonies in America. Of these, the most important were the English dissenters and their numerous codenominationalists in America. Located perforce on the left of the English political spectrum, acutely alive to ideas of reform that might increase their security in England, they were, for the almost endemically nonconformist colonists, a rich source of political and social theory. It was largely through nonconformist connections, as Caroline Robbins' recent book, *The Eighteenth-Century Commonwealthman* (1959), suggests, that the commonwealth radicalism of seventeenth-century England continued to flow to the colonists, blending, ultimately, with other strains of thought to form a common body of advanced theory.

In every colony and in every legislature there were people who knew Locke and Beccaria, Montesquieu and Voltaire; but perhaps more important, there was in every village of every colony someone who knew such transmitters of English nonconformist thought as Watts, Neal, and Burgh;

later Priestly and Price—lesser writers no doubt, but staunch opponents of traditional authority, and they spoke in a familiar idiom. In the bitterly contentious pamphlet literature of mid-eighteenth-century American politics, the most frequently cited authority on matters of principle and theory was not Locke or Montesquieu but *Cato's Letters*, a series of radically libertarian essays written in London in 1720-1723 by two supporters of the dissenting interest, John Trenchard and Thomas Gordon. Through such writers, as well as through the major authors, leading colonists kept contact with a powerful tradition of enlightened thought.

The body of doctrine fell naturally into play in the controversy over the power of the imperial government. For the revolutionary leaders it supplied a common vocabulary and a common pattern of thought, and, when the time came, common principles of political reform. That reform was sought and seriously if unevenly undertaken, there can be no doubt. Institutions were remodeled, laws altered, practices questioned all in accordance with advanced doctrine on the nature of liberty and of the institutions needed to achieve it. The Americans were acutely aware of being innovators, of bringing mankind a long step forward. They believed that they had so far succeeded in their effort to reshape circumstances to conform to enlightened ideas and ideals that they had introduced a new era in human affairs. And they were supported in this opinion by informed thinkers in Europe. The contemporary image of the American Revolution at home and abroad was complex; but no one doubted that a revolution that threatened the existing order and portended new social and political arrangements had been made, and made in the name of reason.

Thus, throughout the eighteenth century there were prominent, politically active Americans who were well aware of the development of European thinking, took ideas seriously, and during the Revolution deliberately used them in an effort to reform the institutional basis of society. This much seems obvious. But, paradoxically, and less obviously, it is equally true that many, indeed most, of what these leaders considered to be their greatest achievements during the Revolution—reforms that made America seem to half the world like the veritable heavenly city of the eighteenth-century philosophers—had been matters of fact before they were matters of theory and revolutionary doctrine.

No reform in the entire Revolution appeared of greater importance to Jefferson than the Virginia acts abolishing primogeniture and entail. This action, he later wrote, was part of "a system by which every fibre would be eradicated of ancient or future aristocracy; and a foundation laid for a government truly republican." But primogeniture and entail had never taken deep roots in America, not even in tidewater Virginia. Where land was cheap and easily available such legal restrictions proved to be encumbrances profiting few. Often they tended to threaten rather than secure the survival of the family, as Jefferson himself realized when in 1774 he petitioned the Assembly to break an entail on his wife's estate on the very practical, untheoretical, and common ground that to do so would be "greatly to their [the petitioners'] Interest and that of their Families." The legal abolition of primogeniture and entail during and after the Revolution was of little material consequence. Their demise had been effectively decreed years before by the circumstances of life in a wilderness environment.

Similarly, the disestablishment of religion—a major goal of revolutionary reform—was carried out, to the extent that it was, in circumstances so favorable to it that one wonders not how it was done but why it was not done more thoroughly. There is no more eloquent, moving testimony to revolutionary idealism than the Virginia Act for Establishing Religious Freedom: it is the essence of Enlightenment faith. But what did it, and the disestablishment legislation that had preceded it, reform? What had the establishment of religion meant to prerevolutionary Virginia? The Church of England was the state church, but dissent was tolerated well beyond the limits of the English Acts of Toleration. The law required nonconformist organizations to be licensed by the government, but dissenters were not barred from their own worship nor penalized for failure to attend the Anglican communion, and they were commonly exempted from parish taxes. Nonconformity excluded no one from voting and only the very few Catholics from enjoying public office. And when the itineracy of revivalist preachers led the establishment to contemplate more restrictive measures, the Baptists and Presbyterians advanced to the point of arguing publicly, and pragmatically, that the toleration they had so far enjoyed was an encumbrance, and that the only proper solution was total liberty: in effect, disestablishment.

Virginia was if anything more conservative than most colonies. The legal establishment of the Church of England was in fact no more rigorous in South Carolina and Georgia: it was considerably weaker in North Carolina. It hardly existed at all in the middle colonies (there was of course no vestige of it in Pennsylvania), and where it did, as in four counties of New York, it was either ignored or had become embattled by violent opposition well before the Revolution. And in Massachusetts and Connecticut, where the establishment, being nonconformist according to English law, was legally tenuous to begin with, tolerance in worship and relief from church taxation had been extended to the major dissenting groups early in the century, resulting well before the Revolution in what was, in effect if not in law, a multiple establishment. And this had been further weakened by the splintering effect of the Great Awakening. Almost everywhere the Church of England, the established church of the highest state authority, was embattled and defensive—driven to rely more and more on its missionary arm, the Society for the Propagation of the Gospel, to sustain it against the cohorts of dissent.

None of this had resulted from Enlightenment theory. It had been created by the mundane exigencies of the situation: by the distance that separated Americans from ecclesiastical centers in England and the Continent; by the never-ending need to encourage immigration to the colonies; by the variety, the mere numbers, of religious groups, each by itself a minority, forced to live together; and by the weakness of the coercive powers of the state, its inability to control the social forces within it.

Even more gradual and less contested had been the process by which government in the colonies had become government by the consent of the governed. What has been proved about the franchise in early Massachusetts—that it was open for practically the entire free adult male population—can be proved to a lesser or greater extent for all the colonies. But the extraordinary breadth of the franchise in the American colonies had not resulted from popular demands: there had been no cries for universal manhood suffrage, nor were there popular theories claiming, or even justifying, general participation in politics. Nowhere in eighteenth-century America was there "democracy"—middle-class or otherwise—as we use the term. The main reason for the wide franchise was that the traditional English laws limiting suffrage to freeholders of certain competences proved in the colonies, where freehold property was almost universal, to be not restrictive but widely permissive.

Representation would seem to be different, since before the Revolution complaints had been voiced against the inequity of its apportioning, especially in the Pennsylvania and North Carolina assemblies. But these complaints were based on an assumption that would have seemed natural and reasonable almost nowhere else in the Western world: the assumption that representation in governing assemblages was a proper and rightful attribute of people as such—of regular units of population, or of populated land—rather than the privilege of particular groups, institutions, or regions. Complaints there were, bitter ones. But they were complaints claiming injury and deprivation, not abstract ideals or unfamiliar desires. They assumed from common experience the normalcy of regular and systematic representation. And how should it have been otherwise? The colonial assemblies had not, like ancient parliaments, grown to satisfy a monarch's need for the support of particular groups or individuals or to protect the interests of a social order, and they had not developed insensibly from precedent to precedent. They had been created at a stroke, and they were in their composition necessarily regular and systematic. Nor did the process, the character, of representation as it was known in the colonies derive from theory. For colonial Americans, representation had none of the symbolic and little of the purely deliberate qualities which, as a result of the revolutionary debates and of Burke's speeches, would become celebrated as "virtual." To the colonists it was direct and actual: it was, most often, a kind of agency, a delegation of powers, to individuals commonly required to be residents of their constituencies, and, often, bound by instructions from them—with the result that eighteenth-century American legislatures frequently resembled, in spirit if not otherwise, those "ancient assemblies" of New York, composed, the contemporary historian William Smith wrote, "of plain, illiterate, husbandmen, whose views seldom extended farther than to the regulation of highways, the destruction of wolves, wild cats, and foxes, and the advancement of the other little interests of the particular counties which they were chosen to represent." There was no theoretical basis for such direct and actual representation. It had been created and was continuously reinforced by the pressure of local politics in the colonies and by the political circumstances in England, to which the colonists had found it necessary to send closely instructed, paid representatives—agents, so called—from the very beginning.

But franchise and representation are mere mechanisms of government by consent. At its heart lies freedom from executive power, from the independent action of state authority, and the concentration of power in representative bodies and elected officials. The greatest achievement of the Revolution was of course the repudiation of just such state authority and the transfer of power to popular legislatures. No one will deny that this action was taken in accordance with the highest principles of Enlightenment theory. But the way had been paved by fifty years of grinding factionalism in colonial politics. In the details of prerevolutionary American politics, in the complicated maneuverings of provincial politicians seeking the benefits of government, in the patterns of local patronage and the forms of factional groupings, there lies a history of progressive alienation from the state which resulted, at least by the 1750s, in what Professor Robert Palmer has lucidly described as a revolutionary situation: a condition "in which confidence in the justice or reasonableness of existing authority is undermined; where old loyalties fade, obligations are felt as impositions, law seems arbitrary, and respect for superiors is felt as a form of humiliation; where existing sources of prestige seem undeserved . . . and government is sensed as distant, apart from the governed and not really 'representing' them." Such a situation had developed in mid-eighteenth-century America, not from theories of government or Enlightenment ideas but from the factional opposition that had grown up against a succession of legally powerful, but often cynically self-seeking, inept, and above all politically weak officers of state.

Surrounding all of these circumstances and in various ways controlling them is the fact that the great goal of the European revolutions of the late eighteenth century, equality of status before the law—the abolition of legal privilege—had been reached almost everywhere in the American colonies at least by the early years of the eighteenth century. Analogies between the upper strata of colonial society and the European aristocracies are misleading. Social stratification existed, of course; but the differences between aristocracies in eighteenth-century Europe and in America are more important than the similarities. So far was legal privilege, or even distinction, absent in the colonies that where it existed it was an open sore of festering discontent, leading not merely, as in the case of the Penn family's hereditary claims to tax exemption, to formal protests, but, as in the case of the powers enjoyed by the Hudson River land magnates, to violent opposition as well. More important, the colonial aristocracy, such as it was, had no formal, institutional role in government. No public office or function was legally a prerogative of birth. As there were no social orders in the eyes of the law, so there were no governmental bodies to represent them. The only claim that has been made to the contrary is that, in effect, the governors' Councils constituted political institutions in the service of the aristocracy. But this claim—of dubious value in any case because of the steadily declining political importance of the Councils in the eighteenth century—cannot be substantiated. It is true that certain families tended to dominate the Councils, but they had less legal claim to places in those bodies than certain royal officials who, though hardly members of an American aristocracy, sat on the Councils by virtue of their office. Councilors could be and were removed by simple political maneuver. Council seats were filled either by appointment or election: when appointive, they were vulnerable to political pressure in England; when elective, to the vagaries of public opinion at home. Thus on the one hand it took William Byrd II three years of maneuvering in London to get himself appointed to the seat on the Virginia Council vacated by his father's death in 1704, and on the other, when in 1766 the Hutchinson faction's control of the Massachusetts Council proved unpopular, it was simply removed wholesale by being voted out of office at the next election. As there were no special privileges, no peculiar group possessions, manners, or attitudes to distinguish councilors from other affluent Americans, so there were no separate political interests expressed in the Councils as such. Councilors joined as directly as others in the factional disputes of the time, associating with groups of all sorts, from minute and transient American opposition parties to massive English-centered political syndicates. A century before the Revolution and not as the result of anti-aristocratic ideas, the colonial aristocracy had become a vaguely defined, fluid group whose power—in no way guaranteed, buttressed, or even recognized in law—was competitively maintained and dependent on continuous, popular support.

Other examples could be given. Were written constitutions felt to be particular guarantees of liberty in enlightened states? Americans had known them in the form of colonial charters and governors' instructions for a century before the Revolution; and after 1763, seeking a basis for their claims against the constitutionality of specific acts of Parliament, they had been driven, out of sheer logical necessity and not out of principle, to generalize that experience. But the point is perhaps clear enough. Major attributes of enlightened politics had developed naturally, spontaneously, early in the history of the American colonies, and they existed as simple matters of social and political fact on the eve of the Revolution.

But if all this is true, what did the Revolution accomplish? Of what real significance were the ideals and ideas? What was the bearing of Enlightenment thought on the political experience of eighteenth-century Americans?

Perhaps this much may be said. What had evolved spontaneously from the demands of place and time was not self-justifying, nor was it universally welcomed. New developments, however gradual, were suspect by some, resisted in part, and confined in their effects. If it was true that the establishment of religion was everywhere weak in the colonies and that in some places it was even difficult to know what was orthodoxy and what was not, it was nevertheless also true that faith in the idea of orthodoxy persisted and with it belief in the propriety of a privileged state religion. If, as a matter of fact, the spread of freehold tenure qualified large populations for voting, it did not create new reasons for using that power nor make the victims of its use content with what, in terms of the dominant ideal of balance in the state, seemed a disproportionate influence of "the democracy." If many colonists came naturally to assume that representation should be direct and actual, growing with the population and bearing some relation to its distribution, crown officials did not, and they had the weight of precedent and theory as well as of authority with them and hence justification for resistance. If state authority was seen increasingly as alien and hostile and was forced to fight for survival within an abrasive, kaleidoscopic factionalism, the traditional ideas nevertheless persisted that the common good was somehow defined by the state and that political parties or faction—organized opposition to established government—were seditious. A traditional aristocracy did not in fact exist; but the assumption that superiority was indivisible, that social eminence and political influence had a natural affinity to each other, did.

The colonists instinctively conceded to the claims of the well-born and rich to exercise public office, and in this sense politics remained aristocratic. Behavior had changed—had had to change—with the circumstances of everyday life; but habits of mind and the sense of rightness lagged behind. Many felt the changes to be *away from*, not *toward*, something: that they represented deviance; that they lacked, in a word, legitimacy.

This divergence between habits of mind and belief on the one hand and experience and behavior on the other was ended at the Revolution. A rebellion that destroyed the traditional sources of public authority called forth the full range of advanced ideas. Long-settled attitudes were jolted and loosened. The grounds of legitimacy suddenly shifted. What had happened was seen to have been good and proper steps in the right direction. The glass was half full, not half empty; and to complete the work of fate and nature, further thought must be taken, theories tested, ideas applied. Precisely because so many social and institutional reforms had already taken place in America, the revolutionary movement there, more than elsewhere, was a matter of doctrine, ideas, and comprehension.

And so it remained. Social change and social conflict of course took place during the revolutionary years; but the essential developments of the period lay elsewhere, in the effort to think through and to apply under the most favorable, permissive, circumstances enlightened ideas of government and society. The problems were many, often unexpected and difficult; some were only gradually perceived. Social and personal privilege, for example, could easily be eliminated—it hardly existed; but what of the impersonal privileges of corporate bodies? Legal orders and ranks within society could be outlawed without creating the slightest tremor, and executive power with equal ease subordinated to the legislative: but how was balance within a polity to be achieved? What were the elements to be balanced and how were they to be separated? It was not even necessary formally to abolish the interest of state as a symbol and determinant of the common good; it was simply dissolved: but what was left to keep clashing factions from tearing a government apart? The problems were pressing, and the efforts to solve them mark the stages of revolutionary history.

In behalf of Enlightenment liberalism the revolutionary leaders undertook to complete, formalize, systematize, and symbolize what previously had been only partially realized, confused and disputed matters of fact. Enlightenment ideas were not instruments of a particular social group, nor did they destroy a social order. They did not create new social and political forces in America. They released those that had long existed, and vastly increased their power. This completion, this rationalization, this symbolization, this lifting into consciousness and endowing with high moral purpose inchoate, confused elements of social and political change—this was the American Revolution.

Winthrop Jordan

14 FAMILIAL POLITICS
Thomas Paine and the Killing
of the King, 1776

This exploratory paper attempts a probe into the problem of who killed George III and why. It seeks as well to inquire into the subliminal sources of popular political influence. It also raises indirectly the problem of how and indeed whether historians should explore such arcane instances of homicide. Granted any report concerning the death of George III in 1776 may be said in one sense to be greatly exaggerated. Nonetheless one can propose that in 1776 George III was killed in his American provinces vicariously but very effectively by an anonymous hand and that this act of murder constitutes a legitimate subject for historical inquiry. The American Revolution has been occasionally placed upon the couch for a brisk session of psychiatric analysis; the resulting diagnoses of American independence as a rejection of the British father have not been difficult. But they have also apparently not been wholly persuasive to the rather large number of historians who think that generalizations about a major historical event ought somehow to be tied to what "facts" are known about it.

If one looks at these "facts," and particularly at the public discussion during 1775 and during the first six months of 1776 about separation from Britain, one becomes impressed by the way Americans strummed persistently upon certain themes: that there was the utmost necessity for union among the colonies, that the British government had mounted a conspiracy to deprive American colonials of their rights, that Americans were threatened with outright enslavement, that Great Britain and especially the British government was steeped in corruption and degeneracy. These are familiar. Yet one theme which one might reasonably expect to find usually arose only implicitly: American patriots simply assumed that an independent America would be republican, that monarchy would come to an end in America once independence was declared. Perhaps this assumption is unsurprising, though historians do need some explanation as to why such an age-old, traditional institution as monarchy did not receive much discussion, pro or con. What is more arresting is that the one piece of political writing which everyone at the time acknowledged to have by far the greatest influence on the public mind contained a forthright attack upon monarchy itself. There were not many such attacks, and Thomas Paine's *Common Sense* was easily the most extended and the most vehement.

Taking American history as a whole, one can make a very good case for the proposition that, with the possible exception of *Uncle Tom's Cabin*, *Common Sense* was demonstrably the most immediately influential political or social tract ever published in this country. Its impact was noted by numerous contemporaries. In a famous comment, George Washington observed that "by private letters, which I have lately received from Virginia, I find 'Common Sense' is working a powerful change there in the minds of many men."[1] Abigail Adams, in thanking her husband for sending a copy wrote: "tis highly prized here and carries conviction wherever it is read."[2] A contributor to the *Connecticut Gazette* lavished extravagant praise upon the still anonymous author: "you have declared the sentiments of Millions. Your production may justly be compared to a land-flood that sweeps all before it. We were blind, but on reading these enlightening works the scales have fallen from our eyes; even deep-rooted prejudices take to themselves wings and flee away. . . . The doctrine of Independence hath been in times past, greatly disgustful; we abhorred the principle—it is now become our delightful theme, and commands our purest affections."[3] One of the earliest historians of the Revolution, a participant himself, explained that the pamphlet "produced surprising effects. Many thousands were convinced and were led to approve and long for a separation from the Mother Country. Though that measure, a few months before, was not only foreign from their wishes, but the object of their abhorrence, the current suddenly became so strong in its favour, that it bore down all opposition. The multitude was hurried down the stream. . . ."[4] It is certain, moreover, that *Common Sense* was widely read: some 120,000 copies were sold in the three months following publication in January, 1776. To match this figure for the American population today, the press run of a brief book would have to reach ten million.

It ought to be inquired, then, why *Common Sense* was so influential when it advanced a line of argument which American patriots did not seem interested in pursuing. Indeed it might be asked, more broadly, why this rambling, disorganized, and at times rather dull pamphlet was so popular and effective in disposing Americans to accept a final separation from the mother country. Part of the answer lies in Paine's racy, epigrammatic phraseology, in his discovering to Americans that "Government, like dress is the badge of lost innocence," that "there is something very absurd, in supposing a Continent to be perpetually governed by an island," that George III is "the Royal Brute of Great Britain."[5] It is difficult, however, to accept these zesty phrases as being altogether responsible for breaking the logjam of continued public attachment to the mother country. *Common Sense* was not the first public plea for independence, nor was it the only vigorous one. Historians need to look further, or rather more deeply, for some of the sources of its appeal.

A more analytic reading of *Common Sense* suggests how much of that appeal was essentially subliminal. To take one example before looking at Paine's assault upon monarchy, the opening discussion of the origin of government describes the state of nature in terms which implicitly but with the utmost clarity identify the beginnings of human society and government with the early settlement of America; in describing mankind living long ago in a state of nature Paine several times refers casually to those first people as "emigrant" without, of course, saying where these first people had emigrated from![6] At one level of logic this makes very little sense; at another, it makes a great deal.

Paine's discussion of monarchy and hereditary succession is even more heavily freighted with appeals to the unarticulated half-thoughts of his audience. For example, he rested a considerable portion of his case against monarchy on scripture, contending that "Government by Kings was first introduced into the World by the Heathens," that it was not until 300 years after the creation that the Jews, who had been living in "a kind of Republic," "under a national delusion requested a King"; that God warned them of the evils of kings before he permitted them to establish a monarchy; in short, that "Monarchy is ranked in scripture as one of the sins of the Jews."[7] It scarcely needs to be pointed out that there were in America many who would sense in Paine's remarks the force not merely of explicit scriptural injunction but of the analagous experiences of God's chosen peoples.

A similar utilization of the American experience may be found in some of Paine's more prosaic though no less aggressive attacks upon monarchy. As one would expect, Paine played his fire upon the luxury, extravagance, and dissipation which were natural to kingship. What is more impressive, Paine possessed a superb capacity for saying two things at the same time, for striking two blows in one sentence, one above and one below the probable threshold of consciousness of most of his readers. In some countries, Paine wrote, kings have no real "business" to conduct and they were always "sauntering away their lives"; in countries where kings are not absolute monarchs, Paine went on, "as in England, a man would be puzzled to know what *is* his business." Having thus described the King of England as possessed of no legitimate calling, Paine strikes his double blow: "The nearer any government approaches to a Republic," he declared in what was a not inaccurate description of the American colonies before 1763, "the less business there is for a King."[8] In this single sentence Paine had not only rendered monarchy antithetical to the Protestant ethic but also suggested that in America there existed no *need* for a king. With a single stroke he had rendered monarchy both reprehensible and superfluous.

Much the most striking instance of Paine's ability to play upon hidden chords of feeling was his proposal for the symbolic transfer of sovereign power from the king to the people of the American republic. This passage in *Common Sense* is of critical importance and deserves to be read carefully. "But where," Paine asks, ". . . is the King of America? I'll tell you Friend, he reigns above, and doth not make havoc of mankind like the Royal Brute of Great Britain. . . . let a day be solemnly set apart for proclaiming the Charter [of the new republic] ; let it [the charter] be brought forth placed on Divine Law, the Word of God; let a crown be placed thereon, by which the World may know, that . . . in America THE LAW IS KING. . . . But lest any ill use should afterwards arise, let the Crown at the conclusion of the ceremony be demolished, and scattered among the People whose right it is."[9]

We need to listen to the inner meaning of this extraordinary passage. Placement of a crown, the emblem of kingship, upon the charter of fundamental law imparts to the charter the king's power, his sovereignty. But this transfer is, as Paine says, dangerously insufficient. The crown, the king, must be "demolished." How? By breaking the crown, the king, into pieces—pieces which must be distributed among the people in order that they may acquire his power. The king is dead; his power is in the people.

It is scarcely possible to ignore the similarity of this ceremony to one which was and is traditionally performed in Christian churches. But one could for a moment be a good deal more outrageous than merely to suggest that Paine had fashioned a political eucharist. This ceremony was rooted in the prehistoric human past, in the days when men sometimes not only killed their father, the leader of the horde, but ate him in order magically to acquire his power. Admittedly, there seems to be a certain lack of hard data on this point, and no historian can properly feel altogether comfortable with such a lack. Yet a crucial and often overlooked distinction needs to be borne in mind: it is far less important whether one thinks such activities actually transpired than whether or not one thinks that men now and in this historical past act *as if* such prehistoric events took place. Given this distinction, it is possible to say a good many things about prehistoric man but it is not possible to say just any old thing, not if one has any notions about the nature of modern man. With these precautions in mind it is possible to advance quite seriously the following propositions: that human beings have worshipped the spirit of their father in the form of a tree, or, more commonly nowadays, in the form of a tree-like cross, and furthermore, that the story of the original sin of man as recorded in the third chapter of Genesis expresses man's sense of guilt for having eaten his fathers, his gods, by recapitulating these long forgotten crimes in the apparently innocent act of eating part of an apple tree.

Having made these suggestions, it will be well to turn again to Paine's aggressive assault upon monarchy and hereditary succession. The only historical evidence adduced to support the claim that Paine was killing the king has been derived from the internal content of his great pamphlet. Yet there are other kinds of evidence available, other ways of ascertaining the subliminal import of this, or any other important historical document. There seem to be at least three additional ways of getting at the inner meaning of any popular political tract. One is to inquire what needs the tract seems to have met in the people reading it. In the case of *Common Sense* one of these needs is obvious and well known: by January, 1776, after nine months of warfare, after being told by Britain that they were aiming at independence, after the American Prohibitory Act stopped their commerce, the colonists were surely ready for a plea of separation.

It is a good deal less obvious that Americans needed to have their king killed. There are in fact a great many indications that as late as 1776 there persisted within Americans a vague feeling that their king was somehow, in some measure, the legitimate father of his subjects. It is well known, of course, that Americans thought of their relationship with the king as being primarily contractual; they said outright that all political authority, including a king's, was based on compact. Nonetheless, when one attends to the imagery rather than to the explicit logic of American political writing in the Revolutionary era, it becomes clear that the age-old notion that a king stood in a paternal relationship with his people was not altogether dead.

Which may explain, indeed, why Paine called George III a "wretch ... with the pretended title of FATHER OF HIS PEOPLE."[10] It has been convincingly established that this notion existed in England in the late seventeenth century when John Locke spent so much effort attempting to demolish Sir Robert Filmer's contention that the basis of kingly authority was the paternal power which kings had inherited from the first father of mankind, Adam.[11] In 1775 the loyalist Jonathan Boucher actually attempted to resuscitate Filmer. In the same year another loyalist called the king "the provident father of all his people."[12] Such sentiments were not confined to those who remained loyal to the king, for in the years before the Revolution the colonial assemblies were referring to the "paternal Care"[13] of the king, to his "paternal regard,"[14] his "paternal Care and Tenderness,"[15] and were addressing him as "our most gracious Sovereign and Father"[16] and as "the father of all his people."[17] These and similar expressions were proffered by various churches, ministers, merchants, college presidents, and chambers of commerce. Nor were these terms simply pro forma: many addresses to or about the king did not employ them. Moreover, the analogy with parenthood was used in much more extended discussions of monarchy. Jonathan Mayhew, preaching on the anniversary of the execution of Charles I, argued that subjects ought to obey "when their prince exercises an equitable and paternal authority over them"; but that "when from a prince and common father, he exalts himself into a tyrant—when from subjects and children he degrades them into the class of slaves," then they ought to overthrow him.[18]

Utilization of this paternal analogy was by no means confined to rationalist clergymen like Mayhew. At the death of George II in 1760, for example, evangelical ministers like Gilbert Tennant eulogized him as "the *Father* of his People"[19] and urged Americans "to drop your filial Tears over the sacred Dust of your Common Father."[20] And when relations with Great Britain had reached nearly the breaking point in 1774, the Continental Congress solemnly petitioned George III "as the loving father of your whole people."[21] Finally, in the winter and spring of 1776 Americans began to call for independence because, as the freeholders of Charlotte County, Virginia, declared, "King George the Third . . . under the character of a parent, persists in behaving as a tyrant."[22] In light of these expressions there is a special meaning and poignancy in Abigail Adams' comment, made in January, 1776, just after her husband had departed to serve in the Continental Congress, that "Our Country is as it were a Secondary God, and the first and greatest parent." Like her husband, she was among those Americans who had decided well before publication of *Common Sense* that there was to be no "reconciliation between our, no longer parent State, but tyrant State, and these Colonies."[23]

The reasons for the persistence of this imagery are so complex and so tightly interwoven with centuries of political and social change that they cannot be even briefly summarized. The point to be made is that Paine's pamphlet helped meet the need of Americans—a need of which they were not fully aware—to deny their king as their sovereign father. At first their undeclared war against Great Britain seemed to them as it was so inces-santly dominated, "unnatural,"—like any violence between those who stood in the "natural" relation of parent and child. Here again, Paine struck precisely the right chord by calling George III a "brute," that is to say, as existing outside the legitimate arena of human relationships. Paine was able to help Americans to feel less filial and more, as it were, fraternal among themselves.

In addition to examination of the needs of his readers, there is a second obvious avenue for approaching the meaning of Paine's message. The circumstances of Paine's own life dovetail in a rough way with what has been suggested rather bluntly to be his patricidal accomplishments. His father was a Quaker and poor; his mother was an Anglican and the daughter of an attorney; his father was eleven years younger than his mother, and apparently they were not very happily married. Paine's extant references to his parents consist of affectionate ones concerning his father and none at all about his mother. Paine himself was married, rapidly widowed; remarried and soon legally separated; he never had children.

The lower status of his father may well have angered Paine, and his affectionate remarks may have masked a hostility he could not admit. His own inability to get along with women may have been owing to an in-ability to identify with his masculine parent. Armed with these facts it is possible to stretch Paine out on the couch and have at him. It seems, though, that because these data are so susceptible of various interpreta-tions and because so many attempts at this sort of analysis have been so patently disastrous, that one ought to shun speculation and turn to evi-dence concerning Paine's thought which can be interpreted without constant necessity of making completely unverifiable suppositions about what must, psycho- and historiologically, have happened in Paine's past.

For one thing, it is virtually certain that Paine borrowed from another writer most of the ideas he advanced concerning God's scriptural dis-approbation of monarchy. If John Adams' memory was correct, Paine had told him that he got his ideas on this subject from John Milton; certainly two of Milton's political tracts contain the same arguments as Paine's. What is particularly interesting in this circumstance is that Milton's tracts were written in defense of the killing of an English king. In defend-ing the execution of Charles I by Puritan revolutionaries, Milton had insisted that "Fathers and kings are very different things"; Milton's own attempt to "distinguish," as he said, "the rights of a father from those of a king" demonstrated that he rightly sensed that regicide and patricide were felt by many people to be equivalent.[24]

This circumstantial derivation acquires greater force when considered in the context of what Paine himself was writing during the year prior to publication of *Common Sense*. As editor of the *Pennsylvania Magazine* Paine wrote numerous anonymous articles, some of them straightforward essays, such as those in which he attacked duelling and Negro slavery, and defended (with arguments which have a very modern ring) defensive wars. More striking is that Paine wrote repeatedly, in various modes, about two subjects: marriage and the downfall of powerful men. A link between these two themes may be found in his "Occasional Letter on the Female Sex" where he cries: "Man, with regard to them, in all climates, and in all ages, has been either an insensible husband or an oppressor."[25] A similar link, and just possibly some of Paine's own background can be discerned in Paine's fanciful tale about Cupid's prevention of a marriage between a rich old lord of a manor and a shepherdess whose heart belongs to a young village swain. As they walk in the marriage procession Cupid casts the lord and the maiden into a strange sleep during which the two separately experience the unhappiness of living in their mismatched marriage. Finally they break out into unwitting soliloquies, "He exclaiming, she rejoicing; he imploring death to relieve him, and she preparing to bury him."[26]

Even more revelatory of Paine's thinking are his metaphors and fancies concerning men of wordly rank and power. In an essay assailing titles of nobility and official station Paine refers to "the possessors of undue honours" and says that "when their repeated guilt render[s] their persons unsafe, they disown their rank, and, like glow-worms, extinguish themselves into common reptiles, to avoid discovery."[27] Paine similarly applauds the enforced self-destruction of great men in his "Reflections on the Life and Death of Lord CLIVE," where he describes the lordly conqueror of India spreading war, rapine, and devastation before returning to England with glory and riches. Upon his second return, however, Clive is hounded by censure and finally laid low by disgrace and poverty; he sinks into "melancholy" and is "found dead at last."[28] Paine did not have to inform his readers that Lord Clive died by his own hand.

It seems reasonable to suppose that Paine's delight in fancying that men of power could be pressured into destroying themselves constituted a displacement of his desire to do the murderous work himself, a desire which was of course not consciously admissible. This displacement of aggressive hostility wears only the thinnest possible disguise in Paine's astonishing fantasy about Alexander the Great. Paine begins by saying that while he was walking near the Schuylkill River his mind fancifully crossed the Styx to see how the great conqueror was faring in the "Plutonian world." There he spies the approach of a splendid chariot and inquires which of the richly dressed riders is Alexander. He is told neither, that Alexander is one of the horses, but "*not always*" a horse, "*for when he is apprehensive*

*that a good licking is intended for him, he watches his opportunity to roll
out of the stable in the shape of a piece of dung, or in any other disguise
he can escape by.*" Later, as Paine is about to leave, he sees a bug on his
clothes; he is about to kill it when it screams out, *"Spare Alexander the
GREAT."* Thereupon, Paine continues—and his words need to be read
with care—"holding up the Emperor between my finger and thumb, he
exhibited a most contemptible figure of the downfall of tyrant greatness.
Affected with a mixture of concern and compassion (*which he was always
a stranger to*) I suffered him to nibble on a pimple that was newly risen on
my hand, in order to refresh him; after which, I placed him on a tree to
hide him, but a Tom Tit coming by, chopped him up with as little mercy
as he put whole kingdoms to the sword."[29] Thus ended Alexander the
Great: eaten off of a tree.

It seems not unreasonable to conclude that Paine was a person who
delighted in the destruction of tyrants and that he protected his own self-
image by compassionately nursing a tyrant whom he wished to destroy,
thereby denying that he, Paine, could harbor murderous passions. And it
also seems likely that a person who dwelt upon such fantasies could very
easily undertake, without of course fully knowing it, to kill a living king.

Having dealt as cautiously as possible with the personality of the
author of *Common Sense*, it is time to explore briefly a third way of
getting at its inner meaning. Since the pamphlet operated partly at an
affective, symbolic level, it ought to be helpful to look at the symbolic
content of Revolutionary thought and action. To what extent did such
content dovetail with the suggestions already advanced concerning *Common Sense*? In many ways there seems to be little connection, as for
instance, with the patriots' penchant for numerology and nocturnal
illuminations. There would appear to be more possibilities in the fact that
Americans thought of the colonies as being children of the "mother" or
"parent" (never "father") country and employed imagery of nurture
and maturation. Paine himself used this image. Far more pertinent, however, was the common and revealing utilization of—of all things—the tree.

It is well known that liberty trees and poles served as rallying points
for both the destructive and ritualistic activities of revolutionary crowds.
Precisely *why* is less certain. To gain some insight into the meaning, the
psychic content, of these symbols, scholars can turn cautiously to the
trees which appear in the political literature of the Revolution. One com-
mentator, for example, ridiculed American patriots for "*Assembling in
the open Air*, and performing *idolatrous* and *vociferous* Acts of Worship,
to a Stick of Wood."[30] Perhaps there was a grain of truth in the charge.
Paine himself wrote a poem about the Liberty Tree which the Goddess
of Liberty had planted in America.

The fame of its fruit drew the nations around,
To seek out this peaceable shore.
Unmindful of names or distinctions they came,
For freemen like brothers agree,
With one spirit endued, they one friendship pursued,
And their temple was *Liberty tree.*[31]

While these lines reveal that Paine was a better pamphleteer than poet, they also make clear that it was the *brother*hood of the worshippers which mattered. Who indeed actually assembled about those trees in America but the *Sons* of Liberty, sons who presumably could not have two fathers. In England similar opponents of the government were called not the "Sons" but the "Friends of Liberty."

This suggestion that the tree of liberty in America constituted a new sovereign is perhaps not so tenuous or gratuitous as it may at first appear. The trees which one finds in the political writing of the revolutionary era were used, more or less explicitly, to represent government. In *Common Sense* Paine explained that when men first abandoned the state of nature to form a "government," "some convenient Tree will afford them a State-House."[32] More metaphorically he linked the future development of America's "Continental union" to the growth of an oak tree.[33] A similar association forms the entire basis for a fanciful political tract written by Francis Hopkinson in April, 1776. Through the mouth of a seer living in the remote past Hopkinson describes the peopling of America and then explains: "And it shall be that the king of islands shall send over and plant in the midst of them a certain tree. . . . And the people shall cultivate this tree with all possible care, and they shall live under the shadow of its branches, and shall worship it as a God. But in process of time shall arise a *North* wind, and shall blast the tree, so that . . . it shall become rotten at the heart." Then Hopkinson has a "prophet" with "spectacles upon his nose" (already Franklin was a sage) "cry aloud and say, 'Seeing that this tree . . . is become rotten . . . behold now, let us cut it down and remove it from us: And in its place we will plant another tree, young and vigorous; and we will water it, and it shall grow. . . .'" After carrying on in this vein Hopkinson concludes that "the people shall dwell under the shadow of its branches, and shall become an exceeding great, powerful, and happy nation."[34]

What is even more arresting than these analogies is the protest of loyalists against the prospect of independence. Boucher objected that "We were not lopped off the parent trunk as useless or noxious limbs, *to be hewn down or cast into the fire*; but carefully transplanted here."[35] In a somewhat different vein, Boucher and John Dickinson described "independency" as "forbidden fruit"[36] and as "a tree of forbidden and accursed fruit."[37] Peter Van Schaack lamented that "the people of this country seem determined to lop off every excrescence from the body politic. Happy if they can stop at the true point, and in order to obtain the fruit . . . do not cut down the tree."[38] In short, opponents of independence were metaphorically equating the overthrow of the crown's authority with destruction of a tree or with consumption of a portion of a tree.

A climax in the symbolic destruction of royal authority—and also the acting out of Paine's proposed public ceremony—may be detected in the days following the formal public readings of the Declaration of Independence. In Savannah, Georgia, a large crowd attended "a very solemn funeral procession" in recognition of the demise of King George III; the crowd included "a greater number of people than ever appeared on any occasion before in this province."[39] In New York City, during the evening after proclamation of the Declaration in the presence of Washington and his troops, a crowd led by the Sons of Liberty gathered around the gilded equestrian statue of George III and, as a contemporary described what followed, the statue "was taken down, broken into pieces, and its honor levelled with the dust,"[40] or, as another observer said, "was by the sons of freedom laid prostrate in the dirt."[41] Elsewhere in the city, and indeed in most or all of the thirteen colonies, the king's arms (usually made of carved and painted wood) were taken down and in most cases destroyed. The royal arms in churches and painted on tavern signs were cut down. In Boston even such royal emblems as shop signs decorated with crowns and royal lions were thrown into a bonfire in King Street. In Providence the king's arms were taken from the Colony House and from the Crown Coffee House and burned before a crowd. Patriots in Baltimore carried an effigy of the king through the town and then threw it into a fire. In Worcester it was reported that "the Arms of that Tyrant in Britain, George III" which hung on the court house "were committed to the flames and consumed to ashes."[42] From New York City came a similar report: "the coat of arms of his majesty George III was torn to pieces and burnt, in the presence of the spectators."[43] It is difficult to see how much more effectively, while still safely, Americans could kill their king than to gather about a fire while the emblem of his authority was, as the Worcester report said, "consumed." Yet an observer in Boston described a scene which recapitulated even more vividly the political eucharist which Paine had described: "In the afternoon the King's Arms were taken down and broken to pieces in the street, and carried off by the people."[44] The American people had not only declared their independence but had taken to themselves the power of their king.

This is to say that what our textbooks call the idea of "popular sovereignty" contained within it a substratum of psychic meaning which needs to be considered as both a part of that idea and as having provided a portion of the energy which went into its implementation. To claim more is to claim too much, but to claim less is to ignore an aspect of historical reality.

As for Paine, it can be claimed that he performed a vital service to Americans—but a momentary one: the sons of the Revolution soon lapsed into acclaiming their staunchest leader as the Father of His Country.

Thomas C. Barrow

15 THE AMERICAN REVOLUTION AS A COLONIAL WAR FOR INDEPENDENCE

The current historiographical controversies over the American Revolution owe much to Carl Becker. From Becker's day to the present, historians have debated the question of the existence or non-existence of an "internal revolution" in American society. Some historians, following Becker's lead, search for traces of internal social or political turmoil. Others, disagreeing with Becker, stress the continuity of institutions and traditions during the Revolution. At issue is the basic question of just "how revolutionary was the American Revolution," and in the failure of historians to agree on an answer to that question lies the source of controversy. And so the great debate continues.

Unfortunately, there is no adequate definition of a "revolution." The dictionary description of a revolution as a "total or radical change" certainly provides no effective guideline. Since history is the study of change in human society, locating a revolution according to that formula becomes a matter of appraising just how much change is involved in a given event, which inevitably comes down to a question of where one wants to place the emphasis. In any case, precise definitions are somewhat beside the point. When the word "revolution" is used today in connection with a political system, its meaning, if not its precise definition, is abundantly clear. The image called to mind is inescapably that of the French and Russian revolutions, which have provided us with our classic formulas for revolutionary re-structurings of society. A revolution in these terms represents the replacement of an archaic, repressive regime or regimes with something new, something more open, more flexible, more adaptable. In effect, in the interests of "progress," within the political system stability is replaced by instability until some new synthesis is achieved. Only then is stability restored, at which point the revolutionary drama is closed.

For generations now American historians have struggled to fit their "revolution" into this classic mold. The difficulties they have encountered in doing so are reflected in the present historiographical impasse. It is a problem that might have been avoided had we remembered that the American people were, until 1776, colonials. By its very nature, a colonial society must be, in certain vital ways, unstable. Unable to exercise complete political control, subject to continual external intervention and negative interference, a colonial society cannot achieve effective "maturity"—that is, cannot create and control a political system that will be suited to the requirements of the interests indigenous to that society. A colonial society is an "incomplete" society, and consequently an inherently unstable society. This was as true of American society prior to 1776 as it is today of the colonial societies left in our world. And consequently, if instability is the given fact in American society at the beginning of the imperial crisis, it is hard to see how the classic pattern of "stability replaced by instability" can be imposed upon it. The answer, of course, is that it cannot, that in fact colonial wars for independence or "liberation" are generally different from revolutions of the French or Russian variety. And, after all, the American Revolution was just that—a colonial war of liberation. Given the widespread existence of such wars in today's world, it is odd that for so long a time we have overlooked the full implications of this fact.

Colonial wars for independence have an inner logic of their own. The first problem is to achieve self-determination. Once that is accomplished, it then becomes a matter of organization, about which, naturally, there always will be fundamental disagreement. What course this disagreement will take, and how bitter it will be, will be determined by the nature of the particular society. In former colonies which have emerged into nationhood in this century, the determining factor has largely been the heterogeneous nature of their societies; with little internal unity or coherence, these new nations generally have fallen back at first on authoritarian centralism. When this has proved incapable of solving the complex problems confronting the society, it has been replaced usually by some kind of collective leadership, often based on the only effective national organization in existence, the military. It is at this point that many of the emergent nations of today find themselves.

Americans were more fortunate in their escape from colonialism. Thanks to the nature of the First British Empire, with its emphasis on commercial growth rather than on imperial efficiency, its loose organization, and the high degree of self-government allowed to the colonists,

Americans had developed effective political units which commanded the allegiance of most inhabitants and served as adequate vehicles for the transition from colonial status to nationhood. Given a common English inheritance and a common struggle against British "tyranny," these states made the transition with a minimum of disagreement and dissension. In effect, by 1760 self-government in America, while still incomplete, had gone far. A tightening of English imperial authority after the last war with France brought about a reaction within the colonies toward complete self-determination, which was achieved finally through military success.

Yet, whatever the difference of the American experience from other colonial wars of liberation, certain elements were of necessity shared in common. Within any colonial society there exists an establishment, a group of men whose interests and situation tie them to the existing structure and whose orientation is towards the preservation of the colonial status. When the issue of independence or self-determination begins to be debated, these men are caught in powerful crosscurrents. As natives to the society, they identify to some degree with its problems. At the same time, as beneficiaries of their privileged position within the existing colonial structure, they are not enthusiastic for change. Such men fall back on arguments of moderation, particularly stressing the economic benefits of association with the dominant country and also emphasizing the immaturity of their own society. The gains associated with independence are outweighed for them by the prospects of social and political disorganization. So these men cast their lot with their colonial rulers. Such a man was Thomas Hutchinson. So, too, were many of his Tory associates.

And men like Hutchinson found much to disturb them within American society. Actually, not only was American colonial society subjected to the instability normally inherent in colonial status but there were certain peculiar circumstances which complicated matters further. The melting-pot aspects of American society, the diversity of ethnic, religious, and cultural backgrounds to be found within it, created problems of communication. And, of equal importance, American colonial society was, after all, an artificial creation. Unlike most other historic colonial episodes, the American case was not a matter of an indigenous native society being expropriated and exploited by outsiders. In such instances, the pre-existing patterns of such native societies provide a degree of internal continuity and stability. But the English colonies in North America had at their disposal no such pre-existence. They were created specifically and artificially to perform certain functions in relation to the mother country. Most particularly, from the very beginning their economy was geared to production for distant markets over which they had no control and little influence.

At the same time, while there were sizeable, non-English elements within the colonial population which created special problems, nevertheless the majority of the colonists were of the same national origin as their "rulers." It was not an instance of a conquered native population forced to bow fatalistically before the superior skills and power of an alien culture. Rather, it was a case in large part of Englishmen being governed and exploited by Englishmen. The result was a high degree of friction between governed and governors—an insistence by the colonists on their rights as Englishmen—that gave a special flavor and complexity to colonial politics.

Thoughtful colonials were well aware of and influenced by these problems. Thomas Hutchinson and John Adams—Tory and Whig—disagreed not so much on the question of the eventual independence of the American colonies as on the question of timing. Hutchinson's Toryism sprang in part from his conviction that American society was too immature, too unstable, to stand alone. External force and authority, it seemed to him, would be required for many years to maintain internal order and stability in America. Realistically, he understood that eventually independence was probable; "It is not likely that the American Colonies will remain part of the Dominions of Great Britain another century."[1] But, Hutchinson added, until then, "as we cannot otherwise subsist I am consulting the best interest of my country when I propose measures for maintaining this subjection [to England]."[2] What particularly disturbed Hutchinson about the changes in English policy after 1760 was that they tended to increase the instability and disorder inherent within American society: "Sieur Montesquieu is right in supposing men good or bad according to the Climate where they live. In less than two centuries Englishmen by change of country are become more barbarous and fierce than the Savages who inhabited the country before they extirpated them, the Indians themselves."[3]

John Adams viewed American development in a different way. Contrasting the New World with the Old, he found the former far superior. The settlement of America had produced men who "knew that government was a plain, simple, intelligible thing, founded in nature and reason, and quite comprehensible by common sense. They detested all the base services and servile dependencies of the feudal system . . . and they thought all such slavish subordinates were equally inconsistent with the constitution of human nature and that religious liberty with which Jesus had made them free."[4] The problem was that this purity of mind and behavior was always threatened by contact with the corruption of the Old World. Specifically, subordination of Americans to a distant Parliament which knew little of their needs and desires was not only frustrating but dangerous to the American experiment: "A legislature that has so often discovered a want of information concerning us and our country; a legislature interested to lay burdens upon us; a legislature, two branches of which, I mean the lords and commons, neither love nor fear us! Every American of fortune and common sense, must look upon his property to be sunk downright one half of its value, the moment such an absolute subjection to parliament is established."[5] Independence was a logical capstone to such reasoning, although it took Adams some time to take that final step.

The differences between Hutchinson and Adams suggest that the divisions in American society between conservatives and radicals on the question of separation from Great Britain were related in part to a disagreement over the means to achieve coherence or stability within American society. For one side, continued tutelage under English authority was a necessity until such a time as maturity was achieved. For the other, it seemed that the major roadblock to maturity, to internal harmony and unity, was that selfsame English authority. In effect, it was a disagreement on means, not ends. And disagreements similar to that between Hutchinson and Adams can be found within any society—whether in the eighteenth or twentieth century—which is in the process of tearing itself loose from its colonial ties.

It is possible, too, to suggest certain similarities between American intellectual development in these years and the experience of other colonial peoples. From his study of politics in eighteenth-century America, and particularly from his analysis of the pamphlet literature of the revolutionary years, Bernard Bailyn has concluded that the "configuration of ideas and attitudes" which comprised the "Revolutionary ideology could be found intact—completely formed—as far back as the 1730's" and that these ideas had their origin in the "transmission from England to America of the literature of political opposition that furnished the substance of the ideology of the Revolution."[6] Colonial societies are both fascinated and yet antagonized by the culture of the dominant exploiting nation. They tend to borrow much from their rulers. The English background of a majority of the American colonists in their case made such borrowing a natural and easy process, particularly for those who for one reason or another, identified themselves with British rule.

However, in colonial societies even many of those who are anxious to assert, or preserve, their native interests or culture cannot resist that fascination exerted by the dominant "mother country." These "patriots" borrow, too, but they are likely to borrow from the dissenting tradition within the dominant culture, from the literature of "opposition," to utilize in their own defense the language and literature of those elements within the ruling society which are critical, or subversive, of the governing traditions. In this way the prestige of the "superior" society can be used against that society itself. On the evidence of Bailyn's research, it seems that the Americans followed just such a line of development, fitting the "opposition" tradition into the framework of their own evolving institutions and traditions—a process which was facilitated by the natural connections between the American religious dissenting traditions and the "opposition" traditions of eighteenth-century English society.

Again, once the movement for independence enters its final phase within a colonial society and becomes an open contest of strength, other divisions tend to become obscured. The most determined supporters of the colonial rule are silenced or forced to rely increasingly on the military strength of their rulers to maintain their position. On the other side, the advocates of independence submerge momentarily whatever differences they may have and present a common front. It is a time of common effort, of mutual support within the forces interested in achieving self-determination. At the same time the "patriot" groups develop special organizations capable of coercing those elements within society, often a majority of the population, which are inclined toward neutrality or moderation. Such were the Sons of Liberty in the American Revolution, and the evidence suggests that they performed their work effectively. Partly because of their efforts, and more generally because of the peculiar character of American colonial society and the nature of the imperial conflict, American society weathered the crisis with relative stability and harmony. As John Adams put it, "The zeal and ardor of the people during the revolutionary war, supplying the place of government, commanded a degree of order, sufficient at least for the temporary preservation of society."[7]

With independence come altered circumstances for a former colonial society. Victorious patriots, confronted with the task of creating a permanent political structure, gradually begin to disagree among themselves as to how it can best be done. Since the only effective central direction came previously from the colonial rulers, the problem in each newly independent society is to fit the surviving local units into some coherent national structure. Here the forces of localism and centralism come into conflict. Those men or interests firmly entrenched in their positions at the local level see in increased centralism a threat to their existence and power. On the other hand, those men or interests of a more cosmopolitan nature, geared to extra-local activities and contacts, can see the benefits that would accrue to them through the introduction of the smoother flow of communications and transactions that effective centralization would bring. The disagreement pits the particularism of the entrenched local interests and individuals against the nationalism of the cosmopolitan interests and individuals. In most contemporary emergent societies these latter groups are by far the weaker. Fortunately, in America, the cosmopolitan groups were stronger and more effective, partly again because of the unusual origin and nature of American colonial society. From the beginning the English colonies had been geared to production for European markets; it was the reason for their existence. The result was the development of an economy which had geographical variations but a common external orientation. Merchants and large-scale producers of items for export dominated this society. In the period after independence was achieved, these men provided a firm base for the construction of an effective national political system. Their success came with the substitution of the Constitution of 1787 for the Articles of Confederation.

Historians following the Becker-Beard approach put a different interpretation on the period following the achievement of de facto independence. For them, it was the moment of the triumph of radical democratic elements, within American society. The wording of the Declaration of Independence, the constitutions of the new state governments, and particularly the drawing up of the Articles of Confederation represent for these historians the influence of a form of "radicalism." Yet, as Elisha Douglass has noted, in the formation of the governments for the new states, rather puzzlingly the one political reorganization that was subjected to the most democratic method of discussion and adoption—that of Massachusetts—turned out to be not only the most conservative of all the state constitutions but more conservative, in fact, than the previous system.[8] Somehow in Massachusetts, at least, an excess of democracy seems to have led to an enthronement of conservatism. And, indeed, the new constitutions or systems adopted in all the states were remarkable generally for their adherence to known and familiar forms and institutions.

Obviously, given the disruption of the traditional ties to England, the interruption of the natural economic dependence on English markets, the division of American society into opposing Whig and Tory camps, and the presence on American soil of enemy troops (which occupied at different moments the most important commercial centers), some confusion and dissension was inevitable within American society. What is remarkable is how little upheaval and disagreement there actually was. Had American society been ripe for a social upheaval, had it been comprised of oppressing and oppressed classes, no better opportunity could have been offered. The conservative nature of the American response suggests that something other than a radical re-structuring of society was what was debated or desired.

Again, some historians have interpreted the decentralized political system created under the Articles of Confederation as a "triumph" of radical democracy. However, if instability, associated with colonial status and with the peculiar character of American colonial society, was a recurrent problem, and if inability to achieve positive control of their own political system was a major irritant, then the decentralization of the Articles was a logical development. In effect, if home rule was the issue and the cure, it was only natural that each local unit should seek as much autonomy within the national framework as possible. Seemingly, decentralization was the best method to bring coherence and stability, or maturity, to American society. Each local unit could look to its own needs, could arrange for the effective solution of its own special problems, could work to create that internal balance and harmony of conflicting interests that are the earmark of stability and maturity.

The problem with the Articles was not an excess of democracy. What brought about an effective opposition to them was their failure to achieve their purpose. The history of the states under the Articles, at least in the eyes of many contemporaries, suggested that decentralization, rather than being a source of stability, was a source of confusion and turmoil. James Madison explained the nature of the mistake in his Tenth Federalist. In spite of independence, under the system created by the Articles, wrote Madison, "complaints are everywhere heard from our most considerate and virtuous citizens . . . that our governments are too unstable." The problem, for Madison, was to control faction within society, and the most dangerous type of faction is that which includes a majority. Unfortunately, the "smaller the society, the fewer probably will be the distinct parties and interests composing it; the fewer the distinct parties and interests, the more frequently will a majority be found of the same party; and the smaller the number of individuals composing a majority, and the smaller the compass within which they are placed, the more easily will they concert and execute their plans of oppression." The solution is to enlarge the sphere, because if "you take in a greater variety of parties and interests," then "you make it less probable that a majority of the whole will have a common motive to invade the rights of other citizens. . . . The influence of factious leaders may kindle a flame within their particular State, but will be unable to spread a general conflagration through the other States."[9]

Nor was the opposition to the Constitution less concerned than Madison about order and stability within society. Again, disagreement was fundamentally over means, not ends. The anti-Federalists clung to the former ideas of local autonomy. They were, in fact, not more democratic than their opponents but more conservative. They were afraid of change: "If it were not for the stability and attachment which time and habit gives to forms of government, it would be in the power of the enlightened and aspiring few, if they should combine, at any time to destroy the best establishments, and even make the people the instruments of their own subjugation." The trouble was that the system created under the Articles was not yet sanctified by time: "The late revolution having effaced in a great measure all former habits, and the present institutions are so recent, that there exists not that great reluctance to innovation, so remarkable in old communities . . . it is the genius of the common law to resist innovation."[10] George Clinton agreed with Madison on the dangers of faction: "The people, when wearied with their distresses, will in the moment of frenzy, be guilty of the most imprudent and desperate measures. . . . I know the people are too apt to vibrate from one extreme to another. The effects of this disposition are what I wish to guard against."[11] It was on the solution to the problem, not on the nature of the problem, that Clinton differed from Madison. For Clinton, the powerful central government created by the Constitution might too easily become a vehicle for popular tyranny. It was this same sentiment which led eventually to the adoption of the first ten amendments, the Bill of Rights, with their reservations of basic rights and powers to local units and individuals.

It would not do to carry the comparison between the American Revolution and other colonial wars of liberation, particularly those of the twentieth century, too far. But there is enough evidence to suggest certain basic similarities between the American experience and that of other emergent colonial peoples—enough evidence, at least, to suggest that the efforts of historians to impose on the American Revolution the classic pattern of the French and Russian revolutions have led to a distorted view of our national beginnings. A French Revolution is the product of unbearable tensions within a society. The purpose of such a revolution is to destroy society as it exists, or at least to destroy its most objectionable aspects, and to replace the old with something new. In contrast, a colonial "revolution" or war of liberation has as its purposes the achievement of self-determination, the "completion," or fulfillment of an existing society, rather than its destruction. A French Revolution is first of all destructive; a colonial revolution, first of all constructive. In either case the process may not be completed. In the instance of the French Revolution, the reconstructed society may contain more of the old than the original revolutionaries desired. And, in the case of the colonial revolution, the process of winning independence and the difficulties of organizing an effective national political structure may open the gates to change, may create a radicalism that carries the original society far from its former course; the result may be more destruction than was originally envisaged. Yet, the goals of these two revolutions are fundamentally different, and their different goals determine a different process of fulfillment. The unfolding of the revolutionary drama, the "stages" of revolution, will be quite different, if not opposite.

For John Adams, the American Revolution was an epochal event, a moment of wonder for the world to behold and consider. At times his rhetoric carried him beyond the confines of his innate caution, and he sounded like a typical revolutionary: "The progress of society will be accelerated by centuries by this revolution. . . Light spreads from the day-spring in the west, and may it shine more and more until the perfect day."[12] But, as Edward Handler has noted, "The truth is that if Adams was a revolutionary, he was so in a sense very different than that produced by the other great modern revolutions."[13] Adams did indeed feel that his revolution had a meaning for the world but it was not related to the violent re-structurings of society. Rather its message, for Adams, was that free men can decide voluntarily to limit their freedom in the interests of mutual association, that rational men can devise a system that can at once create order and preserve liberty. The American success was, in contrast to the traditional authoritarian systems of the Old World: "Can authority be more amiable or respectable, when it descends from accidents or institutions established in remote antiquity, than when it springs fresh from the hearts and judgments of an honest and enlightened people?"[14]

Most wars of liberation are not so orderly as that of the American Revolution. Most, at least in this century, have led to increasing radicalism and division within the liberated society. National unity has not been easily achieved. That the American emergence from colonialism had a different ending is significant. A firm basis for unity obviously existed within American society, which, naturally, suggests that the reverse too, was true—that such tensions and divisions as did exist within American society were relatively minor and harmless. It is no wonder that historians determined to find an internal social or political revolution of the French variety within the American Revolution have encountered such difficulties. Nor is it a wonder that the Revolution has become so beclouded with historiographical debates and arguments. The problem has been in our approach. We have been studying, it would seem, the wrong revolution.

NOTES

Some footnotes have been deleted during the editing of the various papers herein printed. Footnote numbers therefore no longer correspond to the original sources. Full citations are contained therein and should be consulted for academic purposes.

INTRODUCTION

1.   Lawrence H. Gipson, *The Coming of the Revolution, 1763-1775* (New York: Harper & Row, 1954), xii.

2.   A. S. Cohan, *Theories of Revolution: An Introduction* (New York: John Wiley & Sons, 1975), 211. Cohan finds fault with four approaches in analysis of revolution: Marxists, Functionalists, Mass Society, and Psychological approaches. Note also: Carl Leiden and Karl M. Schmitt, *The Politics of Violence and Revolution in the Modern World* (Englewood Cliffs, New Jersey: Prentice-Hall, 1968). These men review over twelve definitions of revolution and conclude, "We are content to leave the question open-ended."

3.   William Kornhauser, "Rebellion and Political Development," in Harry Eckstein, ed., *Internal War: Problems and Approaches* (New York: The Free Press, 1964).

4.   D. E. Russell, *Rebellion, Revolution and Armed Forces* (New York: Academic Press, 1974), 56-58.

5.   Karl Marx and Friedrich Engels, *Selected Works*, 2 vols. (Moscow: Foreign Language Publishing House, 1958); Samuel P. Huntington, *Political Order in Changing Societies* (New Haven: Yale University Press, 1968); Barrington M. Moore, Jr., *Social Origins of Dictatorship and Democracy* (Boston: Beacon Press, 1966), and "On the Notions of Progress, Revolution and Freedom," *Ethics* 72 (January 1962); Mark Hagopian, *The Phenomenon of Revolution* (New York: Dodd, Mead & Company, 1974); and Claude Welch, Jr., and Mavis B. Taintor, eds., *Revolution and Political Change* (Belmont, Calif.: Duxbury Press, 1972), introduction.

6.   Harry Eckstein, "On the Etiology of Internal War," in Welch and Taintor, 60-91; Chalmers Johnson, *Revolutionary Change* (Boston: Little, Brown and Co., 1966), and *Revolution and the Social System* (Stanford: Hoover Institution Studies 3, 1964); Alexander Groth, *Revolution and Elite Access* (Davis: Institute of Government Affairs, 1966). See also Russell; and Robert Blackey and Clifford Paynton, *Revolution and the Revolutionary Ideal* (New York: Schenkman Publishing Co., 1976). They claim to prefer an "open-ended" definition (1-10).

7. Huntington, 264.
8. Hagopian, 1.
9. Welch and Taintor, 2.
10. Eckstein, 61.
11. Johnson.
12. Moore, 112; Huntington, 304.
13. Irving Kristol, Martin Diamond, and G. Warren Nutter, *The American Revolution: Three Views* (American Brands Inc., 1975). All three accept Arendt without question.
14. Hagopian, 66-67.
15. Robert E. Brown, *Middle Class Democracy and the Revolution in Massachusetts, 1691-1780* (Ithaca: Cornell University Press, 1965), 401.
16. Robert F. Berkhofer, Jr., "The American Revolution: The Critical Issues," in Nicholas Cords and Patrick Gerster, *Myth and the American Experience* (New York: Glencoe Press, 1973). 1:83.
17. R. R. Palmer, *The Age of Democratic Revolution: A Political History of Europe and America, 1760-1800*, vol. 1 *The Challenge* (Princeton: Princeton University Press, 1959), 213.
18. Berkhofer, 83.
19. Merrill Jensen, *Tracts of the American Revolution, 1763-1776* (New York: Bobbs-Merrill, 1967), xiii-lxx; and the "New Left" school exemplified by Barton Bernstein, ed., *Towards a New Past: Dissenting Essays in American History* (New York: Pantheon Books, 1968).
20. See, for example, Jack Greene, chapter 7 below.
21. Gordon S. Wood, "Rhetoric and Reality in the American Revolution," *William and Mary Quarterly*, 3rd ser. 23 (January 1966): 3-32. Chapter 8 below.
22. Hagopian, 134-50.
23. Kristol, 36.
24. Raymond Tanter and Manus Midlarski, "A Theory of Revolution," *Journal of Conflict Resolution* 11, no. 3 (1967): 264-80.
25. Bernard Cohen, "Science and the Growth of the American Republic," *Review of Politics* 38 (July, 1976): 365-70.
26. Bernard Bailyn, *The Ideological Origins of the American Revolution* (Cambridge: Harvard University Press, 1967), 95-96.
27. Jack P. Greene, "The Role of the Lower House of Assembly in Eighteenth Century Politics," *The Journal of Southern History* 27, no. 4 (November 1961): 453-56.
28. Thomas C. Barrow, "The American Revolution As a Colonial War for Independence," *William and Mary Quarterly*, 3rd ser. 25 (July 1968): 452-64. Chapter 15 below.
29. Clinton Rossiter, *Seedtime of the Republic* (New York: Harcourt, Brace and World, 1953), 57.
30. Jensen, "Democracy and the American Revolution," *The Huntington Library Quarterly* 20, no. 4 (August 1957): 321-41.
31. Bailyn, 7.
32. Jackson Turner Main, "Government by the People: The American Revolution and the Democratization of Legislatures," *William and Mary Quarterly*, 3rd ser. 23 (April 1966): 391.
33. Barrow, 464.
34. John Adams, *The Works of John Adams, Second President of the United States*, ed. Charles Francis Adams, 10 vols. (Boston: Little, Brown and Co., 1950-56), 6:114-15.
35. Jensen, liii.
36. Jeffrey L. Mayer, "The Decline of Revolutionary Democracy: Committee Government in North Carolina, 1774-1776" (unpublished manuscript, 1978), 18. See also Isaac Rhys, chapter 13 below.

37.   Winthrop Jordan, "Familial Politics: Thomas Paine and the Killing of the King, 1776," *Journal of American History* 60 (September 1973): 294. Chapter 14 below.
38.   Wood, 5.
39.   Wood, 32.
40.   Paul Smith, "The American Loyalists: Notes on Their Organization and Numerical Strength," *William and Mary Quarterly*, 3rd ser. 25 (April 1968): 275.
41.   Welch and Taintor, 2.

CHAPTER ONE

1.   Alexis de Tocqueville, *Memoirs, Letters and Remains of Alexis de Tocqueville* (London, 1861), 1:423.
2.   Harry Eckstein, "On the Etiology of Internal War," *History and Theory* 4 (1965): 133.
3.   Samuel P. Huntington, *Political Order in Changing Societies* (New Haven, 1968), 264.
4.   Chalmers Johnson, *Revolution and the Social System* (Stanford, 1964), and G. Johnson, *Revolutionary Change* (Boston, 1966).
5.   Louis Gottschalk, "The Causes of Revolution," *American Journal of Sociology* 50 (1944): 1-8.
6.   Pitrim Sorokin, *The Sociology of Revolution* (Philadelphia, 1925); Lyford P. Edwards, *The Natural History of Revolution* (Chicago, 1927); George S. Pettee, *The Process of Revolution* (New York, 1938).
7.   Carl J. Friedrich, *Revolution: Nomos* 8 (New York, 1966): 6.
8.   Cf. Alfred Cobban, *The Myth of the French Revolution* (London, 1955), and A. Cobban, *The Social Interpretation of the French Revolution* (Cambridge, 1964).
9.   Pierre Goubert, *L'Ancien Régime*, 2nd ed. (Paris, 1969), 257.
10.   Albert Soboul, *The Parisian Sans Culottes and the French Revolution, 1793-94* (Oxford, 1964).
11.   David Landes and Charles Tilly, eds., *History As Social Science* (Englewood Cliffs, N. J., 1971).
12.   George Rudé, *The Crowd in the French Revolution* (Oxford, 1959), and G. Rudé, *The Crowd in History* (New York, 1964).
13.   Harold Lasswell and Daniel Lerner, eds., *World Revolutionary Elites* (Cambridge, Mass., 1965).
14.   Douglas Brunton and D. H. Pennington, *Members of the Long Parliament* (London, 1954).
15.   R. R. Palmer, "Generalizations about Revolutions: A Case Study," in Louis Gottschalk, ed., *Generalization in the Writing of History* (Chicago, 1963).
16.   J. C. Davies, "Toward a Theory of Revolution," in Davies, ed., *When Men Revolt and Why* (New York, 1971).
17.   Eckstein.
18.   Cf. V. Pareto, *Sociological Writings*, ed. S. E. Finer (London, 1966), 55-58.
19.   Charles Tilly, *The Vendée* (Cambridge, 1964).
20.   Manfred Halpern, "The Revolution of Modernization in National and International Society," *Revolution: Nomos* 8 (New York, 1966): 179.
21.   Huntington, 266.

CHAPTER THREE

1.   Carl J. Friedrich, *Man and His Government* (New York: McGraw-Hill, 1963), 644.
2.   Hannah Arendt, *On Revolution* (New York: Viking Press, 1963), 28.

3.   Stephen Marshall, 1641, quoted in Michael Walzer, *The Revolution of the Saints: A Study in the Origin of Radical Politics* (Cambridge: Harvard University Press, 1965), xiv. Walzer's analysis persuaslively illumines the modernizing, revolutionary nature of the Puritans.

4.   George S. Pettee, *The Process of Revolution* (New York: Harper & Bros., 1938), 96.

5.   Pettee, 100-101.

6.   Crane Brinton, *The Anatomy of Revolution* (New York: Random House, Inc., Vintage Books, 1958).

7.   Leon Trotsky, *My Life* (New York: Charles Scribner's Sons, 1930), 337, quoted in Merle Fainsod, *How Russia Is Ruled* (Cambridge: Harvard University Press, 1953), 84.

8.   Cf. Chalmers Johnson, *Revolution and the Social System* (Stanford: Hoover Institution, 1964), 3-22; Harry Eckstein, "Internal War: The Problem of Anticipation," in Ithiel de Sola Pool et al., *Social Science Research and National Security* (Washington: Smithsonian Institution, 1963), 116-18.

9.   Pettee, 12, 100; Brinton, 100 ff.; Johnson, 5 ff.

10.   R. R. Palmer, *The Age of Democratic Revolution* (Princeton: Princeton University Press, 1959), 1:484.

CHAPTER FOUR

1.   Ted Gurr, "Psychological Factors in Civil Violence," *World Politics* 20, no. 2 (1968): 276.

2.   Michael Walzer, *The Revolution of the Saints: A Study in the Origin of Radical Politics* (Cambridge: Harvard University Press, 1965).

3.   Samuel P. Huntington, *Political Order in Changing Societies* (New Haven: Yale University Press, 1968), 265.

4.   Alexander Groth, *Revolution and Elite Access* (Davis: Institute of Government Affairs, 1966), 4.

5.   Lyford Edwards, *The Natural History of Revolution* (Chicago: University of Chicago Press, 1970), 23. This book was originally published in 1927.

6.   George S. Pettee, *The Process of Revolution* (New York: Harper and Bros., 1938), 33.

7.   Groth, 6.

8.   Edwards, 23-27.

9.   Walzer, 1.

10.   James C. Davies, "The J-Curve of Rising and Declining Satisfactions As a Cause of Some Great Revolutions and a Contained Rebellion," in Hugh Davis Graham and Ted Robert Gurr, eds., *Violence in America* (Washington: Government Printing Office, 1969), 2:547-77.

11.   Lawrence Stone, "Theories of Revolution," *World Politics* 18 no. 2 (1966): 165.

12.   Talcott Parsons, "Some Reflections on the Place of Force in Social Process," in Harry Eckstein, ed., *Internal War: Problems and Approaches* (New York: The Free Press, 1964), 65-66.

13.   Edwards, 35.

14.   Albert Camus, *The Rebel: An Essay on Man in Revolt* (New York: Vintage, 1958), 28.

15.   Hannah Arendt, *On Revolution* (New York: Viking Press, 1963), 251.

16.   Arendt, 275.

CHAPTER FIVE

1.   Condorcet, *Sur le Sens du Mot Revolutionnaire, Oeuvres, 1847-1849*, vol. 12.

2.   Thus Jefferson in *The Anas* quoted from *Life and Selected Writings*, Modern Library edition, 117.

3. The quotations are from John Adams in Charles F. Adams, ed., *The Works of John Adams* (Boston, 1850-56), 4:293; and from his remarks "On Machiavelli," *Works*, 5:40, respectively.
4. Quoted from Theodor Schieder, "Das Problem der Revolution in 19. Jahrhundert," *Historische Zeitschrift*, vol. 170 (1950).
5. Quoted from Edward S. Corwin, "'The Higher Law' Background of American Constitutional Law," in *Harvard Law Review* 42 (1928).
6. Tocqueville, op. cit., vol. II, Fourth Book, chapter 8.

CHAPTER SIX

1. For additional evidence see Robert E. Brown, *Middle-Class Democracy and the Revolution in Massachusetts, 1691-1780* (Ithaca, New York: Cornell University Press, 1955).
2. For a full discussion of Beard's work, see Robert E. Brown, *Charles Beard and the Constitution* (Princeton: Princeton University Press, 1956).

CHAPTER SEVEN

1. Merrill Jensen, *The Articles of Confederation* (Madison, 1940), 11.
2. J. Franklin Jameson, *The American Revolution As a Social Movement* (Princeton, 1926), 18.
3. Bernard Bailyn, introduction to *Pamphlets of the American Revolution 1750-1776* (Cambridge, Mass., 1965-), 1.
4. Gordon S. Wood, "Rhetoric and Reality in the American Revolution," *William and Mary Quarterly*, 3rd ser. 23 (1966): 26, 31 (italics added).
5. Wood, 24.
6. Jackson Turner Main, *The Social Structure of Revolutionary America* (Princeton, 1965), 286-87.
7. P. M. G. Harris, "The Social Origins of American Leaders: The Demographic Foundations," *Perspectives in American History* 3 (1969): 159-344.
8. Clifford Geertz, "Ideology As a Cultural System," in David E. Apter, ed., *Ideology and Discontent* (Glencoe, Ill., 1964), 53.
9. See the useful discussion by Edward A. Tiryakian in "A Model of Societal Change and Its Lead Indicators," in Samuel Z. Klausner, ed., *The Study of Total Societies* (New York, 1967), 73.
10. Geertz, 53.
11. Wood, 30.
12. Wood, 27.
13. Wood, 26.
14. James Rule and Charles Tilly, "1830 and the Unnatural History of Revolution," *Journal of Social Issues* 28 (1972): 49-76.
15. E. A. Wrigley, "Modernization and the Industrial Revolution in England," *Journal of Interdisciplinary History* 3 (1972): 225-59. The definitions of "traditional" and "modern" implicit in my passages are derived from this article.
16. E. J. Hobsbawm, "From Social History to the History of Society," *Daedalus* 100 (1971): 39-40.

CHAPTER EIGHT

1. This is the title of a recent essay by Edmund S. Morgan in Arthur M. Schlesinger, Jr., and Morton White, eds., *Paths of American Thought* (Boston, 1963), 11-33.
2. Edmund S. Morgan, "The American Revolution: Revisions in Need of Revising," *William and Mary Quarterly*, 3rd ser. 14 (1957): 14.
3. [William Vans Murray] *Political Sketches, Inscribed to His Excellency John Adams* (London, 1787), 21, 48.

4.   [Daniel Leonard], *The Origin of the American Contest with Great-Britain . . . [by] Massachusettensis* . . . (New York, 1775), 40; Douglas Adair and John A. Schultz, eds., *Peter Oliver's Origin and Progress of the American Rebellion: A Tory View* (San Marino, 1963), 159.

5.   Simeon Baldwin, *An Oration Pronounced Before the Citizens of New-Haven, July 4th, 1788* . . . (New Haven, 1788), 10; [Murray], 48; David Ramsay, *The History of the American Revolution* (Philadelphia, 1789), 1:350.

6.   Thomas Paine, *Letter to the Abbé Raynal* . . . (1782) in Philip S. Foner, ed., *The Complete Writings of Thomas Paine* (New York, 1945), 2:243; John Adams to H. Niles, Feb. 13, 1818, in Charles Francis Adams, ed., *The Works of John Adams* (Boston, 1850-56), 10:282.

7.   William Pierce, *An Oration, Delivered at Christ Church, Savannah, on the 4th of July, 1788* . . . (Providence [1788]), 6; Enos Hitchcock, *An Oration, Delivered July 4th, 1788* . . . (Providence [1788]), 11.

8.   Petition to the King, October, 1774, in Worthington C. Ford, ed., *Journals of the Continental Congress, 1774-1789* (Washington, 1904-37), 1:118.

9.   Samuel Williams, *The Natural and Civil History of Vermont* . . . (Walpole, New Hampshire, 1794), vii, 372-73; Pierce, 8.

10.   Moses Coit Tyler, *The Literary History of the American Revolution, 1763-1783* (New York, 1897), 1: 8-9.

11.   Charles A. Beard, *An Economic Interpretation of the Constitution* (New York, 1935), x, viii.

12.   Carl L. Becker, *The Declaration of Independence: A Study in the History of Political Ideas* (New York, 1922), 203, 207, 133.

13.   Quoted in Philip Davidson, *Propaganda and the American Revolution, 1763-1783* (Chapel Hill, 1941), 141, 373, 150.

14.   Arthur M. Schlesinger, *Prelude to Independence: The Newspaper War on Britain, 1764-1776* (New York, 1958), 34.

15.   Davidson, 59; Schlesinger, 20.

16.   Davidson, xiv, 46.

17.   Schlesinger, 44; Arthur M. Schlesinger, *New Viewpoints in American History* (New York, 1923), 179.

18.   Morgan, "Colonial Ideas of Parliamentary Power, 1764-1766," *William and Mary Quarterly*, 3rd ser. 5 (1948): 311, 341; Edmund S. and Helen M. Morgan, *The Stamp Act Crisis: Prologue to Revolution*, rev. ed. (New York, 1963), 369-70; Page Smith, "David Ramsay and the Causes of the American Revolution," *William and Mary Quarterly*, 3rd ser. 17 (1960): 70-71.

19.   Jack P. Greene, "The Flight from Determinism: A Review of Recent Literature on the Coming of the American Revolution," *South Atlantic Quarterly* 61 (1962): 257.

20.   Greene, 237, 257.

21.   Bernard Bailyn, ed. assisted by Jane N. Garrett, *Pamphlets of the American Revolution, 1750-1776* (Cambridge, Mass., 1965-), I, viii, 60, x, 20.

22.   Smith, 72.

23.   Morgan, "Revisions in Need of Revising," 13.

24.   Adair and Schultz, ix.

25.   Bailyn, 1:87, ix.

26.   [Moses Mather], *America's Appeal to the Impartial World* . . . (Hartford, 1775), 59; [John Dickinson], *Letters from a Farmer in Pennsylvania to the Inhabitants of the British Colonies* (1768), in Paul L. Ford, ed., *The Life and Writings of John Dickinson* (Historical Society of Pennsylvania, *Memoirs* 14 [Philadelphia, 1895]), 2: 348.

27.   [Dickinson], 388.

28.   Morgan, "Revisions in Need of Revising," 7, 13, 8; Greene, 237.

29.   Edmund S. Morgan, *The Birth of the Republic, 1763-89* (Chicago, 1956), 51.

30.   Greene, 258; Morgan, *Birth of the Republic*, 3.

31.   Bailyn, I: vii, ix.
32.   Bailyn, vii, viii, 17.
33.   J. G. A. Pocock, "Machiavelli, Harrington, and English Political Ideologies in the Eighteenth Century," *William and Mary Quarterly*, 3rd ser. 22 (1965): 550.
34.   Sir Louis Namier, *England in the Age of the American Revolution*, 2nd ed. (London, 1961), 131.
35.   Namier, 129.
36.   Bailyn, 1: 90, x, 169, 140.
37.   Bailyn, 1: 22.
38.   John Duche, *The American Vine: A Sermon . . . Before the Honourable Continental Congress, July 20th, 1775 . . .* (Philadelphia, 1775), 29.
39.   Bryan A. Wilson, "Millennialism in Comparative Perspective," *Comparative Studies in Society and History* 6 (1963-64): 108.
40.   Robert E. and B. Katherine Brown, *Virginia, 1705-1786: Democracy or Aristocracy?* (East Lansing, Mich., 1964), 236; Alexander White to Richard Henry Lee, 1768, quoted in J. R. Pole, "Representation and Authority in Virginia from the Revolution to Reform," *The Jouranl of Southern History* 24 *(1958): 23.*
41.   *Virginia Gazette* (Purdie and Dixon), April 11, 1771; (Rind), October 31, 1771.
42.   *The Defence of Injur'd Merit Unmasked. . .* (n.p., 1771), 10.
43.   Jay B. Hubbell and Douglass Adair, "Robert Munford's *The Candidates*," *William and Mary Quarterly*, 3rd ser. 5 (1948): 246, 238.
44.   [John Randolph], *Considerations on the Present State of Virginia* ([Williamsburg], 1774), in Earl G. Swem, ed., *Virginia and the Revolution: Two Pamphlets, 1774* (New York, 1919), 16; *Virginia Gazette* (Purdie and Dixon, November 25, 1773.
45.   *Virginia Gazette* (Rind), September 8, 1774.
46.   Quoted in Bridenbaugh, *Myths and Realities* (New York, 1963), 27.
47.   John A. Washington to R. H. Lee, June 20, 1778, quoted in Pole, 28.
48.   Julian P. Boyd et al., eds., *The Papers of Thomas Jefferson* (Princeton, 1950-), 1:560.
49.   Max Farrand, ed., *The Records of the Federal Convention of 1787* (New Haven, 1911), 1: 56; Bridenbaugh, 14, 16.
50.   John Adams, "Novanglus," in Charles F. Adams, ed., *The Works of John Adams* (Boston, 1851), 4:14.
51.   Arthur F. Bentley, *The Process of Government: A Study of Social Pressures* (Chicago, 1908), 152.

CHAPTER NINE

1.   Charles A. and Mary R. Beard, *The Rise of American Civilization* (New York, 1927), 1:196.
2.   Charles A. Andrews, *The Boston Merchants and the Non-Importation Movement* (New York, 1968), 101. (Originally published in 1916-17.)
3.   *The American Revolution Considered As a Social Movement* (Princeton, N.J., 1926).
4.   *An Economic Interpretation of the Constitution of the United States* (New York, 1913).
5.   Bernard Bailyn, *The Origins of American Politics* (New York, 1967); and Gordon S. Wood, "Rhetoric and Reality in the American Revolution," *William and Mary Quarterly*, 3rd ser. 23 (1966): 25-32.
6.   May 31, 1750, *John Kidd Letterbook*, Historical Society of Pennsylvania.
7.   "The Late Regulations Respecting the British Colonies . . ." (Philadelphia, 1765), in Paul Leicester Ford, ed., *The Writings of John Dickinson* (Historical Society of Pennsylvania, *Memoirs*, 14 [Philadelphia, 1895]): 228, 227.
8.   Richard Waln, Jr., to Nicholas Waln, June 25, 1764, Waln Collection, Box H, Historical Society of Pennsylvania.

9.   *Pennsylvania Gazette* (Philadelphia), November 17, 1767.
10.   To Samuel Galloway, November 7, 1765, Galloway Papers, Library of Congress.
11.   To Denys DeBerdt, March 4, 1768, quoted in Merrill Jensen, *The Founding of a Nation* (New York, 1968), 271.
12.   R. Waln, Jr., to Harford & Powell, April 18, 1769, Richard Waln Letterbook, Historical Society of Pennsylvania.
13.   Isaac F. Harrell, *Loyalism in Virginia* (Philadelphia, 1926); and Arthur Schlesinger, *The Colonial Merchants and the American Revolution 1763-1776* (New York, 1918), 38-39.
14.   Quoted in Fairfax Harrison, *Landmarks of Old Prince William: A Study of Origins in Northern Virginia* (Richmond, 1924), 2:390.
15.   "Probus to the Printer," in *New York Journal*, November 19, 1767; Thomas Clifford to Thomas Penington, June 25, 1768, Clifford Letterbook, Historical Society of Pennsylvania, *Pennsylvania Chronicle* (Philadelphia), October 10, 1768; March 13, 1769; Sachs, *Business Outlook*, 254-56.

CHAPTER ELEVEN

1.   Jean Jacques Rousseau, "Considerations sur le gouvernement de Pologne et sur sa reformation projetée en avril 1772," (printed in J. J. Rousseau, *Contract Social ou Principes du Droit Politique . . .* [Paris, n.d.] , 356).
2.   Edmund Burke, *Select Works*, ed. E. J. Payne, 3 vols. (Oxford, 1904), 1:231-32.
3.   William Douglass, *A Summary . . . of the British Settlements in North-America*, 2 vols. (Boston, 1755), 1:7.
4.   *The Writings of Benjamin Franklin*, ed. Albert H. Smyth, 10 vols. (New York, 1907), 4:4.
5.   Smyth, 51. The italics are Franklin's.
6.   Jonathan Mayhew, *Two Sermons* (Boston, 1763), 71-72.
7.   Mayhew, 73.
8.   *The Writings of John Dickinson*, ed. Paul L. Ford, 14 vols. (Philadelphia, 1895), 1:169.
9.   John Adams and Jonathan Sewall (*sic*) [John Adams, as editor, was mistaken; the author of the Massachusettensis papers was Daniel Leonard] , *Novanglus and Massachusettensis . . .* (Boston, 1819), 9.
10.   *The Papers of Thomas Jefferson*, ed. Julian P. Boyd et al., 15 vols. (Princeton, 1950-), 1:121.
11.   Boyd, 137.
12.   *The Works of James Wilson*, ed. James de Witt Anderson, 2 vols. (Chicago, 1896), 2:553 et passim; 563.
13.   *The Works of Alexander Hamilton*, ed. Henry C. Lodge, 12 vols. (New York, 1904), 1:86.
14.   Hezekiah Niles, ed., *Principles and Acts of the Revolution in America . . .* (Baltimore, 1822), 42.
15.   Niles, 125.
16.   W. C. Ford et al., eds., *Journals of the Continental Congress, 1774-1789*, 34 vols. (Washington, D.C., 1904-37), 2:161.
17.   Thomas Burke to Richard Caswell, April 29, 1777, in *Letters of Members of the Continental Congress,* ed. E. C. Burnett, 8 vols. (Washington, D. C., 1921-36), 2:345.
18.   Thomas Paine, *The Crisis* in *The Life and Works of Thomas Paine*, ed. William M. Van der Weyde, 3 vols. (New Rochelle, N.Y., 1925), 3:77-79.
19.   Paine, 2:342.
20.   Robert Douthat Meade, *Patrick Henry, Patriot in the Making* (Philadelphia, 1957), 325.

21.	Niles, "Oration delivered at Watertown [Mass.], March 5, 1776, by Peter Thatcher, M.A.," 45.

CHAPTER TWELVE

1.	*Virginia Gazette* (Dixon and Hunter), May 26, 1774.
2.	George Mason to Martin Cockburn, May 26, 1774, in Robert A. Rutland, ed., *The Papers of George Mason, 1725-1792* (Chapel Hill, 1970), 1:191.
3.	William Nelson to Lord Hillsbrough, December 1, 1770, in William Van Schreeven and Robert L. Schribner, eds., *Revolutionary Virginia* (Richmond, Va., 1973), 1:85.
4.	Hunter Dickinson Farish, ed., *Journal and Letters of Philip Vickers Fithian, 1773-1774* (Williamsburg, Va., 1945), 148.
5.	W.H.O.,"in *Virginia Gazette* (Rind), June 30, 1774; "D. C.," *Virginia Gazette* (Purdie and Dixon), December 22, 1774; (Purdie), November 10, 1775.
6.	Farish, ed., 251-52, 255. Jack P. Greene, ed., *The Diary of Landon Carter of Sabine Hall, 1752-1778* (Charlottesville, Va., 1965), 2: 817-18.
7.	Greene, ed., 821-22.
8.	*Virginia Gazette* (Purdie), July 14, 1775.
9.	Peter Force, comp., *American Archives . . .* , 4th ser. (Washington, D.C., 1837-53), 1: 787; *Virginia Gazette* (Rind), July 28, 1774.
10.	Force, 4th Ser. 2:76-77; Van Schreeven and Scribner, 1:153-55.
11.	*Virginia Gazette* (Dixon and Hunter), April 15, 1775.
12.	*Virginia Gazette* (Dixon and Hunter), May 6, 1775.
13.	*Virginia Gazette* (Rind), November 11, 1774.
14.	*Virginia Gazette* (Rind), December 14, 1769; (Purdie and Dixon), December 19, 1774; (Dixon and Hunter), January 28, 1775; George Washington to George Mason, April 5, 1769, in Rutland, 97-98.
15.	*Virginia Gazette* (Dixon and Hunter), April 11, 1771.
16.	*Virginia Gazette* (Dixon and Hunter), April 11, 1771.
17.	*Virginia Gazette* (Rind), July 7, 1774.
18.	*Virginia Gazette* (Rind), July 14, 1774.
19.	*Virginia Gazette* (Pinkney), June 1, 1775.
20.	"W.H.O.," *Virginia Gazette*, June 30, 1774; Rutland, 1:211.
21.	Rutland, 1:215-16.
22.	Hugh Mercer [et al.] to Capt. Grayson, April 14, 1775, in Force, 4th ser. 2:387.
23.	Captain Grayson to George Washington, April 26, 1775, in Force, 4th ser. 2:395; Michael Brown Wallace to Gustavus Brown Wallace, May 14, 1775, *Wallace Family Papers, 1750-1781*. Alderman Library, University of Virginia, Charlottesville.
24.	Force, 4th ser. 2:526; Patrick Henry to Francis Lightfoot Lee, May 8, 1775, in Paul P. Hoffman, ed., *The Lee Family Papers, 1742-1795* (microfilm publication, Charlottesville, Va., 1966); *Virginia Gazette* (Purdie), May 19, 1775.
25.	James Parker to Charles Stuart, June 12, 1775, "Letters from Virginia," *Magazine of History* (January 1906), 159.
26.	William Byrd to Ralph Wormeley, October 4, 1775, photocopy in Virginia Historical Society, Richmond; James Madison to William Bradford, June 19, 1775, in William T. Hutchinson and William M. E. Rachal, eds., *The Papers of James Madison* (Chicago, 1962), 1:159.
27.	H. R. Meewaine, ed., "Proceedings of the Committee of Safety of Cumberland and the Isle of Wright Counties, 1775-1776," *Fifteenth Annual Report of the Library Board of the Virginia State Library, 1917-1918 . . .* (Richmond, Va., 1919), 5:11.
28.	Adam Stephens to Richard Henry Lee, August 24, 1774, and February 1, 1775, *Letters to Richard Henry Lee*, American Philosophical Society, Philadelphia (microfilm [M.63.2] Colonial Williamsburg Foundation).

29.   Robert Brent to Richard Henry Lee, April 28, 1776, in Kate Mason Rowland, *The Life of George Mason*, *1725-1792* (New York, 1892), 1:222.
30.   *Virginia Gazette* (Purdie), April 19, 1776.
31.   *Virginia Gazette* (Purdie), May 17, 1776.
32.   Lancaster County Court Order Book, No. 14, July 18, 1776, Virginia State Library.
33.   Clarence S. Brigham, *History and Bibliography of American Newspapers, 1690-1820* (Worcester, Mass., 1947), 2:1105-38.

CHAPTER FOURTEEN

1.   John C. Fitzpatrick, ed., *The Writings of George Washington from the Original Manuscript Sources*, *1745-1799*, 39 vols. (Washington, D.C., 1931-1944), 4:455.
2.   Lyman H. Butterfield, ed., *Adams Family Correspondence*, 2 vols. (Cambridge, Mass., 1963), 1:350.
3.   *Connecticut Gazette*, March 22, 1776.
4.   David Ramsay, *The History of the American Revolution*, 2 vols. (Philadelphia, 1789), 1:338-39.
5.   [Thomas Paine], *Common Sense* (Philadelphia, 1776), 2, 45, 57.
6.   Paine, 3.
7.   Paine, 13-15.
8.   Paine, 27-28.
9.   Paine, 57-58.
10.   Paine, 47.
11.   Peter Laslett, ed., *Patriarchs and Other Political Works of Sir Robert Filmer* (Oxford, 1949).
12.   John Adams and Jonathan Sewell [i.e. Daniel Leonard], *Novanglus and Massachusettensis . . .* (Boston, 1819), 167.
13.   *South-Carolina and American General Gazette*, June 20, 1776.
14.   *South-Carolina Gazette*, January 23, 1775.
15.   *New York Gazette, or the Weekly Post-Boy*, December 5, 1765.
16.   *Boston New-Letter*, August 21, 1760.
17.   *Virginia Gazette* (Purdie and Dixon), May 18, 1769.
18.   Jonathan Mayhew, *A Discourse . . .* (Boston, 1750), 39n.
19.   Gilbert Tennent, *A Sermon, On I Chronicles xxix. 28 . . .* (Philadelphia, 1761), 12.
20.   Samuel Davies, *A Sermon . . . On the death of His Late Majesty, King George II* (New York, 1761), 19.
21.   *Pennsylvania Magazine* 1 (January 1775): 51.
22.   Peter Force, ed., *American Archives . . .* , 6 vols. (Washington, D.C., 1837-1846), 5:1035.
23.   Butterfield, 1:422, 424.
24.   Don Wolfe, ed., *Complete Prose Works of John Milton*, 4 vols. (New Haven, 1955-1966), 4:326-27.
25.   *Pennsylvania Magazine* 1 (August 1775): 362.
26.   Ibid., 1 (April 1775): 158-61.
27.   Ibid., 1 (May 1775): 209-10.
28.   Ibid., 1 (March 1775): 107-11.
29.   Ibid., 1 (February 1775): 61-62.
30.   Quoted in Arthur M. Schlesinger, *Prelude to Independence: The Newspaper War on Britain*, *1764-1776* (New York, 1965), 29.
31.   *Pennsylvania Magazine* 1 (July 1775), 328.
32.   Paine, 4.
33.   Paine, 30-31.
34.   *A Prophecy*, in Francis Hopkinson, *The Miscellaneous Essays and Occasional*

Writings of Francis Hopkinson, Esq., 3 vols. (Philadelphia, 1792), 1:92-97.
35. Jonathon Boucher, *A View of the Causes and Consequences of the American Revolution . . .* (London, 1797), 475.
36. Boucher, 349.
37. Paul Leicester Ford, ed., *The Writings of John Dickinson* (Philadelphia, 1895), 1:491.
38. Henry C. Van Schaack, *The Life of Peter Van Schaack, LL.D. . . .* (New York, 1842), 25.
39. *Connecticut Gazette,* October 25, 1776.
40. *New-England Chronicle,* July 18, 1776.
41. *Maryland Gazette,* July 25, 1776; *Virginia Gazette,* July 29, 1776.
42. Quoted in Edmund F. Slafter, "Royal Memorials and Emblems in Use in the Colonies before the Revolution," *Proceedings of the Massachusetts Historical Society* 4 (1889): 240n.
43. *Maryland Gazette,* August 1, 1776.
44. Quoted in Slafter, 253n.

CHAPTER FIFTEEN

1. Thomas Hutchinson to John Healy Hutchinson, February 14, 1772, *Hutchinson Letterbooks* (transcripts), 27:296-300, Massachusetts Historical Society, Boston.
2. Hutchinson to Richard Jackson, April 21, 1766, *Letterbooks,* 26:227-28.
3. Hutchinson to [?], December 30, 1773, *Letterbooks,* 27:608.
4. John Adams, "A Dissertation on the Canon and Feudal Law" (1765), in Charles F. Adams, ed., *The Works of John Adams* (Boston, 1850-56), 3:454.
5. John Adams, "Novanglus," 4:131.
6. Bernard Bailyn, *The Ideological Origins of the American Revolution* (Cambridge, Mass., 1967), xi.
7. John Adams, Speech to Congress, March 4, 1797, 9:105.
8. Elisha P. Douglass, *Rebels and Democrats* (Chapel Hill, 1955), 211.
9. Jacob E. Cooke, ed., *The Federalist* (Middleton, Conn., 1961), 56-65. Madison considered the question of the appropriate size for political units further in Federalist 14, 83-89.
10. Quoted in Cecelia M. Kenyon, *The Antifederalists* (Indianapolis, 1966), xci-xcii.
11. Quoted in Kenyon, xcii.
12. Quoted in Edward Handler, *America and Europe in the Political Thought of John Adams* (Cambridge, Mass., 1964), 102.
13. Handler, 101.
14. John Adams, Speech to Congress, March 4, 1797, 9:107.